D042620ᴮ

PRAISE FOR *ENTREPRENEURIAL NATION*

"Ro Khanna clearly loves his subject, and has written a wonderfully readable book about America's industrial and technological base. It is a detailed microeconomic look at the considerable strengths and challenges in the tradable part of the U.S. economy. Policy targeted to employment always involves a subtle balance between respecting powerful global market forces on the one hand and identifying investment opportunities and removing self-inflicted handicaps on the other. On this dimension, the book is terrific; full of practical insights that could inform a collaboration between business and government to expand the economy's employment and growth engines, at a time when we need it."

MICHAEL SPENCE, Nobel Laureate in Economics (2001)

"This is a captivating book that adds to the growing discourse on the relevance of American ingenuity and our manufacturing heritage. The real life experiences of U.S. manufacturing firms, many of which we do business with every day, shed a light on how we really get things done. America is about "making stuff" but we do it with great care for our customers and a focus on how we can do more to improve people's lives through collective innovation. It is a collection of captivating stories and real ideas on how to keep America competitive in the 21st Century."

ELLEN KULLMAN, Chair & CEO, DuPont—
one of America's original manufacturing companies

*"*Entrepreneurial Nation *is an excellent reminder of what makes American manufacturing great. Our culture of innovation has created our industrial base and is now threatened on many fronts. Ro examines the many facets of this problem and proposes specific remedies—some controversial and others less so—*

that are intended to put us back on the track of an expanding industrial base. There is something for everyone in this book in that it brings to the surface many facts that are important but have been masked. For example, why the WTO rules penalize U.S. exporting firms operating under our corporate taxation system. An important read for anyone interested in impacting our manufacturing future."

PAUL OTELLINI, President and CEO, Intel Corporation

"Ro Khanna takes on the sages who predict an inevitable demise of making things in America. He lays out a refreshing vision of innovation-based U.S. manufacturing leadership, not just competitiveness. Entrepreneurial Nation *is based on the views and experiences of real manufacturers making real products in America. It prescribes a hefty dose of federal policy changes to empower private-sector innovation in manufacturing. This is a very important addition to a very important debate."*

CHARLES VEST, President Emeritus,
Massachusetts Institute of Technology and President
of the National Academy of Engineering

"Ro Khanna led Commerce's domestic offices that implemented President Obama's National Export Initiative. He was a key player in the policy debate in Washington, and he was in the trenches listening to the perspective of manufacturers across our country. It shows. His book provides a powerful vision of what American companies need to do to thrive and grow in the world market."

AUSTAN GOOLSBEE, Chairman of the Council of
Economic Advisors (2010–2011), President Barack Obama

"I have always believed that America remains the greatest superpower of innovation. Khanna is a leading thinker on how

to make U.S. manufacturing more competitive across this country, whether it comes to making high-technology planes, cars, steel bars, fire suits, or even blenders. The unconventional ideas in this book chart the path America can take to lead the world for years to come."

ELON MUSK, CEO and Founder of Tesla and SpaceX

"Khanna raises the most important question facing the United States today—Can American manufacturing survive? The heroes extolled in his tales are indeed inspiring, but even they will need the help of all the policy changes he recommends and more to stay alive and thrive."

CLYDE PRESTOWITZ, Bestselling Author of
Trading Places, Three Billion New Capitalists, and
The Betrayal of American Prosperity

"Ro Khanna has firsthand experience with our nation's manufacturing economy, and he knows what it will take for us to succeed in the 21st century. Entrepreneurial Nation provides a candid assessment of the challenges manufacturers face from currency manipulation and a rigged trading regime. Khanna draws on the voices of real workers, union leaders, and manufacturers to provide a compelling vision of how to grow our industrial base and create jobs here at home for the middle class."

RICHARD L. TRUMKA, President, AFL-CIO

"Entrepeneurial Nation takes you to the front lines of the fight to revive our economic fortunes and get manufacturing moving again. Over the last three years, Ro Khanna has travelled across the length and breadth of this country, from Pittsfield, New Hampshire, to Witchita, Kanasas, from San Jose, California, to Seminole, Oklahoma. He has met and talked to manufacturers of every stripe, makers of batteries and blenders, of fire suits and *food processors, aerospace parts and drilling rigs. This is a book about their remarkable successes, the challenges they have surmounted and the issues they confront. It is a vivid portrait of the most dynamic force in the U.S. economy, its entrepreneurs. In the process Ro Khanna offers a compelling vision of our economic potential."*

LIAQUAT AHAMED, Pulitzer Prize Winner, *Lords of Finance*

"This is the book I would have written if I was not currently managing a streetcar manufacturing company. Excellent statistics and a fair and balanced approach to the emerging issues of today's manufacturing policies (or lack thereof). I agree with Entrepreneurial Nation *that we must defend our vital manufacturing base. Its message is timely, thorough, and engaging and a must read for those of us who know that manufacturing is critical to the very future of our great nation."*

CHANDRA BROWN, President, United Streetcar

"This is important reading for all interested in the nature and strength of the United States economy in the 21st century. Khanna uses the experiences of fifteen successful manufacturing companies to address several fundamental questions: How can we compete successfully with low-wage countries? What type of manufacturing sector is necessary to maintain leadership in the development of new technologies? What is the appropriate role for government in these matters? What are our educational needs if we are to compete for high-value jobs? Anyone who reads this book will have a better understanding of the United States economy and the actions that will shape its future."

HUGO SONNENSCHEIN, President Emeritus and
Adam Smith Distinguished Service Professor of
Economics, The University of Chicago

ENTREPRENEURIAL
NATION

■ ■ ■

Why Manufacturing Is Key
to America's Future

■ ■ ■

RO KHANNA

NEW YORK   CHICAGO   SAN FRANCISCO
LISBON   LONDON   MADRID   MEXICO CITY   MILAN
NEW DELHI   SAN JUAN   SEOUL   SINGAPORE
SYDNEY   TORONTO

1 2 3 4 5 6 7 8 9 0   DOC/DOC   1 8 7 6 5 4 3 2

ISBN: 978-0-07-180200-0
MHID: 0-07-180200-2

e-book ISBN: 978-0-07-180201-7
e-book MHID: 0-07-180201-0

Interior design by Lee Fukui and Mauna Eichner

Library of Congress Cataloging-in-Publication Data

Khanna, Ro.
  Entrepreneurial nation : why manufacturing is still key to America's future / by Ro Khanna.
    p. cm.
  Includes index.
  ISBN-13: 978-0-07-180200-0 (alk. paper)
  ISBN-10: 0-07-180200-2 (alk. paper)
  1. Manufacturing industries—United States. 2. Economic development—United States. 3. Technological innovations—United States. 4. Entrepreneurship—United States. 5. United States—Commerce. I. Title.
  HD9725.K44 2013
  338'.040973—dc23
                            2012022872

McGraw-Hill books are available at special quantity discounts to use as premiums and sales promotions, or for use in corporate training programs. To contact a representative please e-mail us at bulksales@mcgraw-hill.com.

This book is printed on acid-free paper.

For Mom, Dad, and Vikas,
who have been there for me at every step unconditionally

Contents

■ ■ ■

ENTREPRENEURIAL
— NATION —

Introduction

Against All Odds

■　■　■

The conventional wisdom in Washington is that America is losing its competitive edge. As President Obama's appointee overseeing the U.S. Department of Commerce's domestic offices, I heard such chatter coming out of the Economic Strategic Roundtables. David Rothkopf, a former trade advisor to President Clinton, organized these closed-door, bipartisan sessions every few months, filling them with current and former Commerce and State Department officials. The participants pointed to China and Singapore as models for attracting foreign direct investment and promoting economic development. Envy of Asia lurked underneath the discussions. According to a senior Obama administration official who was present, one well-meaning participant declared, "China is the Google of nations. . . . America is the General Motors

1

of nations. Let's get back in the game." The irony of the analogy, given Google's run-in with China's censorship laws, was apparently lost on him.

Fortunately, amidst all this pessimism, former secretary of commerce Norman Mineta counseled me to listen to voices outside of the Washington echo chamber. He promised that I would learn and contribute more if I traveled across our nation than I would if I traveled halfway across the world. He was right. I spent two years crisscrossing the nation, visiting our Commerce offices in cities and small towns. The mission of these regional offices is to assist businesses in exporting and in increasing domestic manufacturing. My colleagues traveled to Shanghai or São Paulo, while I went to places like Oshkosh, Wisconsin, and Boothwyn, Pennsylvania. Although I didn't mail as many postcards or get as many stamps in my passport as my overseas counterparts, I met some of the most remarkable Americans, who are making the world's best products right here at home.

Despite cheaper labor abroad, currency manipulation, intellectual property theft, and subsidies to foreign competitors, these American manufacturers are winning. Many of them are small or medium-sized businesses that are family owned. Some are large corporations led by executives who still believe that America is the best place to set up a factory. What they have in common is that they're creating jobs in local communities, defying the stereotype of our manufacturing going offshore. In an era when we hear weekly about plant shutdowns, know friends and family members who are being laid off, and are anxious about the career prospects for young people, they are the embers of hope. This book is their story.

The struggle and triumph of cutting-edge American manufacturers is the latest chapter in our national story. Larry Summers, the former director of the White House National

Economic Council for President Obama, put our economic difficulties in a historical context. In a recent speech, Summers reminded his audience that there have always been skeptics. Back in the heyday of the Cold War, the skeptics, influenced by college textbooks such as Nobel laureate Paul Samuelson's *Economics*, were convinced that the Soviet Union's GDP would overtake ours by the mid-1980s based on relative "growth rates in the 1950s."[1] They were wrong. Then, in the early 1990s, the skeptics believed the articles that appeared in prominent business journals predicting that Japan and Germany would be the dominant post–Cold War economies.[2] They were wrong again.

Today, the skeptics are warning that we're losing out to the emerging Asian giants. The manufacturers I met on my travels, however, refuse to accept second place. Whether they're owners, workers on the factory floor, or middle managers, they work hard and refuse to quit. Every day they strive to develop new ways to compete, on their own initiative and by listening to their colleagues' ideas, in a nation that gives them the freedom and the space to do so. If you want to know the secret— the reason it's not wise to bet against America in the long run— it's in their spirit. Their spirit, fostered in a democratic culture that values the creativity of ordinary women and men, sets America apart as the *entrepreneurial nation*.

These manufacturers help explain why, against all odds, our nation held the global lead over China in manufacturing output until 2009.[3] What's extraordinary is that our aggregate output remains competitive with China's, even though the sector constitutes only 10 percent of our economy compared to nearly 40 percent of theirs.[4] We are a global leader, in part, because our labor productivity (the value that a worker produces annually) is more than six times as large as China or India's and significantly larger than Japan's or Germany's.[5] Strong productivity has enabled the United States to increase its manufacturing output over the past 30 years to a greater extent than any other developed nation, more than doubling in size.[6]

By sharing success stories, I make the case that American manufacturers often have an advantage over their competitors in more authoritarian or bureaucratic nations because participatory governance is preferable to top-down governance, even in the business world. The best American manufacturers consider the intellectual contributions of all their employees. As a result, they provide those employees with healthy work environments and encourage them to be critical and divergent thinkers. Their inclusionary approach enables them to make high-value products through customization, economization, and incessant innovation. This bottom-up philosophy also gives rise to organic clusters that drive collaboration and nurture the entrepreneurial spirit in places like Wichita and Silicon Valley.

The most forward-looking American manufacturers, moreover, are exporting aggressively, overcoming archaic World Trade Organization rules that put them at a tax disadvantage. In certain instances, their diverse workforce is an asset for winning customers in a global economy. Some have even adopted sophisticated metrics to justify domestic production, starting a trend toward onshoring. These metrics include improvements in quality measured through customer satisfaction surveys,reductions in labor hours and shipping costs, and increases in speed to market. The metrics help these companies look beyond labor costs, which usually constitute less than 10 percent of a product's total cost, in site selection.

The news, though, isn't all positive. We shouldn't delude ourselves into a false sense of complacency. Although American manufacturing output continues to increase, the sector's growth rate has declined significantly throughout the last decade and has lagged behind China's.[7] And while our share of world manufacturing is declining, China's share is growing. Our leadership is at risk in a world that has become increasingly competitive. Our businesses are facing foreign competitors of unprecedented scale that are the beneficiaries of unprecedented subsidies. My reporting of the competitive advantages of American manufacturers, therefore, is balanced with an account of their policy requests to be better equipped and unleashed. To paraphrase Winston Churchill, if we give them the tools, they will do the job.[8]

For generations, the American people would have considered it self-evident that the nation should support manufacturing. Our founders spoke not only about government safeguarding liberty, but also about government promoting private industry. In 1791, Alexander Hamilton, our first Treasury secretary, presented to the U.S. House of Representatives a "Report on Manufactures" that opens with the observation that the "expediency of encouraging manufactures in the United States . . . appears at this time to be pretty generally admitted."[9] Hamilton went on to note that "not only the wealth, but the independence and security of a country, appear to be materially connected with the prosperity of manufactures." His insight that American manufacturers require the "aid of their own government" in light of the "artificial encouragements" that foreign governments are offering indigenous manufacturers is perhaps truer today in the age of globalization than it was in his own time. Even Hamilton's ideological rival Thomas Jefferson, a proponent of an agrarian economy, came to appreciate this perspective. After conflicts with the British over trade, Jefferson wrote that "experience has taught me that manufactures are now as necessary to our independence as to our comfort" and that America "must endeavor to make everything we want within ourselves."[10]

Hamilton's report influenced perhaps the two greatest American statesmen of the nineteenth century: Henry Clay, the speaker of the House of Representatives and senator from Kentucky, adopted many of Hamilton's recommendations in his "American System" economic plan. This included the creation of a national bank that provided financing to businesses and federal investments in infrastructure to promote industry and agriculture.[11] Abraham Lincoln subsequently invoked both Hamilton and Clay in putting forth his platform that government should promote the development of technology, invest in infrastructure, and provide land grants to educational institutions that promote the "mechanical arts."[12]

Government support for manufacturing continued throughout the twentieth century. In the 1920s, President Calvin Coolidge, though an eloquent advocate of the ideals of limited government, supported policies to promote manufacturing, specifically in aerospace. He signed the Air Commerce Act of 1926, which established an Aeronautics Branch within the Department of Commerce to "promote air commerce."[13] Government funding for aviation escalated dramatically during World War II. President Roosevelt and President Truman authorized billions of dollars for the development of Boeing's B-29 and B-52 military planes, and, according to historian Alan Milward, war spending also led to unprecedented output increases in aluminum, steel, shipbuilding, and munitions.[14] When Japan later became an economic competitor, the Reagan administration confronted its unfair trade practices on "cars, steel and computer chips" and launched Sematech, a program that provided government funding to semiconductor manufacturers to develop technology.[15] President Reagan spoke about "guaranteeing that government does everything possible to promote America's ability to compete."[16] At the turn of the century, President Clinton recognized that to compete in a global economy, America had to "concentrate on high-end manufacturing."[17] His administration increased the loans available to innovative small and medium-sized manufacturers through the Small Business Administration and aggressively enforced trade agreements.

Most recently, President Obama has argued that the financial crisis happened because we got away from "basics."[18] He has called for a renewed focus on manufacturing, emphasizing the need to "build things better, make things better, right here in the United States" to win the future.[19] His belief that "government still has a responsibility" to help American manufacturers compete is consistent with the values that have defined our nation since its founding.[20]

Throughout the book, I'll draw on America's history to show that the policy recommendations of today's manufacturers are grounded in bipartisan precedent. These proposals may be tailored for our time, and in some cases they may go beyond what any administration—including the current one—has introduced. But they bear a resemblance to what has gone before. Whether the calls are for tax and regulatory reform, leveling the playing field, or strategic federal support, they're in line with the economic principles that helped make us an economic superpower. Polling suggests that the majority of American people want a national manufacturing strategy.[21] We don't need to look to the East, which boasts models of excessive state intervention and central planning, to construct one. Rather, we have to listen to those in the trenches and study our own past. As Richard McGregor, the Washington bureau chief for the *Financial Times*, brilliantly puts it, "America's problem is not that it does not work like China. It is that it no longer works like America."[22]

I'll also discuss the libertarian orthodoxy of those policy makers who seek to abandon America's heritage of supporting private manufacturers, such as Senator Rand Paul. Senator Paul and his followers take their bearings more from Ayn Rand and Friedrich Hayek's work than from American governmental documents, letters, or speeches.[23] When Senator Paul claims, for instance, that "Commerce's main function is delivering corporate welfare to American firms that can compete without it" and recommends slashing the cabinet agency's budget in half, he's repudiating economic principles dating back all the way to Hamilton. He's explicitly repudiating the Coolidge and Reagan administrations' use of the Commerce Department to assist industry, whether aviation or semiconductors.[24]

Unfortunately, some contemporary economists are also questioning our manufacturing tradition. Their ranks, which include Jagdish Bhagwati and Robert Reich, claim that manufacturing has become passé, more infatuation and political romance than smart economics. Let America become a service economy, they argue, turning out writers, graphic designers, programmers, bankers, lawyers, and nurses. Bhagwati claims that we shouldn't have "a preoccupation with manufacturing industries . . . at the expense of more innovative and dynamic service sectors."[25] Reich believes that it's not worth "creating or sustaining" manufacturing jobs because they're largely "routine" and can be automated.[26] He, like Bhagwati, would rather we grow our service sector, convinced that it offers more "analytic" and "innovative" jobs.[27]

While their scholarship is worthy of respect, Bhagwati and Reich undervalue manufacturing. They are right that America should be proud of its service economy and should help prepare its citizens to do complex jobs in fields such as information technology, healthcare, and finance. We should not favor manufacturers at the expense of other dynamic growth sectors that will generate, in their judgment, the lion's share of future employment. But we should not forsake manufacturers either. Instead, we should listen to economists, such as Clyde Prestowitz, who have long argued that we ought to be strong in both services and manufacturing. It's not a binary choice.

As I traveled the country, I learned that manufacturers remain at the cornerstone of our economy and our national security, and are indispensable to American greatness. Pundits and politicians alike are, of course, fond of glibly proclaiming our greatness, but this book makes an effort to do the homework, to shine the spotlight on those who help substantiate that claim and who show us the way forward.

1

Spurring Innovation and Economic Growth

■ ■ ■

Andy Grove, the former chairman of Intel, explained to me why manufacturing is essential for American innovation. Mr. Grove is an icon in the technology field, and I felt comfortable addressing him only by his surname. Born to a middle-class Jewish family, he survived the Holocaust and emigrated from Hungary to the United States in 1957 to escape the Soviet invasion. He was the third employee hired by Intel in 1968, and he rose to become its CEO from 1987 to 1998. Under his leadership, Intel's market capitalization grew from $4 billion to almost $197 billion, and the company became the largest computer chip maker in the world.

When Mr. Grove wrote a provocative cover article in *BusinessWeek* warning about the loss of manufacturing jobs,[1] I sent him a note requesting a meeting, not expecting a reply. But Mr. Grove was intrigued that someone in the administration was paying attention, and took me up on my request to meet. So, I became his guinea pig for getting his message across to Washington.

Mr. Grove's office is surprisingly humble. At first, I walked by his two-story building because it had a vacant ground floor. After checking my BlackBerry to confirm the address, I decided to wander upstairs, where I found his office next door to a local travel agency. When I walked in, Terri Murphy, Mr. Grove's sole assistant, greeted me warmly and introduced us, before asking if she could run to the deli to get me a sandwich for lunch. All I could do was insist on paying because of ethics laws. The entire scene was a contrast with Washington, where a bevy of aides typically guard access to the principal and office suites for even undersecretaries and assistant secretaries can be the size of spacious living rooms.

Mr. Grove didn't waste time on pleasantries. He got right to his point: Were we all asleep in Washington? Did we even *track* how many jobs were being offshored every month? I told him sheepishly that we didn't have that statistic. He remarked with some disbelief: "If you don't measure that, how can you possibly expect to keep jobs here?" He then added, "If you don't measure something, you certainly won't achieve results. If you do measure it, you may achieve results."

After expressing his frustration, he asked me what I hoped to get out of the meeting. Sensing that there wasn't much I could say that would give him confidence, I thought the wiser course would be to ask him for his perspective on manufacturing. He's now a professor at Stanford, and he slowly opened up as if I were one of his students.

One of his legacies at Intel, I learned, was requiring that all research and development work be done with real-life manufacturing constraints. He didn't believe that researchers should dream up proposals in their own cubicles without experimenting, in real time, on whether those proposals worked or their cost implications. That's why he mandated that there be a single product team composed of both design and manufacturing. This simple organizational precept helped spur Intel's technological success. Mr. Grove was one of the first leaders in Silicon Valley to recognize that there must be constant dialogue between designers and manufacturers because innovation requires tinkering and trial and error. Steven Johnson, an incisive writer on technology, observes that today, Apple has a similar philosophy, requiring its design and manufacturing groups to "meet continuously throughout the product development cycle, brainstorming, trading ideas and solutions, strategizing over the most pressing issues."[2]

When manufacturing goes overseas, Mr. Grove cautioned from his own experience, design follows. New products are likely to be invented in the places where current ones are being made. Mr. Grove's argument is corroborated in the recent pages of the *Harvard Business Review*. Professors Gary Pisano and Willy Shih, who have written for the *Harvard Business Review*, observe that the offshoring of semiconductor manufacturing to Asia put American companies at a disadvantage in developing solar panels.[3] Once the process for turning "crystalline silicon into wafers" for semiconductors moved overseas, Asian countries had a head start in making solar panels using crystalline silicon and in attracting talented engineers for this new industry to their shores. Andrew N. Liveris, the CEO of Dow Chemical Company, makes a similar point in his recent book *Make It in America,* an account of why manufacturing matters now more than ever.[4] He cites Mr. Grove approvingly, and observes that Dow Chemical has no choice but to build some research facilities close to factories that are outside the United States because the company cannot "afford to separate innovation from manufacturing."

What, then, about Jagdish Bhagwati's claim that the service sector is more innovative? Mr. Grove shrugged at the relevance. The service sector may have more innovation per dollar invested than manufacturing, since manufacturing has high capital costs. That means that our country should certainly provide further incentives for service innovation. But it doesn't follow that we should write off the manufacturing that currently is responsible for the vast majority of our innovative activity. Macroeconomic facts support this view. Manufacturing today accounts for 70 percent of the nearly $250 billion of business research and development spending annually.[5] With that type of private investment, it's no wonder that almost 90 percent of U.S. patents involve a manufacturing component.[6] According to a recent survey by the National Science Foundation, over a two-year period, 22 percent of manufacturing companies reported innovations (defined as new or improved products or processes), compared to only 8 percent of service companies.[7] Manufacturing companies are those that turn raw products into finished goods, whereas service companies perform some activity for a customer.

Mr. Grove's central message is that the bulk of American innovation is rooted in a culture of close collaboration between designers and producers within businesses that encourage experimentation and that this culture is worth preserving for our own economic vitality. Offshoring, even if it is cheaper at times, may not facilitate the same level of breathtaking technological progress that has been America's gift to the world. While we may not want to single out individual manufacturers for special treatment, our nation must retain a threshold of manufacturing capacity if it is to continue to invent new products.[8] This does not mean that our government should implement policies to shift "consumption dollars from services, which Americans want, to goods which they don't want quite so much," as columnist Steve Chapman properly cautions against.[9] Rather, we should provide foundational support for American manufacturers so that they, as opposed to foreign firms, are capable of meeting the *existing* consumer demand for goods. As Mr. Grove observed, the "physical proximity, face-to-face contact, and organizational proximity" of design and production within the open American ecosystem has resulted in unparalleled breakthroughs that have improved the human condition.

When I mentioned the economist Robert Reich's arguments downplaying manufacturing, Mr. Grove smiled politely and said that the Commerce Department should be listening to people who have lived the innovation process. He didn't understand why the Commerce Department wasn't taking the lead in articulating and implementing an American competitiveness strategy. The last such effort was in the mid-1980s. From his perspective, the Commerce Department was a chronic underperformer, led in recent times by political hacks or bureaucrats, from one party or the other, who simply didn't get it. For a brief moment, I had a feeling that he would have fired us all if he could have. Instead, he sought to inspire. He looked at me and asked my age. "Thirty-three," I volunteered. "Your compatriots are in Afghanistan risking their lives. Take a risk in public service. Do something bold for the country. If we don't figure out how to keep manufacturing here, we may see unemployed Americans marching in the streets. Do you know what can happen to a free society when there is mass unemployment?"

I was struck by Mr. Grove's historical perspective. He didn't take what we have in America for granted. He shared ideas, which I discuss later, about providing manufacturers with access to capital and "importing jobs." But more than learning about any specific policy proposal, I left his office convinced that we need to listen to the Andy Groves of this country, including the less famous men and women who actually make products or run businesses.

REBALANCING OUR ECONOMY

While I was out to see Andy Grove, I also visited Stephan Crawford, our local Department of Commerce office head in San Francisco. Stephan is a fun guy to be around. He crams scores of facts into a few minutes of conversation when he talks about his work, and you quickly get the sense that he loves his job. He told me how privileged he is to visit Silicon Valley companies every day and help them increase their market shares. I wish more Americans could meet federal civilian employees like Stephan, because, by and large, they'd be impressed by their passion and competence.

Stephan explained why we need manufacturing if we are to reduce our large trade deficit. Since 1970, our nation has run trade deficits that, in 2009, stood at nearly $375 billion.[10] That means that we're spending $375 billion more helping to fuel economies overseas than we're earning to fuel our own economy. The only way to bring our economy in balance again is to export more and import less. And the way to export more is to make more things in America, because manufactured goods are 60 percent of our total export base.[11] We may be leading the world in manufacturing, but given our country's consumer needs, we need to make even more domestically. It really is that simple. It's more arithmetic than econometrics.

Bhagwati would advise us that we should place greater emphasis on service exports, where we have a comparative advantage, and there's no denying that these should be maximized.[12] Our service industry is made up of financial wizards, software designers, and movie directors who are technologically savvy and, arguably, some of the most creative minds in the world. But the reality is that most international trade is still in goods. In 2009, our total trade deficit with China was more than $220 billion, despite our having a service trade surplus of $6 billion.[13] In other words, we had a goods trade deficit of more than $226 billion. We can't balance our books simply by selling more financial instruments, software programs, and Hollywood movies to the world. The money we earn from so-called knowledge work isn't enough to make up for what we spend buying overseas products. In fact, Nobel laureate Michael Spence and Professor Sandile Hlyatshwayo have pointed out that in order to reduce the trade deficit, we need to expand "value-added" manufacturing activity in the United States in addition to growing our service sector.[14] As they observe, most of the U.S. employment growth over the last two decades has been in the nontradable sector, and we need to find ways to increase our competitiveness in the tradable sector.

Stephan knew the statistics concerning trade because it was a constant topic of conversation with his Chinese counterparts. Several times a year, he would get together for lunch with officials at the Chinese consulate to discuss business trends and plan joint events to strengthen the bilateral commercial relationship. During their conversations, the subject of manufacturing would invariably come up. One of the commercial officers at the Chinese consulate would try to get Stephan to agree that it would be a good thing if the U.S. economy became service-based and China did the manufacturing. This happened year after year, even though the personalities at the consulate changed. You've got to hand it to the Chinese for being on message. Stephan, of course, would make it clear that running structural trade deficits wasn't acceptable.

After every meeting, he would go back to his office motivated to identify new start-up clients with a U.S. manufacturing strategy and to help them grow and export.

CREATING GOOD-PAYING JOBS

Soon after my San Francisco trip, I met John Jelacic, a senior economist at the Commerce Department, who helped prepare economic briefings for senior staff. The high unemployment numbers made these briefings painful. Secretary Gary Locke would often remark that we were the lucky ones, since we had jobs. Many of those briefings felt like being called into the principal's office for a poor report card. Sitting through them, I realized that I had to round out my theoretical knowledge of economics with facts. So I sought out John to get some concrete figures about manufacturing in our economy. John has been in the department analyzing these numbers for more than 30 years. Like many career civil servants, he's careful not to offer an unsolicited opinion. But he was pleased to share the knowledge that he had accumulated over his career, and he helped me analyze public data and prepare statistics for many of my speeches.

John pointed out that the weekly wage in manufacturing is currently more than 20 percent higher than the weekly wage in the service sector.[15] At a time when many Americans are anxious that wages aren't keeping up with rising gas and food prices, manufacturing jobs still provide a pathway to the middle class. The majority of these good-paying jobs are in transportation equipment, chemical products, metal, machinery, electronic devices, plastics, furniture, coal, processed food, and apparel. Some of them are in emerging industries, such as clean tech and biotechnology. This is not to say that manufacturing jobs pay better than service-sector jobs in finance, information technology, or healthcare. But when you take the average salary based on the entire range of jobs in each sector, manufacturing comes out ahead.

In any case, the relevant question is not whether manufacturing workers or nurses will be a "more valuable economic asset" 10 years from now, as thoughtful skeptics of the recent fuss over manufacturing have provocatively asked.[16] We may very well need more nurses than we do autoworkers in a decade, considering the growth of the healthcare sector. However, it would still be foolish for us to cede our competitiveness in manufacturing and sit idly by as other nations aggressively grab these good-paying jobs. Michael Lighty, the public policy director for the California Nurses Association, observes, "Workers in the service sector have a real stake in expanding manufacturing, since it is those jobs that provide living wages and good benefits and fuel spending throughout the economy—particularly in healthcare."

Manufacturing has not always paid well. The "real wages of manufacturers rose by more than 30%" in the 1950s and 1960s after the introduction of collective bargaining and after many strikes in the steel and auto industries.[17] It's no coincidence that Marvin Miller, the brilliant tactician who helped baseball players make more than a meager salary, began his career as a leading organizer for the United Steelworkers of America. Since the hard-fought labor battles in the 1950s and 1960s, the manufacturing wage has been more reflective of the value that workers provide. The labor movement also helped secure healthcare benefits and retirement plans for workers, which are necessary given the physical toll of decades spent on a factory floor.

In recent years, there has been downward pressure on wages because of globalization and lower unionization rates.[18] While wages in other nations have gone up, the real wage, adjusted for inflation, of American manufacturing workers has stagnated. As the *Washington Post* columnist E. J. Dionne pointed out to me, there also has been polarization between high-wage and low-wage manufacturing jobs. Some folks on the high end may be doing better than ever, but the lower-end jobs do not pay as well as they used to. It's no longer accurate to say that all manufacturing jobs can support a middle-class life. That said, the average real wage is only slightly off its 1970s high.[19]

The bottom line is that the American labor market still rewards people with mechanical aptitude. I met many employers who would prefer to hire someone with practical know-how rather than someone who has a general education but no experience. This often comes as a surprise to freshly minted college graduates. In my generation, many people attended schools that emphasized theory but didn't teach us how to put things together or take them apart. We relied on AAA to fix our cars. Our science labs and machine shop classes often faced budget cuts, and there was a view that we could simply think our way to employment. As a result, we lack awareness about the indispensability and complexity of the trades. In fact, in private conversations, union leaders observed wryly that younger staffers in the White House were unable to describe what a machinist actually does.

That's not to say that we should make light of higher education. Many manufacturing jobs, including those of machinists who operate sophisticated tools to make precision metal parts, require computer proficiency and a facility with math. Back to E.J.'s observation, the more education someone has the more likely she is to snag one of the higher-paying manufacturing jobs. Also, the unemployment rate is about half as high for those with college degrees as for those with just some college or a high school diploma.[20] So there's no denying that young people ought to pursue as much education as they possibly can.

But, as a nation, we can't afford to discount the importance of hands-on technical skills. These skills are an asset for engineers, scientists, or even intellectual property lawyers who will participate in the production process. They also may qualify a young person with a natural talent and affinity for making things for a job on a factory floor. These jobs shouldn't be looked down upon as second tier. They are professions—not just vocations—with contributions that are on a par with those of doctors, lawyers, or financiers. If someone has a calling to pursue a craft, we owe him or her the proper public education and our respect.

THE CURRENT STATE OF MANUFACTURING EMPLOYMENT

In the span of a couple of hours, John Jelacic provided me with a basic tutorial on manufacturing employment in America. The sector has been losing jobs. The reason is that the rate of growth in manufacturing output has declined sharply, from nearly 3.5 percent a year in the 1990s to merely 0.8 percent a year since 2000.[21] The lower growth rate hasn't kept pace with increases in productivity. As a consequence, manufacturing jobs, which peaked at 19.6 million in 1979, today stand at about 11.8 million, constituting about 10 percent of our total workforce.[22] Anyone who works at a facility that's engaged in the production of a physical product, whether an engineer, a designer, or a floor operator, is classified as a manufacturing employee. The majority of the workforce is Caucasian, with African Americans constituting about 10 percent and Hispanics about 15 percent.[23] The most dramatic job losses have taken place in this century.[24] Manufacturing is no longer as significant a share of our economy as it once was, declining from nearly 28 percent of our GDP in the late 1940s after World War II to about 11 percent.[25] We now devote less of our GDP to manufacturing than every other industrial nation except France.[26]

If John Jelacic provided a statistical overview, Bob Baugh, executive director of the AFL-CIO Industrial Union Council, brought home for me what these blows to manufacturing mean for American workers.

I confess that I didn't notify my superiors about this meeting. In Washington—a city that is fond of silos—it's unorthodox for a Department of Commerce official to meet with an AFL-CIO representative. Labor unions are supposed to meet with the Department of Labor, even though that agency is limited primarily to the enforcement of laws and regulations. Business executives are supposed to meet with the Department of Commerce, as if only businesses have a stake in economic strategy. That's just how it's always been. One of the common pieces of advice I got from old Washington hands was, "Stay in your lane, young man." If the private sector rewards "out of the box" thinking, Washington often expects regurgitation as the norm for career advancement. Follow instructions; don't make waves; keep your head down—that's the motto among insiders. It's something that I didn't like and never got used to.

Bob Baugh, equipped with a number of articles, including some of his own, met me for lunch at Old Ebbitt Grill, a popular Washington spot adjacent to the White House. While he was more jovial than Andy Grove, Bob reminded me of him in one key respect: both men shared the same sense of urgency. Bob started by letting me know that over the past decade, nearly 57,000 manufacturing outfits have closed, resulting in the loss of nearly six million jobs. Although manufacturing jobs have led the recent recovery, growing at the fastest pace in nearly a decade, they were among the hardest hit by the recent Great Recession.[27]

As Bob sees it, the loss of manufacturing jobs over the past decade is a national crisis. "Our nation cannot bleed manufacturing jobs and expect to have a middle class," Bob declared. This isn't just a labor issue—this is about the American way of life. We discussed that even Jeff Immelt, the chairman and CEO of General Electric, a company that hasn't shied away from outsourcing, has recently embraced this view. Immelt gave a high-profile speech at the Detroit Economic Club arguing that manufacturing jobs are "high-value-added jobs" and should be "no less than 20% of total employment, about twice what it is today."[28]

What Bob finds most concerning are the unfair trade practices of other nations, mainly China. China's regime plays by its own rules, providing indefinite subsidies to state-owned manufacturers, manipulating its currency, and restricting access to its large market. These practices make Chinese exports cheaper and limit American imports, producing what Nobel laureate Paul Krugman considers an "artificial" Chinese trade surplus.[29] By Bob's estimation, China's artificial trade surplus accounts for millions of American jobs lost.[30] In fact, almost half of all the trade cases investigated by the Department of Commerce involve Chinese firms, for which Bob seeks more vigorous prosecution. He wants tough sanctions levied *and* enforced when firms are found to be in violation of international rules. He also wants the Treasury Department to explicitly label the Chinese government's currency manipulation an unfair trade practice. Such a pronouncement would signal to the Chinese that we're serious about the issue, putting soft pressure on the regime to change its behavior rather than risk punitive measures.

Bob's views cannot be caricatured as protectionism, as they reflect a considered judgment that market-distorting policies are hurting the standard of living *both here and abroad*. Paul Krugman has argued that China's cronyism for its elite companies undermines not only American workers but also China's own consumers.[31] Chinese policies may help select exporters, but they lead to lower real wages and higher prices.[32] An American trade policy that takes a hard line against egregious instances of state favoritism or manipulation will benefit not just American workers but also the Chinese middle class. As a nation, we should have no tolerance for xenophobia or for the stereotyping of Asians, such as in Senate candidate Pete Hoekstra's recent Super Bowl ad.[33] But we should stand firm for a fair trading regime that can lift the middle class both here and in the rest of the world.

Bob's punch line came at the end of our lunch. "Do you know that our guys aren't even on your department's advisory committees that are shaping our national economic policy?" I was shocked. Do we not want Bob Baugh and Jeff Immelt exchanging ideas? One of the major reasons that there has been gridlock in Washington is that labor and business aren't at the same table. If we can't bring business and labor together on Department of Commerce committees, what hope is there for the type of Camp David summit between business and labor to discuss the "economic rebirth for the 21st century" that Thomas Friedman envisions?[34] A few of us young guns went up and down the Commerce building arguing that we needed to open up these advisory committees to labor. It takes about 15 "concurrences" to make any change in a Washington agency; 15 individuals have to sign off on anything—even for something as simple as changing one of your subordinates' titles or responsibilities. Despite the cumbersome "concurrence process," the recommendation to open up a few of these committees has reached the secretary of commerce. It's now in the hands of the secretary to recommend the changes to Congress, and for Congress to concur.

THE FUTURE IN AN
AGE OF AUTOMATION

When I suggested to a friend of mine who is a partner at a white-shoe venture capital firm that our country should expand our manufacturing workforce, he remarked, "I would have expected more intellectual honesty from you. A few months in Washington and you're already spewing political propaganda."

My friend went on to make a version of Reich's argument that the decline in manufacturing jobs in the United States is inevitable because of automation. As factories employ the latest technology, productivity improves, and there's no need to employ many workers, so the argument runs. Reich makes the analogy between manufacturing and agriculture, which a century ago employed "almost 30% of adult Americans" and today employs "fewer than 5%." He observes that factories can become fully automated, with only two employees being needed to instruct "400 computerized robots." As he puts it, "Factory jobs are vanishing all over the world."[35]

Reich's observations, however, don't ring true for many contemporary manufacturers. Foxconn, the tech-savvy Chinese company that manufactures many iPhones and iPads, employs *more than a million workers*. In the city of Shenzhen itself, the company has a campus one mile wide and one mile long that houses a 400,000-person workforce.[36] Manufacturing jobs are declining, but they certainly aren't "vanishing" in China, which still has nearly 100 million of them, more than all the G8 nations put together.[37] We are far away from a world in which computers and machines can take care of all our manufacturing.

Even in the United States, there are downsides to blanket automation. It's often cost-prohibitive to automate the final stage of assembly. That's why Boeing, one of America's most highly automated companies, still employs thousands of people for precision work. A number of U.S. corporations, moreover, are beginning to recognize that machines don't always improve productivity. Consider General Electric's Louisville, Kentucky, factory, where water heaters, dryers, and refrigerators are made. The company plans to hire nearly 1,000 new workers in the next couple of years. When I was down there, Earl Jones, a senior executive, shared why: "People often do it better than machines. They can think, and they can make things better." He elaborated that with machines, you have a fixed process. If there are mistakes or changes that need to be made, it's very costly. With a dynamic and portable workforce, on the other hand, it's easier to tweak production to improve a product or prevent defects. During one of his walkthroughs of the Louisville facility, he noticed an individual who was boxing water heaters and asked his floor manager why this function wasn't automated. The manager replied that the worker was faster and was less likely to scratch or dent the water heaters.

We also can't discount the small and medium-sized businesses that create about half of all manufacturing jobs and make up more than 90 percent of U.S. manufacturers.[38] They are often supplying to niche markets or creating new products that don't yet have established demand. Typically, the size of their market isn't big enough to justify automation. So, many small and medium-sized businesses continue to require skilled workers.

A final retort to Reich is that, historically, economists have overestimated how much technology displaces workers. Most famously, John Maynard Keynes predicted in 1930 that technological progress would result in an average workweek of 15 hours, and that we would all be spending most of our time in leisure.[39] Keynes turned out to be spectacularly wrong about this. The manufacturing workweek remains at more than 40 hours.[40] There seems to be an insatiable need for more sophisticated, cooler-looking, and faster gadgets. The time saved through automation probably leads to a larger basket of goods and more experimentation, as opposed to fewer work hours. Put differently, we may need fewer workers to make any given product, but there will be many more products to make.[41]

Recognizing that the brave new world has a place for workers, Peter Drucker, the renowned business guru, estimated that manufacturing was unlikely to "shrink as much as a producer of wealth and of jobs" as agriculture.[42] He understood, as Krugman observes, that complex manufacturing jobs that "can't be carried out by following explicit rules" are "hard to automate."[43] As a consequence, Drucker projected that by 2020, manufacturing in most developed countries would still account for at least "10-12% of the total workforce."[44] That doesn't live up to Jeff Immelt's vision of a 20 percent manufacturing workforce, but it's far more than Reich's minimalist expectations.

Regardless of whether Drucker's projections are the final word, what we can safely say is that there will be millions of manufacturing jobs in the twenty-first century. The question is whether America will get its fair share. As Thomas Friedman observes, many manufacturers have global supply chains, and see their products as "Made in the World."[45] The challenge for our government, then, is to attract as much of that supply chain to be within our borders. Instead of casting all the blame on robots for any decline in our manufacturing workforce, we'd be better served by looking at what types of manufacturing jobs are sustainable in the United States, how we create them, and how we prepare our citizens to fill them. We should take heart from the recent Boston Consulting Group report prediction that by 2015 the United States has the potential to add up to 3 million manufacturing jobs.[46]

PROTECTING OUR NATIONAL SECURITY

When I joined the Obama administration, I didn't think that helping manufacturers had anything to do with national security. That changed during the Gulf oil spill in the spring of 2010. At Commerce, we were scrambling to offer services to businesses and residents who had been affected by the calamity. The experience showed me just how closely our nation's safety is linked to manufacturing.

A few weeks into the crisis, I called to say thank you to Jeff Sponseller, executive vice president of Miller Weldmaster. Miller Weldmaster, a client of our Cleveland office, was supplying oil containment booms to Louisiana to help with the cleanup. Sponseller explained that the company wouldn't have been able to supply these boons in time if it had been manufacturing outside the United States. It was able to set up production of oil boons for Louisiana within five days because it had the knowledge and technology in Ohio. Critics of the need for a strong manufacturing base sometimes argue that we can create the "factories and equipment that we need" if there is a crisis, in much the same way that we have "mobilized for war" in the past.[47] But the reality is that during national emergencies, as the experience with the Gulf oil spill highlights, time is of the essence. When there's a threat to our homeland, we need to have manufacturing capacity in the United States so that we can respond quickly and decisively.

Once I began to pay attention to the national security angle of my work, I visited General Lawrence Farrell, CEO of the National Defense Industrial Association (NDIA). I asked him whether the loss of manufacturing was harmful for our national defense. General Farrell cut right to the point with the authority one would expect from a general. We can't have the world's most advanced military without having a strong industrial base, he said. Although U.S. defense contractors can subcontract routine parts overseas, no other nation is going to hand us the latest technology to update our warplanes and tanks. Just as we restrict the export of sensitive technologies, other nations place similar restrictions on selling certain goods to us. He cautioned about the time it takes to develop technologies that are ahead of the curve. It's naïve to assume that we could develop this capability immediately prior to a war. The best technologies require years to perfect before being operational.

A limited manufacturing base also puts us at risk during wars that have large equipment needs. For example, at the beginning of our misguided foray into Iraq, we didn't have enough small-caliber ammunition. The Lake City Army Ammunition Plant in Missouri was the sole source for such ammunition, and that plant could not meet our army's needs.[48] As a result, we had to rely on Great Britain, Israel, and South Korea to supply our troops with ammunition.[49] There's no guarantee that in future wars, these nations would be in a geopolitical position to come through for us. As a rule, the more defense manufacturing we have in the United States, the more secure we are.

After making his case, General Farrell asked me in good humor, "Why does agriculture, which is 3 percent of our economy, have its own cabinet agency? But manufacturing, which is at least 10 percent of our economy, has no cabinet agency? The best I can do is talk to someone at your rank in the International Trade Administration!" One of my colleagues actually had the title deputy assistant secretary for manufacturing in the International Trade Administration, which is about five levels down from the cabinet and a blip in the gargantuan executive branch bureaucracy.

THE GLOBE MANUFACTURING STORY

As the months in Washington passed and the unemployment rate refused to go down, I found myself channeling Andy Grove, Bob Baugh, and General Farrell; I became an evangelist for manufacturing. Whenever I traveled, I made a point of seeking out interesting manufacturers and paying close attention to what they had to say. The Department of Commerce's engine is with our field staff. While senior staff members in Washington are a good resource for understanding the strategic challenges for the American economy, our field specialists and commercial officers spend the majority of their time helping actual businesses across the country. I would always count the days before I could get on the road.

On one of my trips to New Hampshire, I met Robert and George Freese, brothers who are fourth-generation owners of Globe Manufacturing Company, which was founded in 1887. Anyone who thinks that all garment manufacturing has gone overseas would marvel at the sight of hundreds of men and women operating advanced sewing and cutting machines in Pittsfield, New Hampshire. The Globe factory floor is the largest in the world for making protective clothing for firefighters. As I walked through, it dawned upon me that I was seeing a part of America that most Americans don't get to see. The image of that bustling factory floor in a quaint town during the picturesque New England fall stuck with me and, in some sense, inspired this book.

Two days after 9/11, the entire Globe company came together to do its part for our nation. On Thursday morning, Rob Freese received a call from Captain Dean Cox of Fairfax County Fire and Rescue Department. Captain Cox was in the Pentagon parking lot at the command post, participating in the rescue efforts to extinguish the roof fire in the building, stabilize the support pillars, and remove hazardous debris. Captain Cox told Rob that the company's crews had been able to work through the night because of the Globe coveralls they were wearing. These coveralls had been specifically designed to protect firefighters from environmental hazards, including chemical and blood-borne pathogens, and to keep them warm for long durations during disasters. Captain Cox informed Rob that other crews who didn't have this protective gear were inadequately shielded from weather and chemical elements and were too exhausted to work through the night. He asked Rob how many suits the company had, and Rob said that he would get back to him within the hour.

Rob took a quick inventory, then called Captain Cox back to let him know that the company had 300 suits. Captain Cox immediately said that he would take all of them. Rob told Captain Cox to fax the sizes that he wanted. Captain Cox, after consulting with command staff, said that there was no time to have the suits tailored. He needed them immediately. He said, "We'll take all of them. Have them here by 6 p.m. tonight." When Rob explained that with the airports closed, this would be nearly impossible, Captain Cox simply told him to figure it out and have them there on time.

Globe rose to the occasion. Rob first called New Hampshire Fire Marshal Don Bliss, who arranged for a FedEx

Cessna cargo plane. The plane would receive "mercy flight status" from Manchester, New Hampshire, to Washington, D.C., at a time when all other commercial planes had been grounded. Once Globe had secured a plane, it had to transport the suits to the Manchester airport within a couple of hours. So Rob summoned Globe's few hundred employees, and they began to pack the suits in boxes. The employees used a utility truck, which they managed to borrow from Barnstead Fire-Rescue, and company vehicles to transport the boxed suits to the airport. Because almost every person at Globe lent a hand, they had all the suits at the Manchester airport by 2 p.m. that day.

Then the Globe employees watched with pride as Rob took his seat as copilot on the FedEx plane. Rob remembers that the plane took a direct route to Washington, DC, over the sobering Ground Zero site in New York City. It was the sole commercial aircraft in the sky at the time. The local distributor, Maryland Fire Equipment, was waiting for the plane at the airport, and the suits reached the Pentagon parking lot around 6 p.m., as requested. A new crew of firefighters was able to use them for the night shift. Rob and many employees at Globe still find themselves getting a catch in their voice when they recount the incident. As Rob put it, "I always love my country, but that day was special. I was a proud American that day! We were thankful that we at Globe could rise to the occasion."

Globe came together that day because it has always been more of a family than a company. This struck me when I met Harriet, an elderly lady who was doing quality control. Harriet has been on Globe's factory floor for 40 years and bought her house right next to the company's headquarters. When Rob introduced me to her, he greeted her with the tenderness one would show toward a great-aunt. In fact, Rob and George made small talk with almost every employee we passed on the floor. The workforce constitutes about 10 percent of Pittsfield's total population. As is probably apparent by now, the Freese brothers, whose father was a longtime public servant in New Hampshire, have a strong civic sense. They know that their city depends on them.

How, then, do the Freese brothers keep manufacturing in the United States and beat competitors in Canada and other nations that have cheaper labor, and also compete with other domestic manufacturers? They make and sell high-value products. Quality matters. I can't tell you how many foreign buyers I met at domestic trade shows who were willing to pay for the "Made in America" label because, in their minds, it ensures excellence. But creating high value in today's economy also requires customization, economization, and incessant innovation.

The first advantage that Globe enjoys in creating high-value products is *customization*. As George Freese put it, "You can't develop tomorrow's products behind a desk." Globe takes pride in talking to each customer, listening to that customer's unique needs, and then designing a fire suit that meets those needs. The suits will vary in color, in style, in tailoring in terms of pocket or name placement, and in the types of specialized gear requested for particular environmental conditions. For example, Globe recently added reflective striping on some of its suits to aid in night visibility based on the request of a fire station. The company worked with the client to determine where best to place the striping on the suits. On average, Globe makes only eight suits that are identical, even though there are almost 30,000 fire stations in the United States, many of which are Globe's customers. Globe's approach is the antithesis of mass manufacturing.

Specialized customer service is something that foreign competitors find difficult to match. Globe develops long-term relationships with customers by engaging them throughout the production process. The company is timely and responsive in all its customer interactions. Logistical barriers make it difficult for an overseas company to develop the same kind of customer relationships. Foreign competitors may be able to undercut Globe in price, but they have a hard time gaining the business of those customers who want to have an ongoing say in the product's very design. Customization is one reason that Globe has more than a third of the American market for fire suits.

Globe also creates high value through *economization*. By eliminating waste and reducing labor time, Globe ensures that a product has high value per dollar spent for its creation. People often think that improvements in the production process require heavy investments in the latest technology. But for Globe, the best process improvements come from employee ideas.

Rob Freese encourages every employee to share his or her ideas, and he provides generous rewards for employees whose ideas are implemented. He receives scores of such ideas every year. One of the most helpful suggestions came from Barbara Lee, a stitcher. Barbara suggested that Globe stitchers should use a smaller needle on a new fabric that provides additional protection for firefighters. The new fabric isn't as forgiving as most of Globe's other fabrics, and needle holes on it are much more visible. Prior to Barbara's suggestion, Globe was throwing out the material any time the stitchers made mistakes. Once Globe stitchers began using a smaller needle that made a smaller hole, they were able to restitch any problem areas without having to throw out the expensive material. Barbara's idea saved both time and money, increasing the value per dollar spent of the new fabric fire suits. In Rob Freese's eye, Barbara wasn't some replaceable drone, but someone who was capable of making a contribution.

Perhaps the most important Globe strategy for creating high-value products is *incessant innovation*. As Rob Freese put it, "85 percent of the product that goes out the door did not exist seven years ago." By continually commercializing new products, Globe stays one step ahead of its competition. The idea is to sell products that no other competitor is even making. Cheaper labor costs become irrelevant if a buyer can't find a substitute product in Canada, China, or Mexico.

Globe doesn't consign innovation to a department with a discrete budget and discrete tasks. Rather, it's a way of life for every employee at the company. George Freese, who describes himself as a "typical New England tinkerer," leads this charge. He isn't an engineer by education, debunking the myth that innovation is the exclusive domain of high-tech PhDs. Instead, George has a knack for playing with designs and making things with his hands. He worked with other employees to design fire suits that included a harness with a rope to scale buildings and to escape from high floors. The rope is tucked neatly into a pocket to minimize discomfort for the firefighter, but is still easy to deploy.

Globe also recently brought in Mark Mordecai, who has more than a dozen patents in technical garment solutions, to work with other employees in designing the fire suits of the twenty-first century. Mark's team is working on making suits with advanced sensors that are capable of relaying biomedical data to the command center. The command center could use these data to figure out how best to contain the fire while protecting the safety of individual firefighters on the front lines. Globe is collaborating with North Carolina State, Worcester

Polytech, and the Federal Emergency Management Agency (FEMA) on the sensor projects.

Globe's strategy of customization, economization, and incessant innovation does not in and of itself explain its success. Strategic plans often are not worth the paper they're printed on. I know this from my time in the federal government—creating a strategic plan is the favorite pastime of many Washington bureaucrats. The hard part is executing that strategy. How did Globe get its employees to execute? This question played back and forth in my mind as I walked the factory floor.

As I was about to leave, I met a young lady who was exposing new fire suit prototypes to intense heat to make sure that they held up. I asked her what it was that she liked about her job, and she told me about the day when two firefighters from the Norfolk, Virginia, fire station made the trek to New Hampshire to visit. They were convinced that the Globe suits had helped save their lives during a major fire. The young lady remembered that the two firefighters had taken the time to thank each and every employee personally. "I'm sorry," she said, slightly embarrassed by her show of emotion in front of our small delegation, "I remember them bringing the burnt suits by and the expressions on their faces." And then I knew. I knew why each Globe employee gives it his or her all. They all believe that what they do matters. The young lady's comments captured a defining quality—the "it" factor—of every successful company I visited. Each has a conviction that its work makes a difference in people's lives.

This book, then, looks to manufacturers such as Globe as models of American entrepreneurialism. The claim is not that the specific manufacturers profiled are the nation's best, but rather that they embody the values that set American manufacturers apart. No one can predict with certainty whether these particular manufacturers will succeed in the long run.

What matters, though, is that they are experimenting with how to compete successfully in the global economy, and in so doing, are helping to chart a course for our economic future. Like the 2011 Chrysler Super Bowl ad showcasing Detroit's resilience, their stories touch a nerve and show us that we can still be a "nation of makers."[50] By persevering through adversity, by soldiering on, they renew America's promise for this new century.

2

Taking the High Road

■   ■   ■

When asked about my job at the Commerce Department, my brother liked to joke, "He travels around the country and gives awards to successful American manufacturers. My tax dollars at work!" Highlighting success stories was a small part of my job, but it often got the most attention. The company I was visiting would typically have a large sign welcoming me. I would then be escorted to a conference room, where everyone from the CEO to employees on the assembly line would be gathered, cameras in hand and families nearby, awaiting my remarks. There was often a trip to the factory floor—and the greatest insult to a manufacturer, I quickly learned, was to rush through or skip any part of the tour.

At first, I felt guilty because these companies were going to so much trouble. But, over time, I came to appreciate the importance of my visits. It meant a lot to manufacturers, who didn't choose a life of making fast money, to be acknowledged for serving the national interest. As one of them described it to me, "Somewhere at the bottom of all the Ponzi schemes that we read about, someone has got to make stuff."

I also realized that a growing number of American manufacturers are challenging the idea that outsourcing to Asia is a presumptive competitive advantage. Whenever CEOs told me that they were moving overseas because of their *fiduciary* obligation to investors, I'd gently push back. "Come travel with me for a week and meet manufacturers who are making things here. You may not agree with their judgment, but you should be aware of their way of doing business."

Those who manufacture in the United States are almost defiant in their pride. One of the favorite articles circulating among this group distinguishes between "high road" and "low road" manufacturing.[1] Dan Luria, research director at the Michigan Manufacturing Technology Center, and Joel Rogers, a professor at the University of Wisconsin, argue that "high road manufacturing" is "'advanced' or 'high end' and certainly 'modern' in its use of equipment, marked by relatively high investments in training and new technology, dedicated to continuous process improvement and product innovation, covering some portions of design as well as production, and compensating its workers much better." High-road manufacturers compete in the global economy by creating high-value products—products that have a high revenue-to-cost ratio. In contrast, "low road manufacturing" is "typically low-paying, unsafe, environmentally degrading, marked by little investment in new training or new technology." Low-road manufacturers fall victims to the competitive pressures of globalization because they fail to modernize and simply sell commodity products.

This chapter looks at how American businesses take the high road through customization, economization, and incessant innovation, and analyzes the federal policies that can support them. The discussion centers around two real-life manufacturers that are succeeding: Vitamix and Steel Dynamics.

THE VITAMIX WAY

There's a myth that America can compete only by leading in new industries, such as clean technology or biotechnology. The truth is, though, that American manufacturers compete in many sectors. For instance, have you ever asked yourself where the blenders that make your Frappuccinos, smoothies, and frozen lattes are manufactured? You might think China, Mexico, or South Korea, but it turns out that high-end coffee shops around the world have blenders that are made in Cleveland, Ohio, by a company called Vitamix; the blenders preparing your $4 frozen coffees and smoothies are currently made in the United States.

The Premium Coffee Shop Challenge

So, now you may be wondering whether Starbucks and other leading coffee chains are doing you a disservice by not importing cheaper blenders and, in turn, charging less for their coffee. Is Vitamix to blame for the few bucks you spend every day because of your Starbucks addiction? Absolutely not. If Starbucks were to get cheaper blenders, you would be less likely to buy its coffee, and, to boot, it would be unable to reduce the price. That's the counterintuitive yet persuasive argument that Vitamix representatives make to the executives of the top three coffee chains. Vitamix doesn't just show up at Starbucks headquarters with one of its blenders and assume that Starbucks should buy it because of its technical superiority. Rather, the company *customizes* its blenders to address Starbucks's business needs and enhance the Starbucks brand.

And just how does a company like Vitamix customize blenders? First, it studies the customers and operations of the largest chains. It learns the biggest complaints, challenges, and opportunities that each company has. For example, Vitamix has found that lower-cost competitive equipment does not deliver a consistent brand experience and yields beverages with ice chips. These ice chips make it difficult for the customer to use a straw and, in general, distract from the blended beverage's texture and taste. So Vitamix designs blenders with custom programs that leave no ice chips. Second, high-end coffee shops want customers to linger in their stores longer. Vitamix helps them meet this objective by minimizing the noise distraction of its machines, making its blenders almost half as loud as the cheaper blenders on the market. Finally, all top brands want to reduce wait times for customers. As a response, Vitamix has created technology that enables stores to reduce blend times. The combination of durability, reliability, and reduced blend times results in lower repair and replacement costs, resulting in a lower total cost of ownership over the life of the blender. In sum, the Vitamix blender is actually helping to lower the cost of your frozen treats and smoothies, while making them with less noise, greater speed, and better texture.

Vitamix's example illustrates the benefit of involving customers in the design and fabrication of products. Because Vitamix takes this approach, more than 85 percent of its customers report being "extremely satisfied" or "very satisfied" with its products. Customer satisfaction, not labor cost, is the company's driving metric. Vitamix's value comes not just from making technically good products but also from solving its clients' problems. The company is proof that today's manufacturers also need the vision to be service providers, consulting on design.

Promoting a Service Culture

So far, I've explained Vitamix's business approach theoretically. But providing excellent customer service isn't just a motto for Vitamix; it's the culture. To give you a sense of this culture, let me share a bit about Jodi Berg, the company's president, and the employees at the Cleveland headquarters and manufacturing plant.

Jodi represents the fourth generation of the Barnard family. Her great-grandfather decided to locate the company in Cleveland after participating in the Great Lakes Exposition, the World's Fair in the late 1930s that drew millions of visitors, and the business has grown steadily since then. Under Jodi's leadership, Vitamix has experienced some of the best years in its history, hiring and expanding its facilities.

I met her for the first time in 2009 at the ceremony for the Presidential Export Award, which is given each year to about 25 of the nation's top businesses that excel in making products at home to sell overseas. Instantly, Jodi stood out in a room full of mostly male award winners. I got to experience her brilliance at crafting a value pitch firsthand. When I asked her what makes her blenders special, Jodi didn't talk about durability or horsepower—the type of jargon that would have gone over my head. Instead, she suggested that her blender could help the first lady achieve her goal of reducing childhood obesity. If schools had Vitamix blenders, Jodi explained, kids would be able to get their servings of fruits and vegetables in flavorful concoctions of soups, sauces, and juices. The blenders would make healthy eating fun. When I confessed that I often got pizza on the way home, Jodi suggested that a Vitamix blender would be good for my own nutrition, given my busy and unpredictable schedule. She even began suggesting cooking recipes that I could use. I was half-tempted to order a blender from her on the spot.

Sensing that she had my interest, Jodi handed me a binder to give to the first lady with her plan for a national rollout of Vitamix blenders at schools. I didn't have the heart to tell her that the closest most presidential appointees ever get to the White House residence is when they sign up for one of the publicly available White House tours. Rather, I promised her that I'd do my best and would be in touch.

After a few months of not being able to get the first lady's attention, I called Jodi to check in, lest she think that the Department of Commerce was blowing off a Presidential "E" Award winner. Somewhat sheepishly, I proposed visiting to congratulate her employees. Jodi was enthusiastic that I was offering to come to her home turf, and she volunteered that the company's success has a great deal to do with Clevelanders being "all-around fabulous people." She didn't mind that the first lady wouldn't be accompanying me. So I called up Todd Hiser, our local Commerce official in Cleveland, and told him that I was flying out. We drove together to the Vitamix headquarters, which is in Olmsted Township, right outside of Cleveland.

The facility, encircled by forest, belies the typical image of manufacturing plants as dirty and polluted; the place feels more like a fitness center than a factory floor. The first thing you notice when you park is the long walking trail and the scattered picnic benches. The main building relies mostly on natural lighting, and it is colored beige so that it melds with the surrounding trees. Inside, there's a lunchroom that serves healthy meals, an exercise room supporting various wellness programs with opportunities for cholesterol checks and nutrition classes, and a very open office environment and assembly plant, including a Silver Leadership in Energy and Environmental Design

(LEED)–certified warehouse. The assembly floor has no grime or soot, and its air has some of the freshness of the surrounding woods. As a whole, the Vitamix facility conveys to workers, from the moment they arrive, that they aren't expendable cogs.

I walked through the assembly floor to congratulate each of the employees, and it quickly became apparent that Jodi's sales skills had rubbed off on them. They talked about how the Vitamix blender has improved their own diet: sure, the blender may help make Frappuccinos, but it can also be used to make alternatives to junk and processed food.

The employees, like Jodi, are proud of their city and believe that "Made in Cleveland" still means something. As they see it, Cleveland is the best place to set up shop because Clevelanders are "hard-working," "modest," "decent," "friendly," and "loyal." A worker in her early twenties who had finished eight hours on the assembly line making sure each blender had an appropriate box drew nods of approval when she credited "the midwestern work ethic" for the uniqueness of the Vitamix brand. Pride in local manufacturing isn't just a midwestern phenomenon; it's a trend that's emerging in cities across the country, from New York to San Francisco.[2] This trend has been dubbed "geographic ingredient branding," a sophisticated type of customization.[3] The idea is that the very culture of a city differentiates the products made there, catering to a particular set of customer expectations or preferences.

In addition to displaying pride in their work, Vitamix employees define their roles and responsibilities broadly. I saw some employees contributing to client pitches, while others were engaged in debate about whether a particular change in the production process would improve the blender's quality. Almost all spoke knowledgeably about how different blender designs serve different client needs. These manufacturing employees are technicians, salespeople, and business strategists rolled into one.

Jodi later explained that employees grasp the big picture because they participate in profit-sharing plans and have an upward pathway to become line leaders or production supervisors. They receive healthcare benefits and good wages and have collaborative relationships with management. Evaluation is based not just on how many hours they log but also on their initiative. The company even provides incentives for them to pursue a college education because, as Jodi puts it, "the more active the brain, the better a person functions." Vitamix understands what Robert Reich's theories miss: "knowledge work" is part and parcel of modern American manufacturing, as opposed to a class unto itself.

Living Up to the Vitamix Standard

I suggested to Jodi that she go on the lecture circuit to share how a manufacturing company can compete in a commodity market by creating higher value. But she, like most manufacturers, has her hands full with her own business. This is where the federal government can come in. The Manufacturing Extension Partnership (MEP) is a federal program with 60 centers across the United States and almost 1,400 field staffers that help small and medium-sized manufacturers improve their competitiveness. One of its recent successes is Schramm, Inc., which is based in West Chester, Pennsylvania. The company, as I'll detail in a later chapter, made and exported the drilling rigs that helped save the lives of Chilean miners.

Roger Kilmer, the director of the MEP, refers to the program as the "best-kept secret" in the federal government. He came to see me a few weeks after my trip to Vitamix. When I told him that every manufacturer in this country should spend time with Jodi Berg, he suggested that a reasonable alternative is for them to seek out an MEP professional. MEP professionals aren't recent MBA graduates, but industry veterans who have a track record of modernizing manufacturing plants. They work with manufacturers to improve every aspect of their businesses, from customizing products, to identifying markets, to training employees to craft value pitches.[4] At reasonable fees, the MEP helps nearly 33,000 manufacturers become more competitive every year (a little over 10 percent of the nation's 330,000 manufacturers).[5]

The MEP program isn't the brainchild of liberal Democrats. Rather, it's a program rooted in Hamiltonian philosophy and implemented by Republicans. As Hamilton argued, it's difficult for businesses that are accustomed to traditional practices to make the "transition to new pursuits" quickly or to make the "most obvious improvements."[6] These businesses require the "incitement and patronage of government" to produce "desirable changes."[7] That's precisely what the MEP program does. It helps our manufacturers make the transition to high-value production. The program was established in 1988 by the Trade and Competitiveness Act, signed by President Reagan. Although Democratic senator Ernest Hollings was a "key supporter" of the idea, the "single, most early proponent" was Sherwood Boehlert, a Republican member of Congress from New York.[8] Other early supporters included prominent Republicans and Democrats, such as Representative Don Ritter (R., PA), Representative Manuel Lujan, Jr. (R., NM), Senator Jeff Bingaman (D., NM), and Representative George Brown, Jr. (D., CA).[9]

Despite its Republican origins, today members of the House Republican Study Committee are proposing to eliminate the program entirely.[10] They argue that a "robust commercial market" already provides the services of the MEP program and that we should leave it to the private sector.[11] The cochairs of Obama's deficit commission have also recommended that the program be eliminated.[12] The program costs about $120 million, accounting for less than 0.1 percent of our federal budget. It's the *only* federal program specifically designed to assist manufacturers, and it's frankly part of the Reagan legacy. Yet somehow it's ended up on the chopping block.

Programs such as MEP are under attack in Washington because of a vocal minority—led by former majority leader Dick Armey and Senator Rand Paul—who believe that government programs almost always impede rather than promote economic growth. In Armey's view, only "incompetent" companies need help from the government.[13] Armey, an economist, doesn't invoke conservative American political leaders to defend this position. Both he and Senator Paul label any government initiative to boost private industry as corporate welfare. Rather, he's explicit that his "intellectual gantry is substantively the Austrian School of Economics," particularly Ludwig von Mises and Friedrich Hayek.[14] He also credits Ayn Rand as being foundational to his political perspective.[15] Armey now chairs a political organization called FreedomWorks that's pushing the ideology of thinkers like von Mises, Hayek, and Rand. Incidentally, FreedomWorks was an early backer of Senator Paul.

The Austrian School of Economics and Ayn Rand's objectivist worldview may be nice in theory, but here's the reality on the ground: China's government isn't sitting on the sidelines. Neither is India's, nor Brazil's, nor Japan's, nor Germany's, nor South Korea's. In some cases, foreign governments are providing their manufacturers with rent, land, worker training funds, capital infusions, and on-site consultants. In other cases, foreign governments are collaborating with companies on research and technology development. So the real question is whether our government can afford to unilaterally sit it out. No one is suggesting that we engage in tit-for-tat behavior and provide ongoing market-distorting subsidies, artificially devalue our currency, or select winners and losers. But that shouldn't stop us from supporting promising American manufacturers in developing the basic strategies that they need if they are to compete. Regardless of the utopian visions of Frederick Hayek and Ayn Rand, practical statesmen such as Hamilton and even Reagan have understood that ideology must never trump national interest, and that our nation has a stake in helping our businesses—particularly our small businesses—navigate the global economy.

But what about the cochairs of President Obama's deficit commission, who argue that MEP isn't necessary because "similar programs are provided by the private sector"? This stance is misleading. Most small businesses cannot afford the rates charged by companies like McKinsey, Monitor Group, or Bain. I've yet to meet a small business owner in this economy who has extra cash lying around to retain a private consulting company.

Like Dick Armey, the cochairs also argue that the MEP helps "inefficient companies." Roger Kilmer, the head of the MEP, would dispute that characterization and would point out that its services result in more than $3.6 billion in sales every year, and are responsible for more than 52,000 jobs. That said, the program mustn't take on any company that's a lost cause, one lacking a path to profitability. The program is designed to help manufacturers *make* improvements, *not* to provide them with indefinite life support. Regionalization is also paramount. MEPs shouldn't be micromanaged by a centralized Washington bureaucracy. Rather, the office directors of MEP centers across the country should be empowered to meet the local needs of manufacturers.

In general, customer survey results show that manufacturers that enroll in the MEP program recognize its value and go on to succeed. Most of them advocate that the government should open more MEP centers to serve a greater percentage of the nation's manufacturers, including those located away from urban centers. That's why President Obama proposed significant increases for the program in both his 2011 and 2012 budgets.[16] If anything, President Obama doesn't go far enough. What's required is for Washington to double funding for the MEP program so that every competitive American manufacturer has access to the program's services. Such an investment would still pale in comparison to the investments that Japan or Great Britain is making in helping to improve the competitiveness of its manufacturers. (Japan invests $2 billion annually in its Kohsetsuhsi centers, and the United Kingdom $400 million in its Technology Strategy Board.[17]) The MEP program is the least we can do for our manufacturers in light of what the rest of the world's countries are doing for theirs. It is not a magic wand. But, at its best, it can guide these companies to become the Vitamix of their respective industries.

STEEL DYNAMICS SHINES

The last 50 years of global competition in steel can be summed up simply: we, with limited exceptions, opened our markets to the world, while the rest of the world closed their markets to us. Our steel production during World War II was so dominant that we've had open markets for most of the twentieth century. The rest of the world, though, chose a different course. Almost every other country heavily subsidized its steel and engaged in protectionism. Both Japan and Germany subsidized their steel during their respective heydays, which lasted up through the 1980s. They also had an advantage in building, with our support, their postwar steel industry from scratch. Therefore, they were able to adopt certain new technologies earlier than we did, such as a basic oxygen furnace that reduced the time it took to produce steel compared to "traditional open hearth technology," which we were using until recently.[18] Today, China, our largest competitor, provides "its steel companies with financial subsidies, cash grants, land grants, conversions of debt to equity, debt forgiveness, preferential loans and tax incentives."[19]

If China isn't playing fair, then what's the state of U.S. steel manufacturing? That's the question I posed to Tom Sneeringer, a senior executive at U.S. Steel. Tom has devoted his life to the steel industry. He visited with the hopes of finding an ally in the administration and shared that the road for American steel companies has not been easy. Still, there are reasons for cautious optimism.

Tom explained that during the beginning of this century, the market was flooded with cheap steel imports, forcing companies to race each other to the bottom in terms of pricing. Many steelmakers, including giants like Bethlehem Steel, declared bankruptcy, resulting in thousands of jobs being lost and retirees losing their healthcare benefits.[20] At this point, President George W. Bush issued a temporary 20-month tariff to slow the influx of cheap, subsidized imports and allow the steel industry the time to restructure.[21] With the cooperation of visionary union leaders such as Leo Gerard, consolidated companies that adopted the latest technology and business practices emerged.[22] The industry saw a few years of very strong productivity growth.[23] Then, during the Great Recession, many of our mills went idle again because of declining demand, and thousands of steelworkers stood in food lines once more and faced personal bankruptcy.[24]

Today, the industry is slowly rebounding. In fact, nearly 80 percent of the steel that Americans buy every year is now made in the United States.[25] The price of steel is nearly three times as high as it was in 2001, and a larger percentage of American mill capacity is being utilized.[26] While China produces nearly 500 million tons of steel a year compared to our 80 to 100 million tons, the vast majority of China's production is for its own market.[27] We get only 2.2 percent of our domestic steel from China, only 1.8 percent from Japan, and 0.74 percent from Germany.[28]

A Modern Hero Starts Steel Dynamics

If you want to understand why American steel is back, it is because of people like Keith Busse. Keith has helped to shape the modern American steel industry. In fact, he's something of a celebrity in Indiana and in the steel world (you know someone is good when his competitors, in this case Tom Sneeringer, mention him positively).

If you suggest that he came from limited means, Keith will correct you and say "abject poverty." Even though he was "accepted at Purdue University" to become an engineer, his family couldn't afford the tuition. He put himself through school to get an accounting degree by "pumping gas and unloading tires and batteries."[29]

But Busse didn't give up on his dreams of making things and becoming a businessman. As a hobby, he bought a gun store that was making a few thousand dollars a year and turned it into a million-dollar business. At the same time, he accepted an entry-level position at Nucor, a steel manufacturer, and worked hard climbing "through the ranks."[30] While he was there, he helped build the first minimill for flat-steel products in Crawfordsville, Indiana, which was a historic accomplishment for the industry.

Minimills allow steel companies to make steel from recycled scraps instead of raw materials. For many decades, they were used only for long-steel products, such as beams that go into skyscrapers and railroad rails. After the Crawfordsville plant was completed, though, minimills began to be used to make flat-steel products that go into automobiles, tractors, and appliances.

Busse's insights from nearly two decades ago, when he was leading that project, still resonate: "I sometimes think Rome is burning and we don't see it. Sometimes it seems that everybody coming out of school wants to go to Wall Street or be a lawyer. Many in this country are gravitating to service jobs. We're a nation of ambulance chasers! How can you fix something if you don't know it's broke?"[31]

After nearly 21 years at Nucor, Busse, along with two of his colleagues, left to found Steel Dynamics in Fort Wayne, Indiana. Today, Steel Dynamics is the nation's fifth largest producer of carbon steels, with annual revenues of $8 billion and nearly 6,000 employees. During the Great Recession, Steel Dynamics weathered 2009 with minor losses and actually posted profits in 2010 and 2011, unlike most of the other U.S. steelmakers. It's arguably the most profitable American steel company in terms of margins. Steel Dynamics isn't unionized, but its workers are among the best paid in the steel industry. Bob Baugh, the head of the AFL-CIO Industrial Union Council, recognized Keith Busse as an advocate for a prosperous America.[32] He explained that the union or nonunion status of a firm doesn't get in the way of the common work of creating domestic manufacturing jobs.

The Most Productive People

Keith Busse is in his element when he's around cars that he loves. The evening before my visit to the Columbia City, Indiana, mill, Keith invited me and some of my Commerce colleagues to join him for pizza and beer at the Auburn Cord Duesenberg Museum in Auburn, Indiana. The museum, which used to be an automotive factory, is a national treasure, featuring some of the first cars and luxury vehicles ever made. Our tour guide explained that during the early 1900s, Indiana rivaled Michigan as the automobile manufacturing center of the nation. One of the museum's sections had Keith's Corvette collection on display. Keith confided that he'd wanted to own these cars since he was in high school. Back then, he would fix them for rich high school kids who had no idea how they functioned. Today, he owns more than 45 of the most gorgeous collectible Corvettes, painted in bright and bold colors.

Keith and I had spoken on the phone once before. Though he was a hard-nosed industry veteran, Keith always took a warm tone with me. Perhaps he considered our conversations to be an opportunity to pass down knowledge to my generation about what he and his colleagues have been through to preserve the American steel industry.

"I think we rested on our laurels for too long after World War II. The lightbulb didn't go off until the mid-1980s that we'd failed to modernize. At that time, much of our product was being imported from Europe and Asia. That's when we started building minimills and using recycled scrap. These minimills, along with a new operating culture, helped us gain a competitive edge."

Keith emphasized that Steel Dynamics *economizes* production in its flat-steel minimills, thereby creating high-value products while lowering costs. The company is always striving for ways to improve efficiency. The key metric is labor hours. It takes Steel Dynamics about 0.25 labor hour to make a ton of steel. It has helped set the standard for others in the American steel industry, which has come a long way. Four decades ago, it took the average American steel company about 6 hours per ton of steel. Today, the American average is about 2 hours per ton of steel, slightly better than the Germans and Japanese, who are between 2 and 3 hours. How do the Chinese fare? Keith estimates that the Chinese are probably closer to 8 to 10 hours per ton of steel. That means that Steel Dynamics is about 40 times more productive than the average Chinese steelmaker.

Keith credited business strategy and technology, in part, for this advantage. On the strategy front, Steel Dynamics was shrewd in acquiring a scrap metal processor to supply materials to its mills. By integrating the supplier of necessary materials, the company ensured the stability of its supply and lowered the price of inputs. On the technology front, in the mid-1990s, Steel Dynamics was at the forefront of developing thin slab casting. The company continues to have the most modern tools in its mills.

But, as Keith put it, "anybody can buy the tools." What truly distinguishes Steel Dynamics is "world-class employees who are the most productive people." It also helps that Keith has created a culture that rewards productivity. These employees are able to multitask, as opposed to being assigned a single task or a single function. Keith pays them well: $30 an hour plus benefits as a base wage and generous bonuses. He boasted that they're the best wage earners in the steel universe. They're also driven by incentives: if they perform well and reduce production time, then their pay reflects that. If the company makes profits, they see more take-home pay. The company didn't lay off a single worker during the economic downturn; instead, it reduced hours. Steel Dynamics's philosophy is that the investment in its labor force makes business sense. As Keith put it, "We ask our employees to tell us what we are doing wrong and to speak up if they think we are not making the right manufacturing decisions."

When I asked whether Keith could foresee the production process being fully automated, he laughed politely. It must have come across as an almost nonsensical question to someone who has spent his life worrying about the safety of real men and women who are exposed to 3,000-degree heat in the mills. "Steel is always going to require people," he replied. "I doubt we are going to get much leaner than today. You reach a point of diminishing returns with automation." He went on to note, "Steel Dynamics has nearly 6,000 employees, and we'll always need people running cranes, melting, casting, or operating the computers that manipulate the production process." He then got a bit reflective, "In this country, Dick, Mark (his cofounders), and I had the freedom of opportunity. We chased the American dream and took the risk of building a steel mill. We hope to continue to grow, to employ even more people, to build new mills. We may never need as many people as U.S. Steel, but we'll continue to create jobs."

Introducing Superior Products

Keith is an *incessant innovator*. He's always thinking ahead. He's mindful not to make the mistake of the dominant steelmakers of World War II, who assumed that their companies' current advantage would last forever. He monitors how much the company innovates every year and how quickly it markets new products.

As its latest example, Steel Dynamics recently invested almost $20 million in its Columbia City facility to make rail for train tracks. It's the only American rail-making mill. We wore hard hats, earplugs, eyeglasses, protective gloves, and an overcoat as we walked through the mill, which stretched a few miles. Every hundred feet or so were signs saying "danger" or "caution: radioactive material." There were a smattering of

American flags hanging from casters or cranes. The first thing we observed was the melting of scrap into molten iron. There were large electrical furnaces shaped like pillars that heated the scrap, with orange sparks flying. The workers were in a pulpit, a viewing room that had a few flat-screen monitors and large windows, directing the machinery. They explained that during the melting, there sometimes is a mini-explosion because of water in the scrap, and the windows get smashed and the entire building shakes. Making steel is not for the faint of heart. We saw the molten steel being poured into casters, washed with water at a pressure of 3,000 pounds per square inch, rolled, flattened, and saw cut. There were men holding "torches," which are *Star Wars*-like lasers heated to 3,000 degrees, cutting the steel bars to the proper size. The bars were melded together and shaped to become rails.

Steel Dynamics's Columbia facility can make 240-foot rails, which is revolutionary. Usually, railroads will buy a 1,600-foot rail string to lay on a track. This means that Steel Dynamics requires only 6 welds to make the string. In contrast, conventional steel producers can make only 80-foot-long rails, requiring 19 welds to produce a 1,600-foot string. The welds are typically the weakest points on the track, most susceptible to derailment and wear and tear.

By reducing the number of welds, Steel Dynamics is able to provide railroads with rail that's safer and that has less maintenance cost. This is particularly important at a time when our nation is considering expanding and upgrading our railroad infrastructure. The demand for freight transport is expected to double by 2035, from 19.3 billion tons to 37.3 billion tons, and rail expansion is necessary to prevent our highways from becoming more congested.[33]

It's no easy feat to produce rail strings that are three times as long as the industry standard. The Columbia City plant requires specialized cranes and material-handling systems. The welding plant also is three times longer than standard, requiring four times the capital expenditure. Steel Dynamics's decision to make this up-front investment at a time when most other steelmakers were struggling to stay out of the red demonstrates its commitment to innovation. Steel Dynamics did not hoard its cash, as many other Fortune 500 corporations have done, to ride out the volatile times.[34] Instead, with typical daring, Keith Busse's company stuck by its philosophy that "introducing superior products" to the market is the smart long-term bet.

Standing Up for American Steel

So what business threats keep Keith Busse up at night? His primary concern is China. The weakness of the yuan allows Chinese steel companies to charge an artificially low price in the United States. As a result, China can sell cheap consumer products made of Chinese steel, reducing the domestic demand for American steel. But the greater danger is if China faces a downturn. As Keith explained to me, China's capacity is almost 600 million tons of steel a year, but it is producing only 500 million tons. China's steelmakers, therefore, are focused largely on supplying the country's own market. But what happens if Chinese demand falls, and the country is left with excess capacity? The proper course for China would be to restructure and close its older, inefficient mills. But no one believes that the Chinese would do that. The worry, then, is that they would dump their excess steel into the United States.

China has already announced an aggressive "going abroad" strategy, flush with subsidies, to establish an overseas presence for its steel industry.[35] As an initial response, the U.S. Commerce Department has imposed duties on Chinese steel pipes to prevent Chinese companies from building market share by selling at prices below fair value. The Chinese complained about these duties whenever they came for bilateral meetings. At one holiday party, I learned what these bilateral meetings were like. After having had a few glasses of wine, a senior administration official involved with the Chinese trade talks told some of us how Ambassador Ron Kirk used the James Baker style of negotiation with his Chinese counterparts. James Baker was the former secretary of state under President George H. W. Bush, and his brand of diplomacy is legendary. The method was crudely described as luring a puppy with a bone and sweetly saying, "Aw, come here, boy, come here, boy," and then as soon as the puppy is within arm's length—*BAM*—knocking the daylights out of him. Put more academically, our negotiators can often lull their counterparts with a false sense of comfort before making their points or demands.

Ambassador Kirk apparently used a mild form of the Baker method on the Chinese. First, he asked what U.S. trade practices the Chinese found objectionable. China immediately complained about our duties on steel. Big mistake. Ambassador Kirk is said to have pounced: "Well, there are at least five steel plants in the United States that will be operated by Anshan Iron and Steel Group, a Chinese company. How many U.S. firms are able to operate steel plants in China? Zero. You don't allow even one of our steel companies to do business in your country." The Chinese reportedly didn't bring up steel again in that meeting; the point had been made. China should be the last nation with the moral authority to lecture the United States about our actions concerning the steel industry. Keith Busse would have approved, and would have urged our negotiators to be equally firm on the currency issue.

Keith's other concern is access to scrap metal. According to his rough estimates, we export nearly 40 percent of our scrap. In one sense, this is positive: our scrap metal industry generates export revenue that helps lower our trade deficit. However, much of our scrap is going to Turkey, China, and India, and scrap metal is becoming more scarce. If the Chinese and Indian automobile markets continue to grow, there may be additional scrap in the future. The numerous automobiles that will eventually be produced in these countries will lead to more global scrap. But that's not the situation now.

Today, the increasing demand for scrap metal is pushing the price up, raising costs for manufacturers. As a consequence, several countries, such as Russia, China, and the Ukraine, are placing high export taxes on their scrap, claiming that it's important for their strategic interests.[36] Busse doesn't expect that we'll do the same. Rather, he asks for basic reciprocity: America should seek the elimination of export taxes that prevent our manufacturers from accessing raw materials that are necessary for production.

For Keith, international trade issues aren't simply economic abstractions; they're his lived experience. He once went to Russia at the invitation of Boris Yeltsin's government to explore the possibility of a joint venture with a Russian mill. To get to the mill, his bus had to ascend a mountain covered with snow. Hundreds of miles away from civilization, the bus broke down. Some of Keith's colleagues feared for their lives; they were afraid that the Russians had orchestrated a conspiracy to steal their money. Keith dismissed these fears as paranoia. He remained calm, got off the bus, and worked on the spark plugs that had caused the problem. During those couple of hours, Keith didn't think of himself as a multimillionaire or as an official guest of the Russian state. Instead, he remembered the times in high school when he'd fixed his rich buddies' cars. After fiddling with the spark plugs, Keith shut the hood and tried the ignition. The bus miraculously started. By saving the day,

Keith sent a message to his counterparts about American ingenuity and resolve. His toughness without pretension is the disposition that our nation should adopt in trade negotiations.

THE TAKEAWAY

KEYS TO THE HIGH-ROAD STRATEGY

Vitamix and Steel Dynamics are outstanding models for how American manufacturers can compete in a global economy, despite the pressure of cheaper labor abroad, by taking the high road of customization, economization, and incessant innovation.

Vitamix demonstrates the value of customizing products. The company didn't sell generic blenders to Starbucks, but rather customized its blenders to meet Starbucks's business needs. The lesson is that American manufacturers can win out over foreign competitors by engaging their customers in the initial design and production of products. In order to customize, manufacturers must have a creative and engaged workforce, which Vitamix cultivates by providing a healthy work environment and encouraging all of its employees to be active participants in the production process.

Steel Dynamics illustrates the value of economization and incessant innovation. The company can afford to pay $30 an hour wages to its workers because it has higher productivity than its foreign competitors. Meanwhile, it's able to make up for the wage differential with foreign competitors by dramatically lowering the number of labor hours per ton of steel produced. The company also makes innovative products, such as rails that have fewer welds. The strategy of being the first to introduce new products to market gives Steel Dynamics a leg up on its foreign competitors.

Finally, the Vitamix and Steel Dynamics stories suggest that the federal government has a role to play in helping manufacturers become more competitive. Through programs such as the Manufacturing Extension Partnership, the government can assist small and medium-sized manufacturers in developing strategies to customize, economize, and innovate. More fundamentally, the federal government must demand that other nations have a fair currency value and allow reciprocal access to raw materials and to their markets. Even the best American manufacturers need a level playing field if they are to have a fighting chance.

3

The Air Capital
of the World

■ ■ ■

When I told some Washington friends over dinner that I was headed to our Commerce office in Wichita, Kansas, they made good-natured remarks about how I should watch out for tornadoes and bring back plenty of *Wizard of Oz* paraphernalia. I hope these world-traveled and well-educated friends of mine have the privilege of visiting Wichita someday. Because if they do, the first thing they'll notice when they land at the airport is a big sign saying, "Welcome to the Air Capital of the World."

Wichita has an Oz museum, to be sure, but it also happens to be the world's top-ranked aerospace manufacturing hub.[1] The city is home to Spirit AeroSystems, the world's largest supplier of commercial airplane parts and Boeing's primary supplier. It also has attracted Airbus, Boeing's European competitor, which decided to build its largest North American facility in Wichita to design and make many of its wings.[2] Cessna Aircraft Co., Hawker Beechcraft Corp., and Bombardier Lear-jet, global leaders in making private jets, are all Wichita-based companies. In addition to these heavy hitters, Wichita has developed a "network of more than 200 precision machine shops" that are aerospace subcontractors and supply some component airplane parts.[3] You can imagine why Wichitans are fond of saying that almost every plane you fly on has a part that is made in their hometown.

CARROL ANDERSON AND THE U.S. AEROSPACE LEAD

You can't understand Wichita without appreciating the contribution of machinists such as Carrol Anderson. Carrol is the late father of A. J. Anderson, who heads up Commerce's Wichita office. A. J. has a big frame, carries his weight well, and drives a truck. He'd moved back home to Wichita to be closer to his mother. A. J. took me to see representatives of the local machinists before my evening speech, and it was at that meeting that he opened up to me about his father.

I had decided to meet with the machinists after reading the Brookings Institution's "State of Metro America" report, which happened to be the latest buzz at Commerce. The report points out that Wichita has nearly 22 percent of its workforce in manufacturing.[4] That is nearly *double* the national average and represents about the percentage that Jeff Immelt has recommended for the nation. Nevertheless, because of the economic downturn, machinists were facing tough times. Around the country, almost 30,000 machinists had lost their jobs, and in Wichita alone, nearly 13,000 aerospace workers had been laid off.[5] How could a Commerce official go to

Wichita without meeting with some of the workers and their representatives?

So my team in Washington communicated to A.J. that a stop at the machinists was a must, and he was happy to oblige. On the day of the meeting, A.J. and I drove up to a building that could have been mistaken for a local warehouse. Steve Rooney, the president of the local District 70 machinists union, and Ron Eldridge, the national aerospace coordinator for the machinists, greeted us at the front door. Then they escorted us to a sparse conference room with a rectangular wooden table surrounded by hard chairs.

Steve began by letting me know that the comments coming out of the administration and Congress bashing private jets weren't helpful.[6] What bothered him most, he said, was the hypocrisy. While politicians scolded auto executives for flying on private jets, they still used them for their own fund-raisers and travel. Ron chimed in, "A business jet is a tool like a computer is a tool. It's not simply for CEOs. It's also used by a company's logistics folks, by their engineers, and by their accountants to get to places efficiently." Steve and Ron were convinced that the Beltway rhetoric was a contributing factor, along with the poor economy, in the nearly 30 percent decline in private jet orders that had cost thousands of machinists their jobs at companies like Cessna and Hawker Beechcraft.

"Our guys are used to layoffs, but Washington is making things worse," Steve continued. I asked how anyone could be used to getting laid off. Steve explained that aerospace machinists are aware of the cyclical nature of the business. A typical machinist who has a 30-year career may experience four or five layoffs in his lifetime. So, the machinists save up in the good years to survive the year when they may not have a job. I was a bit incredulous. "You mean they know they will be laid off and plan for it?" I asked. Steve and Ron nodded their heads, as if what they were was saying was common industry knowledge.

The talk about the lean years struck a nerve with A.J., who'd been quiet until then. His job was to take notes. He was there as staff. No matter how much I tried to get our office directors to relax during my visits, they were sticklers for protocol. So, it took guts for him to speak up and, more so, to share something personal.

"I remember we couldn't move into a nicer house because Dad might have to take a lower-paying job should he be laid off," he said. "We had to stay in our place, even though it was below what my father could afford. There was always the chance of a layoff."

"What was your father's name?" Ron asked. "I know all the guys who have been with us."

"Carrol Anderson. He worked for years as a mechanic at Boeing before it became Spirit."

"The name sounds familiar," said Ron.

A.J.'s memories of his father and his childhood came flooding back. "We sometimes ate noodles for both lunch and dinner in the layoff years. But you never fully understood how bad money was because parents hide that sort of thing from a kid."

As A.J. recounted memories, Ron and Steve looked at him intently. Neither of them interrupted the momentary periods of silence. They no longer were asserting their grievances against Washington, but were instead processing information about one of their own. They had let their guard down once they knew that A.J.'s father was part of the family.

Carrol Anderson worked for Boeing's Wichita facility for nearly 34 years straight, with the exception of the layoff years. He worked mostly in the departments of Experimental and also Modification, helping to build military planes and Boeing's newest commercial planes. The last thing he worked on before retiring in 1989 was a modification of Air Force One. A.J. remembers seeing it flying around town during test flights, and telling folks that his dad had helped build it. He drove around with friends following the plane in the Wichita sky.

After recalling his father's work on Air Force One, A.J. realized that we were running behind schedule and declared somewhat abruptly, "I am afraid we need to get to our next appointment." Ron handed a card to me and to A.J. "Let's stay in touch," he said to both of us. For my part, I assured Ron that I would do whatever I could to raise their issues in Washington.

When we were back in his truck, A.J. apologized for not having been "professional" at the meeting. I told him not to be ridiculous. If anything, I wanted to learn more about his father. He shared a few more details on our drive to my evening engagement. Carrol, I learned, supported the union, but was generally opposed to strikes because he also recognized that the Boeing machinists were the "best paid in the world." He appreciated the good pay and benefits and knew that it was "one of the best jobs a machinist could have." And so he worked hard from early morning to late in the evening on most days. One winter day stands out. His father came home exhausted, his clothes smelling of fuel. Carrol had been out in the cold the entire day, working.

"I think I knew then that I didn't want the same life," A.J. said, his voice filled with the mix of pride and sadness that overcomes a son who understands, later on, the hardships that his father endured to put food on the table.

It's not just A.J. who owes a debt of gratitude to his father; our nation also does. Wichitans like Carrol Anderson have helped propel America into the lead over every other nation in aerospace manufacturing. Today, America's aerospace industry produces nearly $200 billion a year, which is 48 percent of the world's total output, according to Ronald Green, a senior economist at the Department of Commerce who has spent nearly three decades analyzing such data.[7] This is more than all the nations of the European Union, which, put together, account for only 39 percent of the world's output.[8] The fact is that European nations, even taking Airbus into account, are a distant second to the United States. As for other countries, they barely register as of now. Canada is at around 6 percent, while both China and Japan are at around 4 percent, Brazil is only at 2 percent, Israel is at about 1 percent, and South Korea is at about 0.2 percent.[9]

If every American sector were like aerospace, we would be running huge trade surpluses instead of trade deficits. The industry's trade surplus was nearly $50 billion in 2009.[10] Aerospace helps provide a counterweight, albeit an insufficient one, to the oil and gas sector, which puts us $200 billion in the hole every year, over half our total trade deficit.[11] Remember Stephan Crawford, San Francisco's office director, and his exhortation that we need to grow our manufacturing exports to have any chance of reducing the trade deficit? Aerospace is exactly the type of industry that would get him excited. Stephan would love Wichita.

THE CLUSTER EFFECT

Carrol Anderson and his colleagues, as we have seen, deserve a lot of credit for Wichita's success. Their resilience in the face of layoffs cannot be taught in a textbook or mandated by the state. But individual initiative, while necessary, is not sufficient on its own. Economic history teaches us that the place where someone works also matters. In that respect, Carrol was fortunate to work in Wichita, because he was part of one of America's paradigmatic clusters.

The concept of clusters was on my mind when I landed in Wichita. About 10 days earlier, I had been on a panel with Harvard University professor Michael Porter, perhaps the leading authority on competitiveness, and Lawrence Lessig, the most influential thinker on cyberspace. The panel's topic was strategies for improving American innovation and productivity. To be honest, sitting in Ames Hall at Harvard Law School with these two world-renowned scholars was one of the more intimidating experiences I had during my stint with the Obama administration. Just a decade earlier, I would have been one of the students in the auditorium being subjected to the professors' Socratic method. The academic world now seemed removed. The rambling, three-part questions, the professors' adoring groupies, and the majestic portraits of long-dead luminaries staring down at me were reminders of a past life.

Nonetheless, my trip to Harvard made me aware of the importance of clusters, and on my way to Wichita, I read with interest articles and books that the professors' research assistants had recommended. Professor Porter introduced the cluster concept in the late 1990s. He defines a cluster as "critical masses in one place of linked industries and institutions—from suppliers to universities to government agencies—that enjoy unusual competitive success in a particular field."[12] This is consistent with Lessig's thesis that firms in the same industry benefit when they have spaces for collaboration.[13] Lessig would argue that clusters enjoy a productivity and innovation advantage, in part, because of the collaboration they foster among linked entities.

Lessig's work is related to Steven Johnson's account of "fourth quadrant" innovation, which occurs in places that have "liquid networks" where ideas "collide, emerge, recombine," and where entities can "borrow from one another."[14] Clusters have some fourth-quadrant aspects. For example, companies that are connected to one another in a cluster share best practices and develop common approaches to training their workforces. Their employees meet both in civic associations and in social settings, exchanging ideas about developing new technology in the industry. Although clusters are made up of private firms that often are competitors, these firms don't put up hard walls against one another. While they don't adopt the "open source" environments that are common in academic settings, they recognize that having some spaces for the free flow of ideas and collaboration enhances competitiveness.[15]

Wichita is a real-world example of cluster theory. The city has a network of companies, local universities, government, and nonprofit agencies that collaborate on shared objectives. When it comes to developing Wichita's human capital, the aircraft companies work together. They recognize that 40 percent of the Wichita aviation workforce will be eligible for retirement in the next five years.[16] So, they've partnered with the National Center for Aviation Training on training and internship programs with the hope of turning out 6,000 new skilled workers every year. They also collaborate on research and development. Specifically, they work with the National Institute for Aviation Research at Wichita State University, which is considered by many to be the definitive authority on innovation and research on aircraft structure in the world. Finally, the companies find common cause on many federal issues, such as seeking a presidential visit to the area, increased funding for training, or assistance for laid-off workers during down times.

It's not just the collaboration, though, that would impress a visitor to Wichita. It's the constant conversation about the aerospace industry. The city lives and breathes airplanes. There are associations such as the World Trade Council of Wichita where aerospace leaders meet monthly to compare notes. But the exchange of ideas is not limited to these meetings. Discussions about the latest advances in the industry also take place over lunch at Larkspur, located in the heart of the Old Town district, or at the Scotch & Sirloin after work. You overhear snippets of conversations in shopping centers about Washington's unfair bashing of private jets or how Wichita needs to prevent companies from moving down to Mexico. In other words, there's definitely a fourth-quadrant dimension to the Wichita cluster.

Unfortunately, the public at large isn't aware that Wichita is a center for competitive excellence. Other clusters around the nation also suffer from a lack of mainstream recognition, including Vermont's cheese industry, northeast Ohio's plastics industry, and South Carolina's automobile supplier industry.[17] These clusters deserve our attention, not our indifference. At a time of increasing skepticism about our competitiveness, they remind us of what we do well as a nation and the types of local environments in which entrepreneurialism thrives.

IT'S IN THE BLOOD

A key anchor of the Wichita cluster is Spirit AeroSystems, which was one of A.J. and my first stops after he had picked me up from the airport. The company has more than 10,800 workers who occupy almost six million square feet of manufacturing space. The only way to see the plant is in a vehicle resembling a golf cart. Buck Buchanan, who was the chief operations officer, drove A.J. and me around, carefully staying within the demarcated lanes that crisscross the facilities.

The plant is awe-inspiring. There are rows of gargantuan, aqua blue fuselages, the long body of airplanes, surrounded by fastening machines. Some of the workers are running these machines, while others are on stepladders doing detailed handwork on a part of the body. Then there are folks bonding the composite that goes into the fuselages, and forklift and crane operators moving the composite materials. At the far end of the facility, a team is responsible for the transport of the completed fuselages to the adjacent rail station. The fuselages, I learned, travel by rail from Wichita to Boeing's Renton plant in Washington State. All the current Boeing planes—the 737, 747, 767, 777, and 787—have sections designed and built by Spirit.

During our ride, Buck Buchanan provided me with a brief history of the Wichita aerospace industry. He didn't read about it in books, but rather learned it from his father, who spent nearly 42 years working on the factory floor that Buck now oversees. Buck began his career at the same facility, working on light structures, on the subassembly of component fuselage parts, and on the 737 structures value chain. He didn't parachute into leadership, but worked his way up doing the jobs of those who now report to him.

There was some serendipity in Wichita's becoming an aerospace hub, Buck acknowledged. In the early 1900s, the city discovered oil, and several of the city's residents made fortunes. These Wichitans assisted Clyde Cessna, Walter Beech, and Lloyd Stearman in setting up aircraft companies. Buck explained that in addition to oil money, the city's strong winds made it a good place to build airplanes. Every kid growing up in Wichita knows about Cessna, Beech, and Stearman—they're Wichita's modern founders. Cessna founded what is today Cessna Aircraft, Beech founded what is Hawker Beechcraft, and Stearman founded Stearman Aircraft, which became a subsidiary of Boeing and today is Spirit AeroSystems.

Uncle Sam also had a role in Wichita's rise. The government commissioned the aircraft manufacturers to make many of the military planes used in World War II. The folklore is that there was a B-29 being built in Wichita every 40 minutes. The B-29s were the most advanced bombers of their era and were used in the Pacific Theater, including the mission to drop the atomic bombs that ended the war with Japan. As a consequence of their wartime roles, Boeing, Cessna, and Beech became brand-named companies, attracting a talented workforce from across the nation. After the war, some of the workers left to start their own firms, often with seed money from these giants, which is how the network of smaller aerospace companies in the city got started. There's a saying in Wichita, "Small fortune aviation starts with a big one."

Geography, entrepreneurial pluck, and government procurements may have given rise to Wichita's cluster. But I was curious about what has kept it going for more than half a century. "How have you resisted offshoring?" I asked.

Spirit has lowered costs by reducing "high-touch labor," defined as those workers that do manual work on the fuselage. The workers that it employs are largely using sophisticated technology and machines to build the planes. It also has gotten better at anticipating Boeing's demand for an entire year. As a result, there's more predictability in the company's production targets, which prevents large inventories or large numbers of underutilized workers.

The transformation of the dynamic between "engineering and manufacturing" has also been critical to Spirit's success. Traditionally, in the aerospace industry, the engineers would come up with a plan, and then the manufacturers would have to figure out how to build it. This relationship has been, in Buck's words, "turned on its head." Today, the manufacturers articulate how they would like to build, and then the engineers follow their specifications. Spirit has created "integrated product teams" with manufacturers in the lead. Sound familiar?

Andy Grove would certainly approve. I wasn't surprised that leading manufacturers, be they in aerospace or semiconductors, converge on similar organizational structures.

Buck also credited Spirit's relationship with the machinists union. The two sides negotiated a 10-year contract, which isn't the norm as far as labor agreements go. Typically, unions don't want to be bound to terms for such a long duration. The contract also provides a significant amount of flexibility, so that Spirit can ask workers to perform multiple tasks. Spirit, for its part, committed to keeping the facility in Wichita for the entirety of the contract.

Thomas Buffenbarger, the machinists' international president, made the case for the contract: "The thing that upsets [some of our members] is the 10-year deal. But I'm afraid that's what it's going to take to stabilize the industry. If our economy is going to experience severe roils, then people are going to need some stability. The best thing the union can do is to help the company survive and grow in order to protect the members. The best thing we can do is make sure they've got a job."[18] When I got back to Washington, I went straight to the fifth floor of the Commerce building to tell the secretary's team about the business-labor relationship in Wichita. It became another argument for opening up the Commerce advisory committees to labor, which by now many in the building knew was my pet cause.

Although smart business strategy and creative labor contracts have helped keep Spirit at the top, Buck ultimately gives the credit to the quality of the Wichita workforce. "Our folks are the most engaged, hardest-working in the world." "Even compared to China?" I inquired. "Yes. I've spent time in most places. I have a simple test when I walk onto a floor. How many hands do I see moving and how many mouths do I see moving? We have a lot of hands moving and no mouths moving. You don't see that in other places. In Brazil or China, I don't see the same engagement, the same focus."

Buck recognizes the importance of Wichita State University and the National Center for Aviation Training in helping to prepare his workers, which is why Spirit joined with other aircraft companies to fund these institutions. But institutions can't teach the intangibles. "We have a history and tradition of hardworking individuals," Buck emphasized. "Those values are passed down. There are high expectations working here." When I pressed for more, Buck paused. "I know what you are getting at. All I can say is, it's in the blood here, if you will."

That's not to say that Buck doesn't have some concerns about the next generation. He worries about an impending labor shortage. The city needs to develop a pipeline of talent. "There is a different expectation of what spells success from when I grew up," Buck reflected. "Working with your hands is not as cool as it used to be. It's less appealing now." Nonetheless, he's convinced that the institutions for aerospace training will succeed in their goal of turning out 6,000 new workers a year. When I asked the grounds for his optimism, Buck didn't hesitate, saying, "These jobs promote good pay and are still the best in the area."

The challenge is how to get that message out. In the age of Facebook, YouTube, and Twitter, Wichita's oral tradition may no longer be sufficient. The city, and for that matter the nation, may need a public relations campaign, one that goes viral, debunking the outdated image of manufacturing jobs as "dirty, dangerous, and dumb." Today's young people who are interested in aviation have a great opportunity. They can experience the magic of building planes without enduring the same workplace extremities because of the modernization of the factory and equipment. And they can make a good living while doing so. This isn't to say that they will have an easy road in turbulent economic times. Every generation has to earn its stripes. Previous generations in Wichita made history by helping to defeat Japan in World War II. Today's generation can make its mark by helping America stay ahead in the economic competition of the twenty-first century.

AN UNLEVEL PLAYING FIELD

The world may be flat, with increasing trade across continents and culture, as Thomas Friedman famously proclaimed, but it's not level, given the current global trading regime.[19] Picture a slanted world map as a metaphorical playing field. American companies, which receive little government help, have a starting position near the bottom and must move up this inclined field to sell their products. On the other end, Chinese companies start at the highest elevation because of an explicit state-sanctioned strategy of "indigenous innovation" that provides massive subsidies.[20] This may lead to inefficiency and unsustainable government spending in the long run, but it provides a short-term advantage for favored Chinese companies. Imagine Brazilian companies as being positioned somewhere in the middle, given the country's geography and the relative size of its subsidies. What's astounding is that despite this rigged contest, Wichita companies are winning when it comes to selling airplanes, scoring the most sales in different markets.

Many Wichitans, however, aren't sure how long they can continue to compete in the face of foreign subsidies. A. J. and I discussed these concerns at Cessna's corporate headquarters with Mark Paolucci, a licensed pilot and the former senior vice president of sales and marketing at Cessna, and Eric Salander, the company's chief financial officer. We met in Eric's corner office, which is decorated with pictures of his family spread across his desk and on many bookshelves. Slender and stylish, he chooses his words carefully. Mark, on the other hand, doesn't hold back. He's outgoing and connects effortlessly with people, including the receptionists, janitors, and administrative assistants. When we shook hands, he described himself politically, half-jokingly, as "to the right of Genghis Khan." Both he and Eric were passionate about their company, their city, and their country and shared a similar perspective.

They began by providing a brief overview of Cessna. The company remains the leading designer and manufacturer of light and medium-sized business jets in the world, providing employment for more than 8,000 Americans. Over the years, the company has sold nearly 200,000 aircraft, the most in general aviation history. Nearly half of the business jets currently flown around the world are Cessna jets. They're easily identified by the Citation brand, and most are made at the Wichita facility. The Citation Mustang, the newest light jet, is made at the nearby facility in Independence, Kansas.

Cessna's global dominance notwithstanding, Jack Pelton, the company's former CEO, is "scared to death" about the threat posed by Embraer, a Brazilian company.[21] Mark and Eric both acknowledged that, unlike other foreign competitors, Embraer understands how to build planes. What bothered their sense of fairness, though, is that the Brazilian government built Embraer's business, providing the company with a factory and the funds to develop the latest technology. Today, Embraer's biggest leg up is its access to a constant source of cheap financing from the Brazilian government. The Brazilian government also expedites any certification issues for Embraer, and, given our bilateral agreements, the Federal Aviation Administration (FAA) automatically recognizes Brazilian certification. This means that Embraer, using reciprocity, can often get U.S. certification more quickly than Cessna can!

As a result of these advantages, Embraer has gained almost a 15 percent market share in private business jets as of 2009, recently winning a key contract from NetJets, one of Cessna's best and biggest buyers.[22]

Although Embraer is the immediate threat, China's subsidization of its aviation industries poses a longer-term problem. Mary Saunders, my former colleague at the Department of Commerce who is the deputy assistant secretary for manufacturing, testified about the recent Chinese forays into the aviation sector.[23] In 2008, China established the Commercial Aircraft Corporation of China Ltd. (COMAC), heavily subsidizing Chinese aircraft companies and making it very difficult for outside companies to sell into the market without signing joint venture agreements. Given China's record of supporting industries such as steel, clean technology, and telecommunications through its "indigenous innovation" program, there's reason to be "scared," as Jack Pelton puts it, about what its massive subsidies will mean for U.S. aircraft companies in the future. Mark and Eric spent more of their time talking about Brazil's current unfair practices, but that may be a harbinger of what lies ahead once China becomes interested not just in passenger planes but in general aviation.

What, then, can the U.S. government do to give companies like Cessna a fair shot? Mark and Eric argued that the U.S. International Trade Commission and the Department of Commerce's Import Administration must be more aggressive in investigating the subsidies that foreign aircraft companies are receiving and in documenting the negative effect that these subsidies are having on U.S. manufacturers and the world's consumers, and then they should impose countervailing duties to pressure other nations to end these subsidies.

Governor Sam Brownback, who hails from Kansas, recently requested the relevant federal agencies to step up their enforcement.[24] This isn't a call for protectionism—rather, it's making sure that other nations play by the same rules. Even President Reagan, a staunch defender of free trade, was willing to impose restrictions on Brazil, the European Union, and Japan to stop their predatory and unfair practices when it came to motorcycles, computer electronics, steel, or automobiles.[25] He emphasized, "We have the authority to counter unfair trading practices by initiating investigations, entering negotiations, and taking active countermeasures if those negotiations are unsuccessful."[26] He made it clear that "our trading partners should not doubt our determination to see international trade conducted fairly with the same rules applicable to all."[27] In the same tradition, President Obama recently proposed in his 2012 State of the Union address the creation of a "Trade Enforcement Unit" to investigate the unfair trading practices of foreign competitors.[28] Hopefully, this unit will be more assertive and effective than current agencies in penalizing companies such as Embraer that skirt the international trading rules.

But Mark and Eric will also tell you that it's not enough for the U.S. government to play sheriff. Our government should also provide manufacturers with access to capital, so long as it's within the World Trade Organization's (WTO) legal framework. When I asked them their top priority, they emphasized the importance of making financing cheaper, echoing CEO Jack Pelton's public testimony.[29] The irony, in their mind, is that while Brazil and China are financing their jet makers, our federal government is bashing private jets.

There's precedent for the federal government supporting large-scale aviation manufacturers. As I alluded to in the introduction, President Coolidge's Commerce Department "provided financial assistance" to aviation companies, limited to aid for navigational equipment and to defray certain costs of technology development.[30] President Coolidge explicitly credited his government for the "remarkable progress" of the aviation industry, noting that the rapid growth took place *after* he had established an "Assistant Secretary for Aeronautics" in the War, Navy, and Commerce Departments.[31] Moreover, President Roosevelt and President Truman continued supporting the development of aviation through government contracts and support for research.[32]

In the modern global economy, our government must strike a delicate balance when supporting manufacturers such as Cessna. On the one hand, it shouldn't intrude in the management of private businesses or provide subsidies. Any state that embraces such a role places too large a burden on a nation's treasury and facilitates cronyism. The reality is that despite propping up state-favored companies, China and Brazil actually lost manufacturing jobs at a faster rate than the United States prior to the financial crisis because of the closure of inefficient state-owned businesses.[33] Their constant state involvement proved to be counterproductive. They may create short-term wins in certain industries, which cost Americans jobs, but it's at the expense of their own consumer welfare and allocative efficiency. In fact, a recent article in *The Economist* observed that the most dynamic companies in China fueling much of the growth are in the Zhejiang province, where the state has neither meddled in private business nor provided ongoing subsidies.[34] This is no surprise. As Hamilton put it, ongoing government support for manufacturers is "questionable policy" because the state shouldn't be subsidizing a business when there are "natural and inherent impediments to success."[35] In modern lingo, the state shouldn't prop up companies that can't compete in the marketplace.

That said, our belief in free markets isn't undermined if the government makes capital available to privately run companies through loan guarantees for discrete projects that support jobs. This is what Andy Grove recommends. He calls for the creation of a "scaling bank" to provide loans to companies that are investing in new plants or new technology domestically.[36] Andrew Liveris, chairman of Dow Chemical, similarly proposes the creation of an "Economic Growth Bank" with a bipartisan board that includes industry representatives, economists, and engineers.[37] This bank would make capital available to companies such as Cessna that have already attracted a threshold level of private investment and are critical for our national industrial base. The money could go out on a first come, first served basis for any manufacturer that qualifies, as opposed to having government bureaucrats making bets on particular companies. As President Clinton suggests, this national bank's role could simply be as a loan guarantor with existing TARP money, thereby spurring private banks to make the actual loans.[38]

Alternatively, the government could consider offering tax credits to companies such as Cessna for large capital expenditures or temporary tax holidays for 5 or 10 years on revenues from new U.S. factories.[39] This would give companies an incentive to invest in the United States instead of hoarding their cash. The free-market solution of a limited-duration, tax-free zone for manufacturing is likely preferable to direct government loan guarantees.

The call for an economic bank or tax credits is consistent with Hamilton's view that providing "public money" to manufacturers on a "temporary" basis is worthwhile if it leads toward the expansion of our industrial base, increasing both our nation's "wealth" and its "independence." There's a difference between a government that throws money at a company to make it profitable, as China and Brazil have a propensity to do, and a government that provides companies with loans or tax incentives to encourage them to expand. We can make limited interventions in the marketplace to help companies grow and to create jobs within our borders without betraying our free-market heritage. To quote Hamilton, "In matters of industry, human enterprise ought doubtless to be left free in the main, not fettered by too much regulation, but practical politicians know that it may be beneficially stimulated by prudent aids and encouragements on the part of the government."[40]

Regulatory reform is also necessary to help manufacturers such as Cessna. There's no excuse for Embraer's getting FAA certification with greater ease than Cessna. The delays in certification put Cessna at a disadvantage by increasing the time to market for its latest innovations. The company has no problem meeting high standards. Safety is paramount. And yet it has found the bureaucracy to be, at times, unresponsive and slow.

To expedite certification, Mark and Eric suggested that the FAA increase staffing. What's unfortunate is that Senator Rand Paul is proposing to do precisely the opposite, calling for drastic cuts in the FAA's budget.[41] Justifying the cuts, Senator Paul stated, "It's irresponsible as legislators to stand up here and say more, more, more, more. We can't do it. We are talking about the consequences of a massive debt."[42] It's easy to attack a faceless bureaucracy while standing on the Senate floor, but what Senator Rand has not adequately considered is the impact of those cuts on the competitiveness of aviation companies.

We owe it to our manufacturers to staff regulatory agencies properly, and then to demand the highest level of customer service from our regulators. We need to train agency employees to use the latest technology and to work faster and more efficiently. If companies can implement net promoter scores that reflect customer surveys measuring satisfaction, then our federal regulatory agencies should be judged by the same metrics.

DREAM BIG AGAIN

Over the past decade, under the leadership of both Republican and Democratic administrations, Commerce has encouraged its local offices to colocate with regional agencies to foster collaboration. For example, our Commerce office in Wichita is housed in the same building as the Workforce Alliance of South Central Kansas, a nonprofit agency that assists employers and workers with training, skills matching, and long-term planning. A.J. works closely with Keith Lawing, Workforce's executive director, sharing information and leads about clients. Keith has the luxury of thinking about the region as a whole. His mission is to help workers prepare for the jobs of the future.

Keith's organization administers the nearly $7 million National Emergency Grant that the U.S. Department of Labor awarded the region to help laid-off workers.[43] The grant money covers about 1,100 laid-off workers, paying for their training courses, transportation, daycare, résumé preparation, and job searches. The money, however, is inadequate considering that nearly 13,000 workers were laid off in the last two years. And retraining doesn't make up for the economic and emotional pain of being laid off for middle-aged workers.[44] But, at least, from Keith's perspective, it was something positive coming out of Washington.

Keith was disappointed, though, that the Department of Labor had rejected a request to train workers whose hours had been cut. Many of the aerospace companies reduced the hours of their employees to avoid layoffs. Some of these employees wanted to use their spare time for training, but the department allocates funds for the unemployed only. In Keith's view, this is a reactionary policy. He argued that in today's age, we need to invest in employees *before* they are laid off so that they can develop skills, such as proficiency with computers and machines, that are most attractive to employers.

When I asked whether all the laid-off workers were preparing for aviation jobs, Keith made it clear that they were not. They were training for different fields depending on their interests. Keith is steadfast in his commitment to aerospace and aware of its long-term need for more skilled workers, but he also sees the benefits of diversification. Invoking Cessna, Beech, and Stearman, Keith told me that he'd like Wichita to dream big again. Its strong winds can help spawn a wind turbine industry. Manufacturing the high-end plastics that are critical for aerospace can give rise to a medical technology industry, which depends on similar materials. Keith believes in Wichita, the place, more than in any particular industry. The talent, work ethic, and community that made the city the "Air Capital of the World" can make it the capital for new industries as well in the twenty-first century.

Keith's vision for Wichita stayed with me well after our brief meeting. I remembered the conversation while I was sitting at the gate, waiting for my plane back to Washington. Was there anything our government could do to help the city build for the future? I was aware of business writer Vivek Wadhwa's insight that "top-down" efforts to create new industry clusters rarely work. Washington can't just pour funds into an area and hope to create, or even maintain, a cluster by constructing a tech park or commissioning a study.[45] Entrepreneurs drive clusters—not Washington bureaucrats.

At the same time, Washington shouldn't turn a blind eye to the struggles and dreams of Wichitans. The government can assist Wichita entrepreneurs, at least on the margins.

When I got back to Washington, I talked to the secretary's team. The administration, I was told, has a proposal for investing $75 million in a Regional Cluster Initiative that can potentially help places like Wichita.[46] Although there's disagreement about the level of funding, the idea has, in principle, received some support from congressional appropriators.[47] But the devil is in the details. First, Congress needs to authorize the money. If the money is there, then there's the question of implementation. Grants that have numerous Washington mandates won't have an impact. Grants, however, *can* make a difference if they are disbursed to existing local institutions such as Wichita State that collaborate with companies that "have passed the market test."[48] They can, for instance, help support an open platform for universities and companies to share knowledge, facilitating the commercialization of technology developed in research laboratories.

The idea of providing innovation grants is not original. Hamilton argued that our government should support institutions and associations that promote manufacturing and commerce but have "slender funds." Grants to such local entities, in Hamilton's judgment, could have an "immense" impact in leading to new inventions and industrialization that would improve the material condition of society. The Defense Advanced Research Projects Agency (DARPA) grants represented a successful twentieth-century application of Hamilton's theory. DARPA provided federal grants to MIT, Stanford, and Xerox's Palo Alto Research Center.[49] These institutions worked with entrepreneurs in their regions to develop the "core technologies that led to the internet" and to many of the features of modern-day personal computers.[50]

Wichita, not Washington, drives our manufacturing success. I have great confidence in Steve Rooney and Ron Eldridge with the machinists, Buck Buchanan with Spirit, Mark Paolucci and Eric Salander with Cessna, Keith Lawing with Workforce, and A. J. Anderson with our local Commerce office. The question is whether Washington will do its part by

representing Wichita's interests on the world stage and channeling resources effectively to the city's innovators.

BOTTOM-UP CLUSTERS

The federal government didn't mandate that airplanes should
be built in Wichita, nor did it pour billions of dollars into building
industrial parks. Rather, visionary entrepreneurs helped establish the aviation industry in Wichita, and in doing so they created
a uniquely American culture that fostered collaboration—one
that continues to thrive today.

Bottom-up clusters, like the ones seen in Wichita, take
years, if not generations, to develop. Central governments can't
simply throw money at a region and expect that it'll emerge as
an industry cluster. Rather, regional leaders typically work to
establish such clusters over decades. They set up companies,
civic associations, and educational institutions that encourage
experimentation and the exchange of ideas. Regional leadership is critical for America's manufacturing growth—in fact,
I'd argue that bottom-up clusters like Wichita are one of the
key components that provide American manufacturers with
a competitive advantage over many of their foreign counterparts, as they allow our manufacturers to operate in the best
ecosystems for innovation in the world.

Once they emerge, though, these bottom-up clusters need
the support of the federal government. They need federal resources for job training, research, or commercialization programs. Most important, they need Washington to stand up for
their interests in a global economy and ensure that other nations are not rigging the game through unfair subsidies or protectionism.

4

Making the World's Next Big Thing

■ ■ ■

"Great place," President Obama said, tapping me on the shoulder as he worked the rope line in Fremont, California. The shout-out from the president of the United States in my own community is something that I'll never forget. Anyone who acts as if talking with the president isn't a big deal either is lying or has forgotten the sense of wonder and excitement that probably drew him into public service. I, for one, wasn't above trying to sneak myself into a few photographs.

I'm sure one of the reasons that the president praised Fremont was simply to be gracious to me and the other Bay Area residents who were in attendance. But he also seemed moved by his experience meeting executives of the clean technology companies that have sprung up in Silicon Valley over the last decade, and witnessing a new generation of American manufacturing.

What most people don't realize about Silicon Valley is that it's still a place that hosts a lot of manufacturing. Entrepreneurs may jot down ideas on the back of napkins at cafés, but they then make the prototypes close to where they live. In fact, the concentration of manufacturing workers in the San Jose, Sunnyvale, and Santa Clara area is almost 20 percent of the total workforce.[1] This is the third highest concentration of manufacturing workers in the nation, only slightly below the concentration in Wichita.[2]

If the Wichita cluster centers around airplanes, what's Silicon Valley's claim to fame? This isn't an easy question. The Valley is home to companies that specialize in semiconductors, personal computers, web browsers, e-commerce portals, search engines, and now social media and clean technology. New industries don't displace existing ones, but rather add overlapping layers to the Valley. Despite the Valley's sector diversity, venture capitalist John Doerr believes that it has a unifying identity. Doerr started as an engineer at Intel in the 1970s, alongside Andy Grove. He went on to back, as a venture capitalist, the founders of Intuit, Sun Microsystems, Google, and Silver Spring Networks. Technically brilliant and a marketing genius, Doerr is fond of saying that Silicon Valley specializes in making the world's "Next Big Thing."[3]

Silicon Valley emerged as a groundbreaking technology hub during World War II, when our government provided Stanford University with funding for research and development in aeronautics and electronics, funding that continued through the Cold War.[4] Eventually, Stanford established an industrial park and collaborated on joint projects with the first semiconductor and personal computer companies. A number of other educational institutions in northern California, such as Berkeley, Cal State East Bay, and Santa Clara University, also built strong links with these companies. The collaboration among government, educational institutions, and industry created an environment that attracted the best and the brightest from around the country and the world.

These linked institutions were the preconditions for Silicon Valley's rise. But what has made Silicon Valley a great place is a culture of "collective learning," where information is "exchanged openly."[5] The Valley promotes the free flow of ideas that cyberspace scholar Larry Lessig and technology writer Steve Johnson champion. You can observe this firsthand as a casual visitor. At University Cafe in downtown Palo Alto, Woodside Bakery in Atherton, or P.F. Chang's in Fremont, you are almost certain to overhear debates about which form of renewable energy is most scalable. After visiting these restaurants, you can attend an event organized by The Indus Entrepreneurs, a network of thousands of Valley entrepreneurs and executives. The presenters will probably share best business practices, talk about emerging industry trends, and offer advice on how to get a start-up off the ground. If you want to experience more, you can check out a roundtable sponsored by the Silicon Valley Leadership Group, the South Bay Labor Council, the Bay Area Council, or Environmental Entrepreneurs and discuss what policies would most benefit the region, the nation, and the world.

The Valley's interconnectedness helps explain why its players gravitate toward common enterprises. When a few technology optimists turned their attention to solving the world's energy problems, they reached out to their networks to recruit others to join them in this mission. Look at the background of most of the executives at today's clean tech companies in the Valley. Many of them come from semiconductor, personal computer, or Internet companies and changed the trajectory of their careers because of the vision of their peers. In this sense, the Valley shapes how people understand the world and their role in it. Individuals don't just share information; they share dreams. If you're in an environment where social conversation revolves around how a particular technology can improve the lot of humankind, you're likely to want a turn at the plate, swinging for the fences.

And there's no shame in striking out. This is Vinod Khosla's central insight about the Valley. Vinod cofounded Sun Microsystems, worked for years alongside John Doerr at Kleiner Perkins, and today is one of the world's most respected clean tech investors. During one of my trips back home, I stopped by to update Vinod about my job. I explained that I was traveling across the country, helping the businesses that are the pillars of our economy. The bureaucracy, though, was frustrating. Vinod attributed Washington's slowness to the high cost of risk. In large bureaucracies, the penalties for failure are high. You don't make it to the next GS level (the career stepladder for federal employees) or get a step increase if you have a negative mark in your file. That's why bureaucracies temporize or resist change. The difference in the Valley is that failure is generally embraced and experimentation encouraged. Our discussion reminded me of Vinod's widely publicized remarks a year earlier, when he described, almost poetically, the Valley's culture:

> I like to say that I've had one luxury in my life and that
> is the freedom to fail, being in an ecosystem here in the
> valley that allows me to fail. And get up and try again.
> And this ability to fail, this freedom to fail, is what has,
> in my view, given me the ability to succeed. It's given me
> the ability to explore ideas. There was a recent article
> that called me a "risk junkie" but it's easy to be a risk

junkie if the consequences of failing aren't that high. And they aren't in this ecosystem and that's what makes the valley such a *great* place. So, I like to say that vision is about more shots on goal, more at bats at the plate. That's really all I want to say.[6] (Emphasis added.)

In this chapter, I profile innovators working for Serious Materials and some of the Valley's civic associations. My intent is not to anoint certain companies as clean technology leaders, but to provide a glimpse into the Valley's entrepreneurial ethos. There's no guarantee that the companies discussed here will succeed. In fact, I address the failed Solyndra experiment head on.

Nonetheless, innovators in the Valley are displaying a boldness that represents the best of America's manufacturing tradition. Robert Kennedy's favorite quotation applies: they "dream of things that never were and ask why not." But their dreams are little solace for the unemployed. I also share the frustration of Silicon Valley's jobless. The jobs problem, if it is not solved, is the largest threat to the fabric of the place, hindering businesses from attracting the engineering talent or public support necessary to continue making the "Next Big Thing."

THE TRIPLE BOTTOM LINE

Kevin Surace does not mince words. "China continues to execute a war against us," he e-mailed me as a follow-up to a series of conversations about how the United States was faring in the clean tech race. "An economic and industrial war. And they win every single battle as we sit by helpless. Our Senators and House members are arguing about salamanders while Rome burns."

Kevin is the high-profile CEO of Serious Materials, one of the nation's leading "green buildings" companies.[7] His company has attracted the attention of Democrats and Republicans alike, with words of praise from President Obama, President Clinton, and Governor Schwarzenegger. He has been on the cover of *Inc.* and has been featured in *Fortune* and at a TED conference.[8] From these articles and presentations, you'd gather that he's an environmentalist who is intent on reducing carbon emissions. You'd also probably guess that he has a talent for selling stuff and leading people. What doesn't fully come through, however, is Kevin's belief in America.

This belief is what gets Kevin up in the morning; it's rooted in his upbringing. Kevin has never forgotten where he came from. He was raised in upstate New York in the 1960s in a small suburb of about 5,000 families. His father was both an Army and a GE man. He remembers a time when almost every product you saw in a store and every piece of equipment in a building was labeled "Made in the U.S.A." As he puts it, the "world used to come to our door" to buy the best products.[9] He wants his grandkids to feel that kind of pride in America.

So, he shares his PowerPoint presentation with everyone he meets. Although they are stamped with the Serious Materials logo, the slides are as much about the country as they are about the company. The first few slides discuss the relative decline in American manufacturing since the 1970s and our large trade deficits. The next slides present a way out: America must dominate energy efficiency manufacturing. Kevin argues that increasing energy costs will drive businesses and consumers to remake every part of their built environment, including windows, walls, floors, cabinets, rooftops, pipes, and lighting structures, in a manner that maximizes efficiency. The market is huge. Serious Materials is focused on making windows and drywall, but there is room for thousands of American manufacturers, both new and existing, to invent and make new kinds of building materials.

Serious Materials's transformation into a clean tech company is a typical Valley story. Kevin readily admits that his interest in energy efficiency came about because of his collaboration with Marc Porat. In the 1990s, Marc and Kevin had already founded two information technology start-ups together: General Magic and Perfect Commerce. When Marc recruited Kevin to Serious Materials in 2002, the company wasn't in the clean tech space. Its focus was on making fairly traditional, soundproof drywall. But then, around 2005, the two of them began participating in the conversations with their peers about climate change. By this time, Al Gore had become a fixture in the Valley. Both Marc and Kevin recognized that the American public was becoming much more aware of the issue. They resolved to link their company's purpose to the broader goal of reducing CO_2 emissions by making drywall and windows that have less energy seepage and that require less energy to manufacture.

To this day, the culture of the Valley shapes the company's triple-bottom-line philosophy: Serious Materials sees a concern for the environment, profits, and social responsibility as equally important. The triple bottom line concept didn't originate in the Valley, but it has taken hold there. Andrew Savitz, formerly a lead consultant on sustainability at PricewaterhouseCoopers, originally popularized the concept. Savitz wrote a sweeping book giving concrete examples of how major corporations can improve profits by caring about sustainability and their communities.[10] Since then, many Valley executives have embraced the triple bottom line as the right metric for success. They judge their colleagues by that standard and push one another to meet it. They center their companies to create "shared value" along the three axes, striving to meet Professor Michael Porter's recent call that corporate America build "economic value in a way that also creates value for society."[11]

So, how does Serious Materials measure up when it comes to the triple bottom line? During one of our longer meetings in Silicon Valley at Faz Restaurant, a popular Mediterranean spot, Kevin shared his outlook. He began with the environmental impact of his company's work. Energy efficiency in buildings, he declared, is the "low-hanging fruit." To make his point, Kevin asked me what I thought was the biggest contributor to CO_2 emissions. I guessed automobiles. It turns out that I couldn't have been further off the mark. Almost 52 percent of CO_2 emissions are tied to the built environment, 40 percent from the energy needed to run our buildings and 12 percent from the energy used to make the materials. Comparatively, automobiles account for only 9 percent of the emissions worldwide.

"What about renewable energy?" Kevin prodded. "How much of our energy do you think we get from solar?" This time I didn't take the bait and just asked him for the numbers. Apparently, 80 percent of our energy supply still comes from oil, coal, and natural gas, while solar and wind are still less than 2 percent given their comparative costs.[12] Kevin clarified that he's a strong proponent of continued investment in renewable energy sources and believes in their potential. But it's not enough to find new supplies of energy. We need to "lower demand." Serious Materials is helping the environment by reducing our demand for energy.

Serious Materials is also having success along the economic axis of the triple bottom line, with opportunities for big profits. Ambitious executives in the Valley like Kevin don't talk in millions. They always talk in billions. They're never bashful about their desire to make a lot of money, as profits demonstrate that an initiative is sustainable over the long run. According to Kevin, the total market for selling new windows around the world is $100 billion, and that doesn't even take into account all the old windows that need to be replaced. From his perspective, every person should be buying energy-efficient windows because of the savings on their energy bill. The risk for the company is that people aren't willing to pay the 20 percent higher up-front cost for the long-term savings, or that they think that better insulation, not efficient windows, should be their first priority.[13] So, Kevin's task is not just to make a better window. In many ways, that's the easy part. His job is to sell the American people on the value proposition.

The company manufactures its products in the United States to maximize profits, Kevin stated bluntly. Drywall and windows are very large and heavy to ship. With the increase in fuel prices, the costs of shipping from Asia would add about 30 percent to a drywall board or a typical window. This outweighs any savings from cheaper labor overseas. Domestic manufacturing also happens to be green and good for the community, highlighting the "shared value" that Kevin considers the sweet spot for his company.

What irks Kevin, though, are the subsidies that foreign competitors in the building material space receive from their governments. He brings up that familiar refrain: China gives its indigenous manufacturers "free land, free factory space, free capital." The subsidies, more than the cheap labor, are what make it difficult to compete on price. Serious Materials's only recourse is to continually improve the formula for its windows and drywall to maximize efficiency and cost savings.

Some critics erroneously assume that Serious Materials is propped up by federal funds, given all the attention it garners from high-level political leaders. But, for the most part, Serious Materials is just receiving a lot of praise; the company is surviving with little financial help from our federal government. Kevin was appalled by a recent John Stossel report implying that Serious Materials had received support because of the company's political connections.[14] Stossel alleged that the company is a symbol of "crony capitalism." Kevin set the record straight. Through a competitive application process, the company qualified for a small manufacturing tax credit of about $500,000 (less than 0.02 percent of the total funds available) from the Department of Energy for purchasing equipment.[15] Every little bit helps, but the grant hardly qualifies as a game changer. Moreover, Serious Materials received less assistance than six of its glass or window competitors. The charge that the company was singled out for special treatment is false, and it is particularly unfortunate considering the sincerity of Kevin's patriotism. Frankly, Kevin isn't interested in securing more federal funds for his company, which has the advantage of competing in a space where shipping costs pose a barrier. He worries about the larger U.S. clean tech industry, particularly renewables and energy monitoring systems, and how they will compete in the face of Chinese subsidies.

Kevin argues that Serious Materials's social impact—perhaps the most meaningful axis in the triple-bottom-line framework—is helping America remain the dominant twenty-first-century economy. "America is still ahead in energy efficiency," Kevin declared. "Solar and wind are mostly gone," but other countries "don't have as much tech in the efficiency areas." Statistics on energy efficiency projects back up his claim. In 2010, the United States had more than 30,000 projects given Leadership in Energy and Environmental Design (LEED) certification by the U.S. Green Building Council, an internationally recognized body. LEED certification provides third-party verification that a building is green, or energy-efficient.[16] (A good example of a LEED project is Serious Materials's recent initiative to insulate all 6,500 windows in the Empire State Building.) In comparison, the United Arab Emirates, which came in second, and China, which came in third, each had only a few hundred projects that were LEED certified. The market for energy efficiency is here. The big projects are here. There's no doubt that because of companies like Serious Materials, we have a head start in the emerging energy-efficiency space.

Serious Materials is also helping the American economy by creating jobs. Kevin worked with Carl Rosen, the president of the Western Region of the United Electrical Workers, to re-open a windows manufacturing plant in Chicago. The previous owner had declared bankruptcy, committed fraud, and laid off hundreds of workers. Kevin and Carl managed to get the plant running again to make energy-efficient windows, and so far the company has reemployed about 50 of the laid-off workers. Kevin encouraged me to reach out to Carl, which I did a few weeks after our dinner.

Carl may sit on the opposite side of the table from Kevin during certain negotiations, but they share a commitment to keep manufacturing here. He's convinced that, as costs of production are slowly climbing overseas, "any smart company can figure out how to manufacture here at a good profit by investing in technology and people." What makes his collaboration with Kevin successful is Serious Materials's underlying perspective that the "union is an entity that can be of assistance, as opposed to being managed." When there's a shared attitude of teamwork, Carl suggested, unions can do a lot to help. They can make sure the right skilled workers are in the right job, help establish a good public image for the company, and improve the production process. Another way Carl's union members provide value is by flying out to train workers in different project locations, such as sending them to New York to help with the Empire State Building retrofitting job. Carl was blunt about the benefits of his union: "You get what you pay for. You have a very dedicated workforce, loyalty, and dedication to see the place functioning." More generally, Neil Struthers, the brilliant head of the South Bay Building and Construction Trades, explains why unions still matter to technology companies: "Almost all the high-tech companies such as Apple, Google, Cisco use us for their work because they do not have the same cost pressures as the public sector, and they prioritize quality."

Even more than the partnership with the United Electrical Workers, Kevin is proudest of Serious Materials's plant in Vandergrift, Pennsylvania. At various moments throughout our dinner, he'd let the word *Vandergrift* roll off his tongue with a slight giddiness. Kevin suggested that I make a trip out there. When I told him I wasn't sure it would fit in with my schedule, he said it would be worth my time to read up on the opening they had there. So I did.

I suspect what moved Kevin about the Vandergrift opening, what may have filled him with hope for his company and his country, are the words of Robin Scott. Robin is a glass technician with two children and "elderly relatives" to support.[17] He had been laid off from a window factory for months before Serious Materials reopened the plant. He expressed what the new job meant to him during brief remarks at the March 16, 2009, opening:

> The way I see it, this is more than just a job to me. It's also doing something—our small part—in this tiny corner of America to move this country forward. . . . I'm not a tree-hugger, by no means. But even I know we have to change. We cannot leave this world the way it is now. So if we can get this green bandwagon rolling here in Vandergrift, well, that's just what I want to see. We can

start here in Vandergrift and create a whole bunch of new jobs—that's even better.[18]

At a time when we read about factory workers at Fox-conn, one of China's largest manufacturers, having to perform largely repetitive work and even, in some instances, being verbally abused, Robin Scott is a reminder of how differently we do things today in America.[19] Our best companies are relatively meritocratic institutions where a worker can be lauded with just as much attention as a manager at the opening of a factory. The Vandergrift facility is an American answer to our foreign competitors' plants.

Kevin's right that we need to step up our game to win the clean tech race. There's no guarantee that Serious Materials will succeed, and we can't underestimate our competition because of its sheer size. But in a deeper sense, no matter how much money an authoritarian government may spend, no matter how brazenly it limits access to consumers as a bargaining chip for demanding technology transfers, it will always lack the credibility to instill in its workforce the sense of ownership that's wired into our DNA. We empower ordinary Americans such as Robin Scott to imagine the future. That is our enduring advantage.

SILO BREAKERS

Silicon Valley rejects silos. When it come to business, those working in the Valley search for good ideas wherever they can find them, regardless of whether they come from a college dropout, a fresh-off-the-boat immigrant, or a technician on the factory floor. This open culture also influences the Valley's approach to policy. Prominent business and labor groups engage each other to craft consensus proposals to grow our manufacturing base.

Take the partnership between Cindy Chavez, the head of the South Bay Labor Council, and Carl Guardino, the head of the Silicon Valley Leadership Group, which represents 325 of the Valley's most respected companies. Cindy is as comfortable talking to a rally for organizing janitors as she is in a corporate boardroom. She builds coalitions that include the perspectives of "labor, business and stakeholders."[20] The few times I went back to the Valley for manufacturing forums, Cindy would tell me to reach out to Carl. When I did so, Carl would ask me whether I knew Cindy's take on a particular issue. They consider each other not just colleagues but friends. I brought up Cindy and Carl's example to my superiors in Washington often, mentioning it along with the business-labor cooperation that I had witnessed in Wichita. My point was, and remains, that Washington policy makers should learn about finding common ground from these *silo breakers* who are willing to extend beyond their core constituency and find common ground with other constituencies that traditionally aren't considered their natural allies.

To be specific, the Valley's approach can help advance the debate on the repatriation of U.S. money that's overseas. Ask members of the Silicon Valley Leadership Group, such as John Chambers, CEO of Cisco, or Tim Guertin, CEO of Varian Medical Systems, about their first priority to create more U.S. manufacturing jobs, and they'll talk about freeing more than a trillion dollars that U.S. companies have stuck overseas.[21] They're referring to the money that American corporations earn from their subsidiaries in foreign countries. Whereas many other nations do not tax companies on their overseas profits, the United States requires that companies pay our corporate tax when they bring overseas earnings back home. We have the second highest corporate tax rate among industrialized nations. Companies don't want to pay this tax, so they often prefer to invest the money they earn overseas in foreign plants to minimize their tax liability. Many Silicon Valley CEOs argue that if the federal government implemented a one-time tax break for the repatriation of this money, they would be able to bring cash back and invest in domestic facilities, hiring more workers.

The historical record for a repatriation tax break is sparse because the hoarding of cash overseas is a relatively recent phenomenon. Repatriation was tried once in 2004, with questionable results. The government allowed corporations to bring back money at a 5.25 percent tax rate, which resulted in hundreds of billions of dollars coming back to the United States. Some of the money did go into domestic capital investment and research and development.[22] But, according to a study conducted in collaboration with economists at the Department of Commerce, most of it went into share repurchases, helping stockholders instead of generating domestic employment.[23] This is why a number of thought leaders at the AFL-CIO and, frankly, in the Obama administration remain skeptical of that policy. Not only would the U.S. Treasury be forgoing revenue by lowering the tax rate, but the benefit to American workers is unclear. Making matters worse, some U.S. corporations, such as Merck & Co., have found ways to dodge the U.S. tax altogether, bringing billions of dollars back home through elaborate schemes without measurable job creation.[24]

Carl Guardino wanted to find a way forward on this issue. If there's a single adjective that describes Carl, it's "mild-mannered." Despite having almost every major Valley CEO on speed dial, he lacks any swagger. He was familiar with Cindy and the South Bay Labor Council's philosophy that any incentives for business to keep manufacturing in the United States must be consistent with three broad principles: "targeting," "standards," and "accountability."[25] *Targeting* means that the benefits go only to firms that take concrete actions to support American jobs. *Standards* means that the benefits go to firms that pay fair wages and benefits. *Accountability* means that firms should provide information to the government about what they've done with the benefits.

With these principles in mind, Carl floated the idea to members of his group about explicitly linking repatriation with a specific obligation to create jobs. He shared with them that Andy Stern, the highly visible former president of the Service Employees International Union, advocates a similar framework.[26]

Varian CEO Tim Guertin then developed the concept of what a jobs-centered repatriation policy could look like, which he described to me when I visited his office. Only those multinationals that expand their total U.S. workforce, measured by the number of people on the payroll, should qualify. The amount of dollars these companies repatriate at a discounted tax rate, moreover, should be directly tied to the number of unemployed workers that they hire *and* keep employed for more than 12 months. These provisions would help overcome the loopholes in the 2004 effort, preventing companies from playing accounting games by using repatriated money to displace money that had already been committed for salaries or domestic investment. Tim also was open to wage and benefits standards and rigorous reporting requirements. He spoke about how he wants his grandchildren to have jobs, and that this idea was more for them than for his own company's future, which would be fine wherever it locates manufacturing.

Critics whose instinct is to poke holes in Tim's proposal are missing the larger theme. Obviously, his proposal needs to be fleshed out. Any legislation will need to ensure that companies aren't given incentives to move operations overseas in anticipation of future repatriation holidays. The Silicon Valley Leadership Group will need to continue the dialogue with its labor friends and the national business community and line up a broad coalition of legislative sponsors. But these people's very efforts expose as false the caricatures in our current political debate of all CEOs as Benedict Arnolds or labor leaders as economic Luddites. The truth is that CEOs of multinationals often care, as citizens, about creating jobs here, and labor leaders understand that the United States needs incentives to attract manufacturing in a global economy. The forward-thinking dialogue in the Valley, which genuinely considers different points of view not as a formality, but to make better policy, gives me hope that different interest groups are capable of working together to promote American economic competitiveness.

LET'S TALK ABOUT SOLYNDRA

You may have read about Solyndra, the solar manufacturer headquartered in Silicon Valley that received a loan guarantee from the Department of Energy (DOE) for $535 million only to go bankrupt a year later. More than a thousand manufacturing and construction workers lost their jobs. The media fixated on the story line of who was to blame for the Solyndra debacle. A number of politicians used Solyndra as a political football, implying that the Obama administration had provided the loan guarantee to reward investors who had close ties to the administration. Lost in many of the headlines was the fact that the DOE began the process of providing Solyndra with a loan guarantee during the Bush administration.[27]

The failure of Solyndra has triggered media and congressional investigations into the proper role of DOE's loan guarantee program. If there is any real evidence of a lack of transparency or ethics, then the individual violators need to be held accountable. However, the political debate should move beyond personal, cheap shots at former DOE officials, aimed at character assassination. We should judge the DOE's loan program based on its entire portfolio. Of course, the DOE is not immune from constructive criticism. Herb Allison, the former Treasury official who conducted a thorough review of the DOE's loan guarantee program, has called for stricter vetting standards for any future loan guarantee applications and an independent risk officer to perform due diligence on any disbursements.[28] The DOE leadership must examine why officials did not heed the warnings of industry experts who were concerned about the scalability of Solyndra's business model months before the loan was approved. They also need to ensure that companies receiving public funds are held to high standards in terms of how they manage taxpayer money and how they treat their employees.

However, whatever shortcomings may exist in the DOE process, Solyndra's failure should not be seen as a failure of the American solar industry. On the contrary, Solyndra made a bold attempt to create a new product that could compete against Chinese solar panels that are being unfairly subsidized. The experiment failed. But in America, we tolerate and celebrate failure, recognizing that it paves the way for future advances. The American manufacturing miracle is possible precisely because entrepreneurs and venture capitalists are willing to gamble on companies such as Solyndra that dare to try something different.[29]

In this section, I discuss Solyndra's business model, and also what went wrong. After reading this section, you may still be angry with the government bureaucrats who made the Solyndra loan and also with Solyndra executives for mismanagement and paying themselves hefty bonuses while the company neared bankruptcy. But I hope you will agree that the ecosystem in Silicon Valley that enables companies such as Solyndra to emerge within five years is a testament to America's innovation culture.

The Solyndra Plan

Ben Bierman was one of the two Solyndra executives, along with founder Chris Gronet, who escorted President Obama on the now-infamous factory tour. Ben was responsible for Solyndra's manufacturing and oversaw the construction of the company's "futuristic" plant.[30] He wears big glasses, is of medium height, and has a round face with a traditional side hair part. He worked for several laser and semiconductor equipment manufacturing companies in the Valley before joining Solyndra soon after it was founded. Since the company filed for bankruptcy, he has been criticized for receiving large bonuses and for mismanagement.

I spoke with Ben on the phone a few months after the president's visit. Although the Commerce Department had no involvement with the Solyndra deal, I was curious about whether Solyndra would manage to defy the skeptics who were already predicting the company's demise. I was hopeful that it would because I knew that thousands of jobs were at stake.

Ben's perspective sheds light on what the Solyndra team was hoping to achieve. He began by providing a brief overview of the U.S. solar industry. He quickly recognized that I knew little about the industry and had had no interaction with the Department of Energy.

As Ben explained, in the early 1990s, the United States produced 40 percent of the world's solar panels and was the undisputed leader.[31] We did the most to develop and commercialize the technology, but then the markets for solar power shifted to Japan, which implemented a "New Sunshine Program" subsidizing solar technology development, and to Europe, where many nations required utilities to buy a percentage of solar energy at a fixed price. So solar panel manufacturers, including U.S. companies such as SunPower and Evergreen Solar, decided to locate manufacturing overseas to serve those markets. At the same time, Asian countries such as China, Taiwan, and Malaysia benefited from having large-scale semiconductor manufacturing and applied that expertise to make the crystalline silicon needed for solar panels.[32] Not only did these countries have a wage advantage over the United States, but they also provided solar manufacturers with free land and financial assistance. China was the most blatant example.[33] Ben singled out China not to gripe, but to let me know the competitive price pressures that his company was facing. As a result of China's aggressive strategy, most of the top 10 solar manufacturers today are Chinese. China has captured almost 55 percent of the global market for solar panels and 25 percent of the current $2 billion U.S. market.[34]

The response from Silicon Valley has been to invest in new technology for solar panels, namely thin film. On the most basic level, thin film reduces the amount of material required to create a solar cell. Thin-film panels are lighter, aesthetically more appealing, and theoretically cheaper to make than crystalline silicon panels. The trendsetter is First Solar, an Arizona-based company with a large manufacturing facility in Ohio, which has catapulted into one of the world leaders for solar panels using thin-film technology. But even First Solar has seen its stock plummet by nearly 85 percent from its peak in the face of the Chinese dumping of solar panels into the U.S. market.

What made Solyndra unique was its cylindrical design for thin-film panels, making them easier to install on rooftops. But they were too expensive to make, and there was no way to scale manufacturing to bring the cost down. Solyndra's panels cost more than the traditional silicon crystal panels that are being made in China with the aid of government subsidies.[35] Ultimately, Solyndra simply couldn't compete on cost.

Although Solyndra failed, it had a plan to reach profitability. Ben argued that the total cost of installing Solyndra's panels on rooftops was less than the cost of installing silicon crystalline flat panels. This wasn't just a theoretical claim. Ben listed Solyndra's well-known customers, including Anheuser-Busch, Coca-Cola, Frito-Lay, and the Seattle Seahawks. Sure, Solyndra's individual panels might cost more than conventional panels. But when you look at the total cost of installing a system on a rooftop, which Ben suggested was the right data point, then Solyndra's system cost less. The savings came mainly from not having to spend money screwing tubular panels, which are resistant to wind, into the roof. Ben was convinced that increased automation, such as robotic vehicles that transport materials throughout the factory floor, would also help Solyndra lower the cost of making an individual tubular panel in the next year or two. Unfortunately, Ben's optimism turned out to be wrong. Still, you can't fault the company for lacking a strategic plan. Before its collapse, Solyndra did install, according to Ben, "nearly 1 million panels on thousands of roofs in over 25 countries on 5 continents."

Despite automation, Solyndra was providing jobs for blue-collar workers. On the factory floor, the ability to run high-tech equipment and operate computers is often more important than a proficiency in trigonometry or calculus. Basic math matters, but beyond that, practical skills count. Ben talked with pride about one of his employees—a young high school graduate who had previously been working at Starbucks during the economic downturn. He operated Solyndra's vacuum deposition system. I barely understood what the machine does, but what I gathered is that it deposits, with precision and no contamination, the thin films that make up the tubular panel. Ben's star employee had mastered how to use the machine and earned his trust. Reflecting on this success story, Ben suggested that the ability to "interface with sophisticated machines" is perhaps the most important skill for a person seeking a job at a twenty-first-century manufacturing plant.

Ben laid out the business case for why Solyndra built its plant in the United States. The U.S. market is growing, which "helps swing things in favor" of manufacturing here. It's one thing to locate offshore to supply to Japan or even Germany, but sending materials to Asia, having them processed, and then shipping them all the way back to the United States is not as cost-effective. Moreover, Solyndra never considered China because of the "politics." It worried that doing a joint venture in China, which is the cost of entry into the country, would result in lost intellectual property.

Singapore, Malaysia, and the Philippines were more flexible and offered generous incentives, such as free land, big loans, and an allowance to train employees. However, the loan guarantee from the U.S. Department of Energy and the clean technology manufacturing tax credits for capital equipment provided some counterbalance. Although these benefits were not as large as those offered by other nations, Solyndra could point to them when justifying its decision to investors. The advantages of a sizable domestic market and better quality control, coupled with the United States' own incentives, tipped the scales to stay. Ben made it clear that its application for a loan guarantee started in the Bush administration and was completed in the Obama administration. There was a bipartisan commitment at the Department of Energy to provide Solyndra with incentives so that it could open its new solar factory in the United States. DOE officials were eager to provide capital financing for Solyndra to stay in the United States because, in their judgment, the company had already met the market test of raising significant private investment.

Solyndra deliberately chose Silicon Valley as the place to set up its factory, despite the higher cost of living there compared to other U.S. locations. There is "no place in the world where you can scale a business as fast," Ben said emphatically. "In five years, we went from an idea on paper to having hundreds of thousands of square feet of manufacturing. This is the best place to incubate technology and bring it to a certain level." The presence of talented engineers, venture capital, corporate legal services, and skilled trades creates an ideal environment for start-ups to get off the ground and perfect the prototype of a new technology. To borrow a metaphor from the automobile world, the Valley offers a zero-to-sixty advantage to start-ups.

Ben seemed nonplussed when I asked whether Solyndra would still be around 50 years from now. He didn't dwell on 50-year horizons. By then, there could be new technologies and better solutions. "Our commitment is to pay back the loan and to be profitable," he said. It might make sense to locate future plants in Oklahoma, Arizona, Michigan, or even overseas to export. Of course, the company was unable to live up to its commitment.

What Went Wrong?

Why, then, did Solyndra not make it through even a few years, let alone 50? There's no definitive answer, but three reasons stand out. For starters, Solyndra never managed to get its costs under control and reduce the burn rate. (The burn rate is the amount of investors' money a company is spending every quarter.) According to a former Department of Energy official, the people on the Solyndra team were so focused on building new factories and new technology that they forgot that they were running a business. In a very low margin business, they should have waited to build a new factory until they had perfected a technology that could compete in the marketplace. Their rationale for building a full-capacity plant was that, in the long run, it would save nearly 15 percent on manufacturing costs because of the efficiency of scale. However, their optimistic projections for the demand for their product turned out to be faulty, and in hindsight, they would have been better off taking an incremental approach to adding manufacturing capacity. The executive team also should not have continued to pay itself high salaries and bonuses while the company floundered.[36] It's debatable whether Solyndra could have survived, but the company never really had a chance. The members of the management team chose the wrong manufacturing model, scaling up prematurely. They were, perhaps, a bit too enamored with their own press and jumped stages before they were ready.

Second, there is the issue of Chinese dumping. China accumulated so much excess capacity that it was selling solar panels into the United States at about 50 percent of the cost of manufacturing them. Solyndra might have survived against fair competition, but it stood little chance against cheap Chinese silicon that was priced far lower than anyone could have forecast. In fact, the Coalition for American Solar Manufacturing, a coalition of seven solar companies, recently filed an antidumping complaint against Chinese manufacturers for "illegally dumping crystalline silicon solar cells into the U.S.

market and receiving illegal subsidies."[37] The Department of Commerce found that China did, in fact engage in the dumping of solar panels into the United States "at prices below their actual cost."[38]

Finally, bad luck also played a role. In 2011, when Solyndra was going through its cash crunch, the financial markets weren't doing well. The company was unable to raise the money it needed to keep afloat, given the tight capital markets. It was facing stiff competition from Chinese solar companies with falling prices and was unable to borrow enough funds to stay afloat. If anything, Solyndra's failure is evidence that our government isn't in the business of providing indefinite subsidies. If Solyndra were a Chinese company, there's a high likelihood that the Chinese government would have continued to pour money into the company to keep it afloat. In the United States, we rightfully do not have such a safety net for companies that don't meet the harsh realities of the marketplace.

Even though Solyndra failed, we shouldn't discount the role of start-ups in creating jobs. The Kauffman Foundation, perhaps the best-recognized center on entrepreneurship, concluded that start-ups have been more successful in creating jobs than large companies. Its study, titled "Firm Formation and Economic Growth: The Importance of Startups in Job Creation and Job Destruction," is based on data from the U.S. Census Bureau. The study concluded, "Existing firms are net job destroyers, losing 1 million jobs net combined per year. By contrast, in their first year, new firms add an average of 3 million jobs."[39] This finding was true for all but seven years from 1977 to 2005.

The study is a wake-up call that we have to do better at giving large corporations incentives to create jobs in this country. But it also means, as Robert Litan, vice president of research and policy at the Kauffman Foundation, points out, that job creation could be "boosted by supporting startup firms."[40] Kauffman Foundation president Carl Schramm goes further by stipulating that "the single most important contributor to a nation's economic growth is the number of startups that grow to a billion dollars in revenue within 20 years."[41] Fortunately, America creates far more new businesses than any other nation in the world, according to the most recent data from the World Bank.[42] The Valley can take its share of credit for this lead.

As with any start-up, there was no guarantee that Solyndra would succeed or have enough demand for its product.[43] But even as a failed experiment, it provides valuable lessons for future entrepreneurs.

Regardless of the outcome, clean technology companies such as Solyndra represent the type of "new undertakings" that Hamilton encouraged our nation to support.[44] Hamilton recognized that nascent industries require government assistance if they are to establish themselves. As he put it, "Bounties are in most cases indispensable to the introduction of a new branch" of industry. The reason is that "undertakers of a new manufacture" have to contend with both the "natural disadvantages of a new undertaking" and subsidies that other "governments bestow" on their competitors. Our federal government should be wary of picking winners and losers, but it can still play a role in the development of clean energy. The government can provide broad-based tax credits to help domestic clean energy manufacturers, and it can take a firmer stand against foreign competitors that engage in unfair dumping.

THE LONG TERM

What are the long-term prospects for the United States developing a thriving solar industry? Despite Solyndra, industry experts remain cautiously optimistic that the new technologies that the United States is developing will take hold in a solar market that is increasing in size. The American public certainly wants us to succeed. Regardless of political affiliation, more than 90 percent of Americans believe that it's important for America to develop and use solar energy.[45] It's probably unrealistic to think that the United States will ever be as dominant in this field as it was in the 1990s. But the hope is that we'll continue to lead the way in crossing new frontiers and developing the latest technology, helping not just our economy but also the planet.

A MAN IS NOT A PIECE OF FRUIT

"You guys love talking about the future. That's nice. But what are you doing to create jobs now?" asked a man in his mid-fifties, to thunderous applause from an angry audience of about 80 community members in Fremont, California. He was reacting to my brief remarks that Fremont could be a hub for new manufacturing in advanced technology industries. I'll admit I was expecting a different kind of reception.

Earlier in the week, our Commerce team had convened a successful symposium on the future of manufacturing in Fremont. The symposium was a response to the closure of the Toyota-owned NUMMI auto plant in Fremont, resulting in the layoff of nearly 4,700 workers. At the event, I, along with Congressman Pete Stark's district director, presented a grant to the city to help it prepare a plan for new manufacturing. We also highlighted many of the innovative clean technology, biotechnology, and high-technology companies that were manufacturing in the area. Speaker after speaker commended our vision. The local papers quoted elected officials who expressed their delight at receiving federal funds. So I figured that the meeting with Fremont residents, many of whom were Obama volunteers and supporters, would be a small victory lap for the administration's initiative to help the region.

What I didn't anticipate was that nearly a third of the attendees would be unemployed. My exchanges with the attendees provided me with an understanding of why the president's approval numbers sagged throughout 2010. People who had walked precincts for President Obama a couple of years earlier were now criticizing his administration openly. Clean technology made no difference in their immediate lives. They weren't impressed with the stimulus money, and they were furious that Washington was providing bailouts to the very bank executives who had got us into the financial mess. The road signs proclaiming America's recovery contradicted their everyday reality. From their vantage point, the administration appeared to be on the side of large corporations and financial institutions, as opposed to that of workers struggling to remain in the middle class. Corporate profits might have been at a record high, but they or their family members still couldn't find work. They had brought their résumés to give to me, hoping that I could forward them to someone—anyone, actually—who could provide them with a job.

One of the most poignant moments of the symposium came when Michael, a laid-off installation manager, had the floor. The 60-year-old spoke about how he was "involuntarily retired" from Macy's when Macy's eliminated its divisional structure in April of 2009.[46] His voice conveyed resignation more than anger. Michael's job was to manage the manufacturing and installation of equipment for Macy's West Coast stores. Since being laid off, Michael had been looking for positions with scores of companies, including those in clean tech. Despite 30 years of management experience, a college degree, and computer skills, he hadn't found anything. He was so desperate that he had even applied to Walmart for a job as a store greeter, placing his name 170th on the waiting list for the position. Time was running out for him, with his savings almost depleted. He lacked health insurance and wasn't old enough for Medicare. His wish in life was to find some work. Was there anything the administration could do to help?

Then there was the testimony from Sergio Santos, the president, at the time, of the local United Auto Workers Union. He talked about how his guys, many of them in their fifties and sixties, were afraid for the future. Some of them had spent their whole careers at the Toyota plant and had expected to retire from their jobs there. All they knew was how to make cars. Now, they had to scramble for something new. "Where are the green jobs for them?" Sergio asked rhetorically. The Brookings report highlighting that the economy has almost 2.7 million clean tech jobs, with wages that are almost 13 percent higher than the median wage, and rapid employment growth in the solar and wind sector had no tangible impact on his or his friends' lives.[47]

When I checked in with him months later, he shared that those who had been laid off were having a very difficult time, visiting food pantries and struggling to make mortgage payments. Sure, Tesla Motors, a dynamic and visionary electric vehicle company, had taken over part of the NUMMI site, with much fanfare from politicians and the press. The company offers great hope for the future of the region and the country. But Tesla hadn't committed to hiring any of Sergio's guys. Rather, Sergio explained that Tesla would probably hire younger employees whom it could mold, overlooking many of his members who had years of experience. Andreas Cluver, a passionate advocate for the Alameda County Building Trades Council, observed that Tesla had not, as of then, engaged his unions to do construction work.

Sergio also cautioned about putting too much stock in the One-Stop Career Center, set up with government funds. Sergio said that his members appreciated the counseling from caseworkers about searching for jobs and fine-tuning their résumés. But, the reality is, "It's not easy to find work as a 50-year-old when you haven't had to look for years." He continued, "You're throwing people out on the streets right before they can retire."

The fate of these workers reminded me of Willy Loman, age 63, who was fired because his company was no longer profitable and, as his boss explained, "business is business." Willy could have been speaking for many laid-off autoworkers at the Toyota plant, "I put 34 years into this firm. . . . You can't eat the orange and throw the peel away—a man is not a piece of fruit."[48]

Chronic unemployment is the underbelly of the Valley; throughout 2010, it hovered over 10 percent.[49] For all the hope that companies such as Serious Materials and Tesla offer, the Valley's future hinges equally on finding a way of lowering this rate. It's not just a moral issue. High unemployment leads to foreclosures; declining revenue for cities such as Fremont, Hayward, and San Jose; poorer school districts; depressed wages because of a "flooding of the labor market"; social tension; and increased crime.[50] It saps the Valley of its positive energy, making it a less attractive place for the most innovative minds to settle and raise families.

There's no easy answer to the problem of the Valley's unemployment. Robert Reich correctly worries about America's "two economies," where many workers are left behind despite increases in corporate profits and the stock market.[51] Part of the solution is to reduce the skills gap. Economists estimate that there are millions of jobs in the United States that could be filled if workers had proper, specialized training.[52] Later in the book, I'll address how to prepare an advanced manufacturing workforce, including the type of additional certifications that employers seek. That said, it's difficult to expect workers who are in their fifties or sixties and without income to enroll in classes based on only a vague hope for future employment. There need to be more jobs available for them.

Many of the proposals discussed throughout this book and summarized at its end can support and give incentives to businesses, including those in the Valley, to create more jobs. If implemented, these ideas, which come from those who live and breathe manufacturing, can lower unemployment in both the Valley and the nation. But they're only a start, not a panacea. What I do know is that we owe a comprehensive manufacturing agenda to workers who have toiled for years and are simply seeking the dignity and security of continued employment.

THE TAKEAWAY

BOLD EXPERIMENTATION

America's culture of risk taking is an intangible asset that accounts for our manufacturing leadership—and no place illustrates that fact better than Silicon Valley. The motto of the Valley is to dare to be different. Whether successful or not, most companies in the Valley are pushing the envelope of what is possible, which means that they're competing not simply on price, but on vision. If they can make products that dramatically save costs over the long term, such as Serious Materials's energy-efficient windows, then the market will pay for the higher value.

In an increasingly competitive world, our manufacturers simply can't afford to rest on their laurels. If an American manufacturer is offering the same product as a foreign counterpart, then there's a strong possibility that consumers will prefer the cheaper foreign alternative. That's why the best American manufacturers are always one step ahead, thinking creatively about how to improve the design and functionality of a product to provide consumers with new value. As the Solyndra example highlights, not every manufacturer is successful in implementing a novel business plan. Still, our manufacturers must take risks in order to evolve industry standards. That is the only way they can compete against foreign companies that have the benefit both of subsidies and of low-wage labor.

The days when American manufacturers could take their global dominance for granted, as they did immediately after World War II, are gone. Those who look at the glass as half empty point out that America's relative manufacturing position has declined since then. But competition, so long as it is fair, isn't something that we need to fear. Stiff global competition is challenging us to imagine the future more boldly. We may need to be more nimble and creative to keep our manufacturing lead, but the hope is that the competition will bring out the best in us, setting the stage for the twenty-first century to be perhaps our nation's greatest era when measured by our contributions to humanity's technological progress.

5

Going Global

■ ■ ■

The legendary football coach Vince Lombardi's insight that the "best defense is a good offense" applies to American manufacturers as well. The most successful ones aren't merely holding their position in domestic markets, but are also seeking buyers in foreign markets. These manufacturers are aware that both 95 percent of the world's consumers and 70 percent of the world's purchasing power are outside the United States.[1] They sell to developed markets in Europe and North America, and also to emerging markets in China, India, and Brazil, which have growing middle classes.

In his 2010 State of the Union address, President Obama announced the National Export Initiative, with a goal of doubling our exports in five years. President Obama followed in the tradition of President Kennedy, who, in 1962, had grasped the "importance of increasing American exports" to "expand our economy."[2] President Reagan also emphasized exports in his 1986 State of the Union address, and exports almost doubled in the next five years.[3] The Clinton administration brought a new focus on "emerging markets," and export growth was robust throughout the 1990s.[4] To this day, people at the Commerce Department speak fondly about Secretary Ron Brown's vision and leadership in export promotion.

Despite the bipartisan focus on exports over the last 50 years, America needs to do better. Currently, only 1 percent of American businesses export.[5] Nearly 58 percent of the companies that do export do so only to one market, most likely Canada or Mexico.[6] They're still reluctant to venture out to Latin America, Asia, or even Europe. It's not surprising, then, that exports make up only 11 percent of the U.S. gross domestic product (GDP). In comparison, exports are nearly 50 percent of Germany's GDP, more than 30 percent of China and Russia's GDP, more than 25 percent of both the United Kingdom and India's GDP, and nearly 20 percent of Japan's GDP.[7] Even Brazil has a higher export percentage than ours by a few points.[8]

Anyone who remembers Econ 101 will understand why we need to increase our exports. A nation's GDP, you'll recall, is equal to consumption plus investment plus government spending plus exports minus imports. During times of large deficits and lower consumer confidence, we need exports to be strong in order to drive economic growth. This was demonstrated in the first year of the president's National Export Initiative. Exports were up 17 percent in 2010, accounting for a significant percentage of that year's GDP growth.[9]

Our 109 domestic Commerce offices were front and center in responding to President Obama's call to double exports. They're the first stop for a business that wants to export but is unsure how to do so. The offices provide matchmaking services, finding potential buyers for an American company that wants to sell overseas. They work with the Export-Import Bank to help secure financing for these transactions at a time when capital is tight. They engage in advocacy, reducing trade barriers and import duties for American products, and promoting American goods to both foreign firms and foreign governments. This advocacy is often overlooked by the media, which focuses on the role of trade agreements in promoting exports. Agreements that open markets for American products while upholding labor standards are, of course, important, but they're just one tool in our arsenal. Any Commerce trade specialist will tell you that her day-to-day work with our embassies to solve a particular exporter's problems is equally critical.

These specialists will also tell you that the biggest barrier to increasing exports is cultural. For more than 50 years, many of America's small and medium-sized business did not look overseas because the domestic market dwarfed any foreign opportunity. Some companies had an "international" department out of obligation. But overseas sales were a secondary consideration, a nice bonus if such sales fell in their lap.

Every day, Commerce trade specialists challenge this culture of complacency by encouraging American companies to step out of their comfort zones. They attend Chamber of Commerce events and business forums, making presentations on why companies must have an affirmative exporting strategy. They put local business executives, who may not be well traveled, at ease with exporting by teaching them how to navigate regulations and sharing anecdotes about social customs that they will encounter. Their greatest service is educational, helping Americans understand the opportunities of the new global economy.

These trade specialists, unfortunately, have few government incentives to offer exporters. The World Trade Organization (WTO) rules prohibit that. When we were contributing ideas to design the president's National Export Initiative, I suggested that we provide a tax incentive to companies that export. Senior trade experts quickly shot down my idea as naïve. They gently mocked me for suggesting something that is a direct violation of the WTO.

Remarkably, the WTO allows countries that have a value-added tax, such as China and Germany, to provide generous tax credits to their exporters (around 17 percent), but prohibits the United States, which has a corporate income tax, from providing any tax credits to its exporters. What's more, U.S. companies must pay the value-added tax to China and Germany when they export, but Chinese and German companies are exempt from paying the corporate income tax when they sell into our market. This makes no sense.

That's why scholars from the Peterson Institute for International Economics, a think tank that has received bipartisan praise, called for revising the WTO's "archaic" distinction between indirect and direct taxes and ending discrimination against U.S. companies.[10] Either the United States should be allowed to offer a tax credit to its exporters, or other countries should be prohibited from doing so. The WTO rules are particularly offensive considering that American markets are far more open than those of our emerging competitors, such as Brazil, Russia, India, and China.[11] Former president Clinton recently argued that removing the unfair burden on our exports is one of the most critical things we can do to "bring manufacturing back."[12]

Of course, reforming the structure of the WTO is a long and arduous process. In the meantime, despite the structural disadvantages, a number of American manufacturers, with help from Commerce trade specialists, are enjoying booming sales overseas that are contributing to their profits and sustaining domestic jobs. This chapter looks at how Schramm,

Inc., Pucker Powder, and A123 Systems are winning the business, and in some cases the hearts, of people around the world.

SAVING THE CHILEAN MINERS

American manufacturers helped save the Chilean miners. In his 2011 State of the Union address, President Obama singled out one of the heroes, Brandon Fisher, who is the owner of Center Rock Inc., a company in Berlin, Pennsylvania. As the president pointed out, Brandon designed the drill bits that were used to drill the escape hole for the miners. Brandon personally traveled to Chile and assisted in the drilling efforts for more than a month. What the president didn't mention in the speech was that another Pennsylvania-based company also deserves credit for the rescue: Schramm, Inc., manufactured the machine that anchored the entire effort.

Schramm's T130XD, now known as the "Miracle" in Chile, looks like a fire engine that has a drilling rig mounted to it. A drilling rig is a vertical metallic apparatus that is used to bore holes in the ground. Brandon's specialized drilling bits were inserted into the T130XD drilling rig to do the job. Schramm had sent Jeff Roten to Chile, and he worked with Brandon during the drilling to make sure that the T130XD was operating to its fullest potential. The two of them were in daily telephone and e-mail communication with Greg Hillier, the product manager, and other senior executives at Schramm, Inc. They strategized on how to overcome obstacles that they encountered during the drilling, such as a metal bar or unusually hardened or abrasive rock.

Team Pennsylvania wasn't the only one trying to reach the miners. The Chileans had orchestrated a three-way race to drill an escape hole. There was an Australian drilling rig called Strata 950 that was being operated to reach the miners, but this rig was comparatively slow and left debris that would have made it difficult for the miners to escape. There was also a Canadian oil-drilling rig, RIG-421, adorned with Canadian flags, that many of the miners' family members had expected would quickly reach the miners.[13] What they didn't anticipate was that the gigantic rig would have difficulty digging the precisely targeted hole that was necessary for the miners' escape.

Fortunately for the Chilean miners, the race wasn't even close. The Chilean government had projected that the drilling would last four months, and that one of the three efforts might succeed sometime before Christmas. So there was astonishment and elation when the T130XD reached the miners in a little over a month and had created a wide enough escape hole in the process. The other rigs, of course, abandoned their efforts once the T130XD achieved this "miracle." The miners were safely returned to the surface by mid-October.

Brandon Fisher from Center Rock and Jeff Roten from Schramm returned back home a few days after the rescue hole had been completed. They weren't interested in seeking the limelight or taking the attention away from the Chilean miners and their families. The Americans had come to do a job. They did it to perfection, and then they got out of the way. It's because of companies like Center Rock and Schramm that "Made in America" still evokes trust in almost every corner of the globe.

Supplying the World from West Chester

The Obama administration sent me to visit Schramm, Inc., to acknowledge the company's accomplishment in Chile. Secretary Gary Locke had presented it with an award at a major exporting conference. But it was left to me to make the trip to West Chester, Pennsylvania, and meet with the employees themselves.

Tony Ceballos, our Philadelphia office director who works with Schramm, picked me up from the Philadelphia train station on a snowy winter day. Dan O'Brien, our deputy national field director, accompanied me from Washington and had persuaded me not to cancel the trip despite the storm. The company had been preparing for the visit for weeks. So we drove through the ice-covered roads to West Chester, which is about an hour west of Philadelphia.

West Chester is a charming small town with Colonial architecture and brick sidewalks. It has a population of about 20,000. The streets are narrow and lined with restaurants, coffee shops, craft stores, art galleries, and the occasional fast-food joint. As we drove through the city, we were puzzled as to where in this town a drilling rig manufacturer could be located. Mapquest had let us down. Tony finally called his contact at Schramm, and he received directions referencing well-known city landmarks, including Green Mount Cemetery and West Chester Henderson High School. Schramm's 27-acre facility was just a mile or so away from downtown.

We were greeted by Ed Breiner, the CEO; Fred Slack, the vice president of business development; and Jim Dolan, the vice president for manufacturing. Ed is an imposing figure, tall and broad-shouldered, and clearly in charge. When he spoke, the others deferred. Fred, on the other hand, has a swimmer's build and is somewhat reserved. He was instrumental in arranging our visit and very welcoming, but he let others do most of the talking. Jim is short, skinny, and balding, yet he exuded charisma because of his passion for manufacturing. A Naval Academy graduate, he had turned around a number of manufacturing plants and was eager to talk about what makes Schramm competitive.

After handing our overcoats to the receptionist, we began the factory tour. The facility was spread out, with separate buildings for different parts of the production. We walked through parking lots covered with slush, with the wind blowing against us. Dan and I looked at each other occasionally, freezing, but we pretended to be unaffected. The last thing we were going to do was ask to go back for our coats and seal our image as a couple of wimps from Washington.

Jim smiled when we entered the main facility, a building about 100 feet high and a quarter mile wide and long, which is the final assembly site for the rigs. "You couldn't walk in this place a couple of years ago," Jim explained. "It was covered with black grime, and had equipment all over." Jim convinced Ed to spend millions of dollars on renovation during the Great Recession, when the company's sales were down. "I had committed to Jim, and so we did it," Ed stated plainly. The renovations have made production more efficient and also improved morale. Workers now enjoy being in the space, and clients can see the towering rigs undistracted by messiness.

As we walked through the other buildings, Jim explained the keys to Schramm's manufacturing strategy. He pointed out that quality control is done on each component part, instead of waiting until the final product. This reduces the likelihood of defects. Jim also obsesses about reducing the time for manufacturing each part. This isn't simply to reduce labor hours—rather, the less time the part spends on the floor, the fewer the errors. However, Jim is perhaps most passionate about customization. Almost every part meets a customer's specifications. Considering that a rig costs up to $2.5 million, Jim believes that customers are entitled to have input not just on the final product but on each of its components. So Schramm workers don't have the luxury of repeating the same production process. They have to think. They tweak the process for every new order, tailoring each component part to meet a particular function.

The latest technology gives the company an additional advantage. Schramm recently installed a new plasma burn table, at a cost of more than a million dollars. The table allows Schramm to cut materials incredibly close to their final shape, dramatically reducing raw material waste. The precision also reduces the weight of the rig so that it falls within highway weight limits, thereby making it more attractive to consumers. Then there's the Integrex, the newest generation of computer numerical control (CNC) machines. A CNC machine accepts raw materials and then, through complex, automated processes, turns out a finished part.

Schramm's most prized asset, though, is its workforce. As Fred put it, "The pride of workmanship runs deep." The company has many long-term employees and little turnover, but Ed is most impressed with the kids who are willing to roll up their sleeves. He spoke with admiration about a young man who grew up on a farm in middle Pennsylvania and is one of the first to arrive at work and the last to leave. No task is beneath him. Those who have only book learning rarely make it in Schramm's culture. Ed's concern is that the nation doesn't have enough young folks who can operate machines or who have an intuitive grasp for solving mechanical puzzles. The company has difficulty recruiting employees with these skills. That's why Schramm has invested in scholarships for students at Penn College of Technology in Williamsport, Pennsylvania, which has graduated some of the company's best workers.

Although he has great confidence in his workforce, Ed hasn't been afraid to seek outside perspectives to improve the company's manufacturing. He has little respect for fancy consulting firms with Ivy League graduates who have insufficient real-world experience. But he spoke very positively about the contributions of the Delaware Valley Industrial Resource Center (DVIRC). DVIRC receives funding from the Manufacturing Extension Partnership (MEP), the federal program discussed at length earlier. It sends an industry veteran to Schramm quarterly to work with the senior management team to implement the latest manufacturing techniques and processes.

Schramm's commitment to manufacturing excellence is rewarded by a global customer base: an astonishing 70 percent of the company's revenue is based on exports. This was true before the Chilean miner rescue. The miner story may have put Schramm on the front pages of newspapers, but the reality is that Schramm has been selling its rigs overseas for years—and not just to Chile but to many other nations as well.

Ed explained that most mining is being done overseas, and so the company gives priority to international sales. Schramm drilling rigs have a reputation for being compact, mobile, and high-performance. The company's brand certainly drives inquiries and orders. But Schramm isn't content to wait for customers to come to it. The company also aggressively seeks to enter new markets and get business. It works closely with trade specialists at the Commercial Service, including Tony Ceballos and Janice Barlow, for export counseling and matchmaking services. These specialists have helped Schramm conduct market research and find buyers in Argentina, Austria, China, and Venezuela. The specialists also facilitated Schramm's participation in trade shows in Brazil and China that led to business.

When I asked what more the federal government could do to facilitate exports, Ed brought up the trade practices of both Brazil and China. Brazil's duties and import documentation requirements are huge barriers to entry for Schramm.

Ed argued that the United States should demand basic reciprocity from Brazil, requiring it to be as open to our companies as we are to its. But what concerned Ed more is China's
state-sanctioned theft of Schramm's technology. Recently,
the Shijiazhuang Zhongmei Coal Mine Equipment Company attempted to copy the T130XD with the help of both the
Shijiazhuang municipal government authorities and Hebei
provincial authorities. This project was authorized as a National Development and Reform Commission (NDRC) priority, with China University of Petroleum in Beijing supporting
it. Thus far, the Chinese effort has not paid dividends. The
copied rigs are of poor quality and haven't captured any of the
global market. Ed is concerned, however, that if the Chinese
put enough money into the copying efforts, they may eventually succeed. "The first time I met a businessman from China,
he talked about technology transfers," said Ed, frustrated by
the lack of transparency in China. He went on to explain how
he'd like the U.S. Trade Representative to investigate and initi-
ate more WTO actions against China for intellectual property
infringement.

The guys in West Chester aren't asking much from their
government. They want us to keep the competition honest and
to continue to provide them with assistance in selling into foreign markets. At stake are not just American jobs but whether
people around the world will have access to the type of technology that has a proven record of saving lives.

Investing in the U.S. and Foreign Commercial Service

The U.S. and Foreign Commercial Service is the principal export
promotion agency of the federal government. It's made up of
109 domestic offices, which I oversaw and whose function I

outlined at the beginning of this chapter. It also has foreign commercial officers in our embassies in nearly 80 nations. The service has nearly 20,000 clients like Schramm, Inc., counseling almost 10 percent of American businesses that are currently exporting. It's responsible for facilitating thousands of export sales worth more than $50 billion each year. The agency achieves these results with a headcount of less than 1,500 individuals and a budget of about $250 million.

Ask almost any businessperson who's retained the Commercial Service, and he or she will tell you that it's a government agency that works. For a fee of several hundred dollars, businesses receive assistance that often translates into six-figure export sales. The service's success is attributable to its culture. It's a bottom-up organization in which the best ideas come from the field, not from Washington bureaucrats. The organization has zero tolerance for paper pushers who are content to check off boxes. Regional managers get rid of such dead weight in the annual performance reviews. The trade specialists who survive show initiative. They offer customized and innovation solutions to help clients increase their global market share, routinely working on a weekend or late into the evening.

Despite this success, for almost a decade the Commercial Service has faced shrinking budgets when you take inflation and rising rent overseas into account. Our nation's lack of support for the women and men who are advancing our economic interests is appalling. When I joined the administration in 2009, trade specialists didn't even have BlackBerries. We scrounged through the budget to provide them. The Commercial Service still requires funding to improve its web portal for exporters, to meet basic travel needs and to ramp up staffing. Some states have stand-alone offices with only one Commerce official to service the entire population! Many overseas posts, such as those in China and Canada, are woefully understaffed, resulting in a waiting list for American businesses that seek assistance in selling into those markets.

Unfortunately, instead of providing the service with more funding, Congress proposed nearly $100 million of aggregate cuts in its budget and that of related export promotion agencies.[14] These cuts are motivated by a sincere desire to reduce our federal deficit. But the service, which supports more than $200 in export revenue for every tax dollar spent, helps grow the tax base.

Consider what other countries are doing when it comes to export promotion. According to economists at the Department of Commerce who have studied this matter, China's Ministry of Commerce has nearly 4,000 individuals dedicated to export promotion, with an estimated budget of $1.5 billion. In other words, China has nearly three times the personnel we do, and six times the budget. Or take Britain. Despite having a significantly smaller population, it has a budget of nearly $500 million and almost 2,400 trade specialists. Similarly, Germany has about 2,700 trade specialists, nearly twice what we have.

Just as we have the best military in the world, we should have the best export promotion agency in the world in an age in which battles are increasingly fought along economic lines. The global economy lacks perfect information and transparent rules. We can't expect our small and medium-sized businesses to fend for themselves while their foreign competitors rely on their national governments to open doors. Our trade specialists are as talented and dynamic as any government employees in the world. But they need adequate resources. Congress should support, at a minimum, a 25 percent increase in the Commercial Service's headcount and budget.

EXPORT ALABAMA: A MODEL APPROACH

There's a misperception that only states near the coast are interested in exporting. Alabama is a great counterexample. Of the states I visited, Alabama stood out for having extraordinary teamwork among state agencies, local chambers of commerce, city governments, educational institutions, and the U.S. Department of Commerce to promote exports. The Export Alabama Trade Alliance, which brings these diverse players under one umbrella, serves as a model for other states across our nation. The alliance works closely with the governor's office to develop and implement a trade strategy for Alabama.

One of the alliance's marquee events is the Governor's Trade Excellence Award reception, where leading Alabama exporters are recognized. A few months after the 2010 midterm elections, I went down to Montgomery to give a speech at this event. I was apprehensive about how I'd be received, considering that the state had just swept Republicans into office at every level. It didn't help matters that the night before my speech, I'd been stranded at the Charlotte, North Carolina, airport because of cancelled flights. After a night without much sleep, I finally managed to get onto an early morning flight to Montgomery, but my baggage didn't arrive when we landed, so I had to borrow a staff member's suit, which was too big for me. As I walked into the State Chambers, I was concerned that I wouldn't make a very good impression on behalf of the president in a state that already was skeptical of his policies.

Thankfully, Governor Robert Bentley, Seth Hamett, the former speaker of the House, and the state's other political, economic, and education leaders in attendance quickly put me at ease. Some made good-natured jokes about my suit (word travels fast in Montgomery). All of them, however, went out of their way to tell me how much they appreciated my coming.

They had recommendations for their favorite barbecue places, and a couple of businessmen even offered to drive me around town and show me their favorite spots. Everyone applauded heartily when I was introduced and when I finished my remarks. The response had nothing to do with what I had said, but more to do with the respect and warmth with which Alabamans treat their guests.

I learned that Nelda Segars, one of our local Commercial Service officials, was referred to as "the Grandmother of Alabama." She knew everyone at the reception, and everyone gushed about her. There were no turf battles between the state and federal agencies, and no one seemed to pay attention to partisan affiliations that day. When it comes to promoting business, Alabama's leaders seem to put their state first and politics second. They view Alabama as an important hub in the global economy, and they speak passionately about doing business in India, China, and Latin America. The state's coordinated focus on exports has borne results. Alabama's exports grew a remarkable 25 percent from 2009 to 2010, more than national exports, which grew about 20 percent.[15]

Scott Green was one of the awardees recognized by Governor Bentley at the event. He and Kathy Green, his wife, founded Pucker Powder. One year later, their relatives Bruce and Karri Goldstein joined them in the venture. Scott goes out of his way to give Bruce and Karri credit for the company's international success. The company sells powdered candy that's dispensed out of a machine into a clear tube, which Scott designed. For the first five years, Scott and Kathy struggled to make ends meet. Kathy worked a number of jobs to keep the company afloat, and Scott focused on the business full time. Today, the business is thriving, with more than 30 full-time employees, an expanded 70,000-square-foot production facility, and more than 20,000 orders annually from around the world. You may have seen these machines on your trip to Disney World, where they're branded as Goofy's Sour Powder.

When I was introduced to Scott, I was told that he was an "inventor." But Scott quickly rejected that label. "The idea of a solitary inventor does not make sense. I get ideas from all over: my employees, my grandmother, my wife, my business partner." He invited me to tour Pucker Powder's facility. So Nelda, the rest of the Commerce team, and I drove about an hour to Irondale, Alabama, to learn what makes the business a global success.

Connecting from Irondale to the Global Marketplace

We were seated in one of Pucker Powder's conference rooms as Scott shared how his company's exports went from "nothing or little" to more than 22 percent of total revenue within the span of a few years. Irondale is a city of less than 10,000 with an Asian population of less than 1 percent and a Hispanic population of less than 3 percent. If Pucker Powder can sell to more than 20 foreign countries, then there's hope for almost every small business across our nation to go global. The key is to know how to get started.

What made the difference for Pucker Powder was an international trade show. After the business had established a strong domestic presence in theme parks across the country, Scott became interested in exporting. He and Bruce Goldstein, the driving force behind the company's sales, visited the Alabama International Trade Center and local Commerce offices, which recommended that Pucker Powder participate in an international trade show. In 2007, Scott and Bruce decided to attend the International Sweets and Biscuits Fair in Germany, the largest trade show in the confectionary industry. The show drew more than 30,000 people and the most sophisticated and largest international clientele for candy. Pucker Powder purchased a booth in the U.S. pavilion with the help of some subsidies from the U.S. Department of Agriculture. At the show, Pucker Powder won its first international customers from Bolivia and France. The company also developed relationships that eventually led to sales in Australia, New Zealand, the United Kingdom, and the Middle East, including to Saudi Arabia, Jordan, and Kuwait.

Scott now recommends that any small business that is interested in exporting participate in a trade show. There, businesses will find distributors who can handle most of the sales, eliminating many of the bureaucratic and cultural challenges of selling overseas. Trade shows are expensive, though. That's why Scott is a proponent of the argument that the U.S. government should help defray the travel and participation costs of small businesses that are attending these shows for the first time. The businesses could, in turn, reimburse the government if they line up a sale at the show. Our Department of Agriculture provides such incentives to food companies. However, the Trade Fair Certification program in the Department of Commerce doesn't have the funding to provide these incentives to American manufacturers more generally. Congress should provide the Trade Fair Certification program with a budget to support new exporters, such as Pucker Powder, that are interested in attending trade shows. This would help grow our exporter base, improving the dismal statistic that only 1 percent of American companies currently export.

The Trade Fair Certification program could also help finance U.S. pavilions in which American companies can set up their booths. When you go a trade show, it's embarrassing how often the British, German, Turkish, Italian, or Egyptian pavilions put ours to shame, because their governments subsidize pavilions that are chic and modern. Our pavilions, while competent, don't have nearly the same draw. This is, in part, because of a resource differential. We leave the financing of our pavilions entirely to private companies such as Reed Exhibitions, which have tight budgets. It's time for our government to make a modest investment in these pavilions the way it does in our embassies. Our pavilions represent our manufacturers abroad, so they should be of the highest quality.

After we discussed the value of trade shows, Scott vented his frustration about the barriers to entry into the Chinese market. Apparently, China's customs officials often don't let food products into the country, ruling arbitrarily based on the political climate that the food isn't safe to eat. Pucker Powder can't take the risk of having its containers returned or confiscated. Moreover, the company doesn't have the resources to pay Chinese authorities for access to the market, as a well-known candy maker did to the tune of nearly $80,000. The only way Pucker Powder can sell in China is by manufacturing in China. As a consequence, China is its only overseas manufacturing location. Pucker Powder supplies the rest of the world, including Brazil, India, and Mexico, from its Irondale facility.

When I asked why Pucker Powder doesn't supply other Asian and Middle Eastern countries from China, Scott replied that consumers in other nations continue to want American products; they won't buy candy that is made in China. The Chinese government may be able to force its own citizens to buy Chinese, but American products "command more money" and prestige in almost every other nation.

Scott was eager to show us the facility to give us a sense of the advantages of manufacturing in America. From the outside, Pucker Powder looks like a tidy warehouse that blends in with homes and shops in a largely residential community. But the appearance is deceptive. As soon as I walked onto the factory floor, I realized that it's a state-of-the-art, high-tech facility. The most impressive area is the printing shop, where Scott and Kathy oversee the customized design of labels for each of the different markets. They make hundreds of different creative labels, each of which appeals to a particular locality. The printing isn't restricted to two-dimensional labeling; the Greens are also innovating by adopting 3-D printing, one of the latest advances in modern manufacturing. They have employees who draw in 3-D parts of the Pucker Powder machine, then send the prototype to a local company that uses it to make the parts. Pucker Powder gets the manufactured parts within a few days and assembles the machine on its floor. According to Scott, the customized labeling and 3-D printing process is far easier if employees are in the same space than if they're trying to communicate across multiple time zones. The Grovian insight of integrating design and production applies to making candy as much as to making computer chips!

Scott hopes that Pucker Powder may become a $300 million company, but it's not money that motivates him and Kathy or their partners, Bruce and Karri. None of them views the company as a traditional candy wholesaler. "Kids are more attracted to the colors than the flavors," Scott observes. "Our own kids aren't allowed to have any candy during the week," he continues. "Candy is a snack," not a daily meal. For the Pucker Powder team, the deeper mission is to foster children's creativity by involving them in making something they like. They love watching kids engage with the Pucker Powder machines, mixing colors and filling their tubes with "candy art." As they see it, they have the best jobs: they get to work each day with employees in their hometown to share their artistry with children around the world.

THE IMMIGRANT ADVANTAGE: UNLEASHING THE BEST AND THE BRIGHTEST

My stump speech concerning the president's National Export Initiative had a two-liner that would usually get laughs: "When we negotiate with China, we send Commerce Secretary Gary Locke, a Chinese American. China doesn't send someone of American origin to negotiate with us!" I'd then go on to share that the deputy secretary at Commerce is an African American, our undersecretary is a Hispanic American, and I, of course, am of Indian origin. Our incredible diversity at Commerce reflected the diversity of our nation, which gives us an edge in a global economy. Immigrant populations, with their global frame of reference, are often most appreciative of the comparative benefits of American manufacturing. Moreover, they understand the local culture, language, politics, opportunities, and challenges of almost every overseas market.

The critical role that immigrants play in domestic manufacturing is evident at A123 Systems, a lithium-ion battery company based in Massachusetts. The company was founded by Yet-Ming Chiang, an MIT professor. Desh Deshpande, a serial entrepreneur who founded an MIT center focused on commercializing technology, is A123's chairman. Although the company has a manufacturing facility abroad, the majority of its manufacturing is domestic. When I visited, Andy Chu, the company's vice president of marketing and communications, explained that the company's leadership prefers keeping production within the United States because the quality of engineering here is the best in the world.

I was pleasantly surprised by this observation. "I keep hearing that China is turning out all the engineers. Is that not true?" I asked. Andy explained that while China graduates a greater number of engineers than we do, engineers in the United States tend to be more seasoned and have greater experience in their field. Specifically, U.S. engineers typically have far more practical knowledge that has been acquired through years of firsthand on-the-job training. As a result, U.S. engineers are more adept at solving problems when they are faced with a new, unexpected situation. Because engineers in China typically have not gained this valuable on-the-job experience, they require more explicit instructions to accomplish a particular task, and sometimes an impasse is created when those instructions do not work. Such has been the case at A123, when in some instances, as Andy pointed out, projects in China would "grind to a halt" whenever the instructions didn't work.

In contrast, A123's American workers, regardless of their ethnic background, are trained to rely more on their experience and acquired analytical skills than on top-down commands or standard operating procedures. If they encounter obstacles, they don't stop what they're doing but instead draw upon their past experiences to resolve the issue. One of the senior engineers present at the meeting credited "Yankee ingenuity" for A123 batteries having a longer life and superior power compared to their competitors' products.

Andy's belief in American manufacturing is not knee-jerk patriotism. He's deeply proud of his Chinese heritage, and he has great respect for the work ethic and intelligence of Chinese workers. But his life story has given him an appreciation of the unique culture and economic system that allow people from all over the world to be the most creative in America.

Andy's parents were born in China and fled from the Communists to Taiwan in the late 1940s. They came to the United States for graduate school in the early to mid-1960s, and Andy was born in Annapolis, Maryland. In the 1970s, Andy's father owned an American Motors car dealership in New Jersey that sold the Pacer and the Gremlin, so, Andy was exposed to entrepreneurship and immigrant values early in his life.

Meanwhile, A123 gave Andy the chance to explore his Chinese roots. He spent more than a year living in China, helping to set up the company's operations there, while also building relationships with customers to promote exports. During this time, his Chinese improved considerably. However, he also observed firsthand the frustrations of working in China and the bureaucratic bottlenecks imposed on creativity. As he put it, "My dad has often said that my brother and I have no idea how lucky we are that we were born in the United States. After spending time in Asia and being able to see things from a different perspective, I am beginning to realize what he meant." Andy is particularly bullish on immigrants contributing to America's future: "It takes a certain personality to make a new life as an immigrant. Imagine if you had to move to a new country, learn the language, adapt to the culture, and make a new life for yourself and maybe your family. This is not for the faint-hearted. It takes self-motivation and resourcefulness. This self-selected population has certain skills that I believe will serve the United States well."

The extraordinary drive and initiative of many immigrants helps explain their entrepreneurial success. Nonetheless, immigrant entrepreneurs also often benefit from the support of our federal government. This is true in the case of A123. Andy credits the federal government's grant of $100,000 to MIT professor Yet-Ming Chiang to develop new battery materials for electric vehicles as essential to the company's founding. The grant was made by the Department of Energy under the Bush administration in 2002. Then, in 2003, A123 was awarded an additional $750,000 from the Department of Energy to demonstrate a cost-effective process for manufacturing electric vehicle batteries. A few years later, in 2006 and 2008, the U.S.

Advanced Battery Consortium (USABC) awarded A123 contracts for the further development of these batteries.

Federal support for A123 continued under the Obama administration. In 2009, A123 was awarded a $249 million grant from the U.S. Department of Energy primarily to build its manufacturing facility in Livonia, Michigan. According to Andy, the facility integrates design and production, and spans "research and development, manufacturing of high-value components such as A123 Systems' proprietary Nanophosphate cathode powder, electrode coating, cell fabrication, module fabrication, and the final assembly of complete battery pack systems."

These bipartisan investments are in the national interest. The stakes are high. For decades, China and Japan's governments have invested in developing advanced lithium-ion batteries. As a result, China currently has 40 percent and Japan 36 percent of the global market, compared to only 2 percent for the United States.[16] Fortunately, the market for advanced batteries thus far has been limited to electric bicycles and consumer electronics. The demand for electric vehicle batteries is new, and it provides the United States with an opportunity to grab market share in a big way. The global market for these new batteries is expected to exceed $50 billion. The investments that the Bush and Obama administrations made in A123 and similar battery companies are intended to help the United States take the lead in this space.

And as it turns out, those investments are paying off. In just a few years, A123 has established itself as one of the global industry leaders, attracting customers like Daimler, General Motors, Fisker Automotive, and BMW. The Chinese are already pleading with the company to share its cutting-edge technology through joint venture agreements. That said, A123's success is by no means guaranteed, and critics have pointed out that the company needs to attract more customers for long-term profitability.

A123 is by no means the only American company driving technological advances in electric vehicle batteries. The reality is that U.S. battery makers, in the aggregate, are filing far more patents than Chinese companies. They are even closing the gap with Japan, which was, until recently, the undisputed innovator in batteries. Our entrepreneurs who represent the best and brightest from around the world are doing their part. The question is whether we, as a nation, will continue to stand with them and make the strategic, diversified, and discrete investments that we have often made to launch, in Hamilton's words, a "new industry."

Overseas Obstacles

A123's diverse leadership helps the company enter into markets around the world. Throughout that process, the company's biggest challenge is overcoming trade barriers, both legal and cultural. While the United States is willing to import batteries from anywhere in the world, other nations aren't as open.

China, for example, requires companies such as A123 to sign joint venture agreements as a condition of selling into the Chinese market. If A123 wants to sell to Chinese consumers, the company must share its technology with a Chinese partner and do a significant portion of the manufacturing in China. Andy Chu and his team explained the creative approach that A123 often takes in negotiations with the Chinese: they're willing to provide the Chinese with access to past technology, but not immediate access to the latest cutting-edge technology. A123's bet is that any intellectual property loss through its

Chinese partner will be slow and that giving away past technology won't put it at a significant competitive disadvantage, even if it did leak out.

As Andy Chu puts it:

> A technological advantage has a finite shelf life—the best a company can hope is to delay the competition. A123, like all good companies, continues to innovate. When a strong partnership is established, part of the attraction to working with A123 is that it can offer its Chinese partners with a steady pipeline of new products and innovations, provided they "re-up" their commitment. By always having something better in the pipeline, A123 is able to forge stronger bonds by offering access to these advancements, provided the arrangement continues to serve both parties. That's a page taken from the Chinese playbook: a strong partnership requires trust, but continues to thrive because both parties have something the other side wants.

In a perfect world, China wouldn't deprive its citizens of access to American goods by imposing joint venture requirements. America certainly doesn't require Chinese companies to sign joint venture agreements in order to sell into our market. However, until the Chinese are persuaded to give priority to consumer welfare, the A123 model of distinguishing between past and future innovation when signing joint venture agreements is instructive for other companies that are seeking to export to China.

Japan also is a difficult market to penetrate, but not because of artificial barriers. The Japanese place a high premium on establishing social bonds as a precondition for doing business, which is different from the situation in the United States.

In America, local manufacturers can seldom rely on cultural affinities to generate sales; rather, it's price and quality that usually drive purchasing decisions. In Japan, relationships come first. As a consequence, Japanese firms have a cultural advantage in supplying to the domestic market.

But this advantage isn't insurmountable for American firms. A123 executives recognized that in order to penetrate the Japanese market, they first had to become part of the Japanese business family. They grasped that if an American company could establish trust in Japan, then Japanese consumers, in turn, were capable of being very loyal. So A123 worked tirelessly to cultivate relationships in Japan, and its efforts have already begun to show results: the company recently entered into a joint marketing agreement with IHI Corporation, a Japanese battery supplier to Toyota, Honda, and Nissan.[17] The lesson for aspiring American exporters is simple: understanding and respecting foreign business practices is critical for success.

Exporting batteries is hard not only to Asia but also to Europe. It's a myth that European markets are open and easy for American companies to penetrate. When it comes to batteries, for example, that is not the case. Germany and France both have nationalistic strategies in the electric battery space, providing generous subsidies to domestic manufacturers. In 2009, Germany passed its "National Electromobility Development Plan," with an overall goal of leading the electric battery market by 2020. To meet these goals, the German Federal Government initiated the Lithium-Ion Battery Alliance (LIB 2015) and provided a budget of more than $80 million to German companies to develop lithium-ion technology. France's Strategic Investment Fund will be investing more than $170 million in the construction of Renault's lithium-ion production facility over the next three years. European nations further restrict imports by creating certification standards tailored toward domestic manufacturers and imposing duties on foreign batteries. As one senior Commerce official studying the electric battery market put it, "These countries will all be damned if they aren't producing the lithium-ion batteries for their national auto producers." The only reason A123 has succeeded in selling to customers such as BMW and Daimler is that the A123 battery is regarded as state-of-the-art.

In one sense, there's never been a better time for American manufacturers such as A123 to export. The Internet and social media have made faraway markets more accessible, and economic growth overseas provides huge market opportunities. But exporting is also more difficult in today's world than it was in the past because of the increasing strength of foreign competition. American goods are not the only game in town; every nation is seeking to build domestic capacity in leading industries. Despite this fierce competition, A123 shows that American manufacturers still have two significant advantages: first, we have a leg up because of our innovative products, and second, our diverse workforce has an insight and a connection into almost every global market. Ultimately, we need to make the most of these advantages if we are to sustain and grow advanced manufacturing in the United States.

THE TAKEAWAY

AMERICAN MANUFACTURERS NEED SOPHISTICATED EXPORT STRATEGIES

The world wants American goods. It's worth repeating that 95 percent of consumers today are overseas. Yet, only 1 percent of American businesses currently export. If we want to grow our manufacturing base in the twenty-first century, we need to step out of our comfort zone of selling only to the U.S. market.

Schramm, Inc, Pucker Powder, and A123 Systems are excellent examples of American manufacturers that are leading the way when it comes to exports. They understand that overseas business doesn't just fall into your lap—securing foreign buyers is hard work. These companies participate in trade shows and trade missions, and they travel abroad extensively to build relationships with customers. They've found that there's great demand for their products overseas, and that "made in America" still has cachet. Their exports helped them weather the U.S. recession because their revenues were coming from markets all over the world.

The federal government also has a role to play in helping American manufacturers export. Most critically, our government should demand that the WTO do away with the unfair practice of allowing countries with a value-added tax (VAT) to provide tax breaks for their exporters while prohibiting America from providing a corporate tax break to our exporters. Moreover, we need to invest in the U.S. and Foreign Commercial Service, which helps our manufacturers make sales overseas. Fortune 500 companies may not need help in getting into India, China, or Brazil, but many small and medium-size manufacturers, such as Schramm, Inc., or Pucker Powder, can use the assistance of trade specialists to navigate complex bureaucracies overseas and identify potential buyers. Our government must be aggressive in advocating for our manufacturers abroad, not only to help create jobs at home but also to raise the standard of living around the world by providing consumers with access to the best products.

6

Importing Jobs

■ ■ ■

n 1972, when Andy Grove went to Malaysia to establish Intel's first foreign operation, the chief minister of Malaysia introduced him to Chet Singh, who headed the state's Penang Development Corporation.[1] "Chet Singh is your one-stop agent," the Malaysian chief minister told Mr. Grove. Whenever Intel had an issue with getting a particular license, permit, road paved, or available tax credit, Chet would take care of it. He stayed in his job for more than two decades until the early 1990s, facilitating Intel's ability to expand its Malaysian presence. Today, Malaysia is home to Intel's largest manufacturing facility outside the United States, with three campuses that employ more than 8,500 individuals.

"The Commerce Department can learn from Chet Singh," Mr. Grove stated. As it stands now, companies opening facilities in the United States have to approach scores of different departments, ranging from sanitation to environmental to fire and police. It can take more than two years for them to obtain all the regulatory permits.[2] As far as incentives are concerned, a company's lawyers have to browse city, state, and federal agency websites, trying to figure out which incentives may apply. Even if these companies have an inclination to stay in the United States out of convenience and patriotism, we don't make it easy for them.

Lately, many of these companies have been using their profits to expand their overseas presence. In 2010, corporate profits were at a record high.[3] The stock market was up more than 11 percent.[4] Yet unemployment persisted. One reason is that in 2010, American companies created 1.4 million jobs in overseas locations (mostly for foreigners), compared to a little less than 1 million in the United States.[5] The top five foreign nations for these jobs were the United Kingdom, Mexico, Canada, China, and Germany.[6] That said, offshoring has been far more prevalent in the service industries than in the manufacturing sector. In fact, in the past decade, more than 90 percent of offshoring has involved nonmanufacturing jobs, including retail trade, healthcare assistance, administration support, and food services.[7] U.S. manufacturers have created about 250,000 jobs overseas in the past decade, but this pales in comparison to the millions of retail and administrative jobs that multinationals have sent overseas.

If anything, several American manufacturers are turning the tables and bringing jobs back home, a phenomenon that can be illustrated through two important case studies. First, General Electric has brought the manufacturing of many refrigerators and water heaters from China back to its plant in Louisville, Kentucky. Second, Sigma has shifted processed meat production, including Mexican-style ham and sausages, from Mexico to Seminole, Oklahoma. This chapter examines the economics underlying each of these decisions to onshore. The hope is that these companies become trendsetters. The chapter concludes by proposing that we ramp up the Select-USA program within the Department of Commerce to attract private-sector investment within our borders.

GENERAL ELECTRIC'S NEW TEMPLATE

General Electric's Appliance Park, which spans 900 acres and has 17 buildings, feels like a college campus. Brian Harris, our local Louisville, Kentucky, Commerce official, drove in circles for nearly 10 minutes as we tried to find the building where Jim Campbell, the CEO of GE Appliances at the time, and Earl Jones, a senior counsel, had their offices. Brian is a Louisville native in his mid-forties who hadn't been to the park in many years. While we were in his car, he recalled friends and acquaintances who had worked there when he was growing up. Almost everyone in Louisville has some connection to the plant, which, at its peak, had nearly 25,000 employees. In the last few decades, though, GE had moved a significant amount of manufacturing to Mexico and China, and the head-count had dropped to about 3,600 employees. As Brian explained, every few years there would be a new round of layoffs, and the city would suffer.

Expanded Metrics

Earl Jones, a perfect gentleman who measures his words carefully, was candid about the evolution in GE's thinking. In the 1980s, GE began looking to Korea, China, and Mexico to outsource manufacturing of water heaters and refrigerators. The company was convinced that its brand would always dominate and focused primarily on reducing labor costs. As a consequence, by the late 1990s, almost 40 percent of GE's products were manufactured outside the United States. However, the model of relying on brand name alone turned out to be insufficient in the twenty-first century. GE began to realize that American consumers were willing to buy appliances from Korean companies, such as LG and Samsung, that were offering new features at equivalent prices. The days of just selling white, boring appliances were over. Consumers cared about styling, and GE had to invent new designs for its appliances and better features. GE knew that this innovative work could be done most efficiently in the United States, where many of the company's engineers and designers resided. Moreover, with rising shipping costs, slowly rising wages in China, and China's modest moves to raise its currency, the cost of manufacturing in China had also increased. So, Jeff Immelt asked the members of his Louisville team to take a look at how they could bring manufacturing of certain appliances back. He challenged them to "break the code."

When I asked whether this means that Jeff Immelt trusts their instinct on where to locate, Jim Campbell chuckled at my naïveté. Jim is a substance guy. He belies the stereotype of a CEO as someone who is broad-shouldered, has a chiseled jaw, and is a glad-hander. He comes across more as your high school physics teacher: he's skinny, wears big glasses, and revels in the nuts and bolts of running a large operation. "I need to go before GE's board and justify what we are doing," he explained. "If I just say I want to bring back manufacturing to the United States, they will say, 'That's nice, Jim, but the next person who will have your job . . .'." GE's board and management expect hard analysis. That's why Campbell and his team came up with an expanded set of metrics to capture the benefits of moving manufacturing onshore.

The focus is not simply on labor cost. In fact, the most significant metric is speed to market. According to Campbell, the cycle time for introducing a new refrigerator or water heater

to the market is significantly reduced when design and manufacturing are both done in the United States. When an appliance was being made in China and there was even the slightest
problem, GE would have to ship it all the way back there to get
the problem fixed. The back and forth between the design and
production teams, separated by thousands of miles, to perfect
a product added months to launch time. As global competition
put pressure on GE to continually innovate its products, the
delay in getting new products to market became an increasing liability. Campbell decided to track the time lost in marketing a new product because of the offshoring of manufacturing.
He wanted a metric that would capture Andy Grove's insight
that there are costs to separating design and manufacturing.
Mr. Grove would have been impressed not just with the in-
tegration but also with the company's rigor in measuring the
benefits.

The company also started to measure customer satisfaction to gauge the quality differential. GE doesn't have as much
control over the supply chain or the production process in
China. So, the company suspected that there was some compromise in quality. But Campbell didn't rely on anecdotal evidence from his engineering team; he was interested in the
perspective of customers. So he instructed his team to survey
customers and quantify the difference in quality that they per-
ceived. Moreover, the company began tracking service calls
to determine the relative number of problems with products
manufactured domestically compared to those manufactured
in China.

In addition to measuring quality, the company quan-
tified all of the costs of outsourcing, making sure that they
were comprehensive and thorough in their approach. Many
of its metrics coincide with those that writer Brendan Koerner identifies in his brilliant, recent article in *Wired*, which

examines why companies have started to "buck the offshoring trend."[8] The people on Campbell's team projected wage increases in China and also the likely appreciation of the Chinese currency in upcoming years.[9] They looked at rising shipping costs and accounted for the inevitable transportation costs associated with fixing a product with defects. They considered the savings on raw materials that would result from an integrated environment of design and sourcing. Such an environment encourages designers to model with a greater sensitivity for input costs because sourcers make them aware of the cost constraints from the beginning. Finally, they assessed the reduction in labor hours that comes from having a skilled domestic workforce that is empowered to make changes within an assembly line to maximize efficiency.

After analyzing the expanded metrics objectively, Campbell's team concluded that there was a business case for moving the manufacturing of refrigerators and water heaters back to Louisville, which they presented to GE's board of directors. To further make their case, they pointed to the federal tax credits for investment in efficient appliances and the Kentucky incentives for creating new jobs. Louisville, they argued, has a favorable business environment for manufacturing. Staying within American shores also protects GE's intellectual property from being copied by competitors. GE's board of directors was convinced; it decided to invest hundreds of millions of dollars in renovating the Louisville plant.

Much is riding on whether GE's Louisville experiment succeeds. We have been losing market share in the appliance industry to Korea, China, and Mexico for decades. And currently, only about 50 percent of appliances sold in the United States are made domestically.[10] But if the GE Appliance Park team can show that it has "cracked the code," that trend may reverse. The goal is for GE to have the overwhelming majority of its manufacturing back in the United States. GE's success may be a harbinger for the three million manufacturing jobs that Boston Consulting projects will be created in the United States in the next decade.[11]

That's not to say that GE hasn't faced its share of difficulties. Just recently, the company faced criticism for not paying corporate taxes. Many also view the company with suspicion because it recently closed its aviation plant in Albuquerque, New Mexico, and chose to offshore wind manufacturing to the United Kingdom and Germany instead of locating it in Albuquerque.[12] But when it comes to GE's Louisville experiment, every American should be rooting for the company to succeed. If GE, one of the world's model companies, proves that onshoring is profitable, other American companies are likely to follow suit.[13] What happens in Louisville matters for the future of American manufacturing.

One Team Reshaping Our Future

"One Team Reshaping Our Future" is more than a GE branding campaign. Everyone, including GE's top management and its union workers, lives by that mantra. Campbell credited the philosophy with providing an advantage over competitors in more hierarchical societies. "When I go to Korea or China, the CEO never takes notes. They have executives whose job it is to take notes." Campbell, in contrast, took his own notes. But, more than that gesture, the way he conducted performance reviews illustrates the company's egalitarian culture. Working teams didn't come to his office to make presentations. Instead, he went out to the factory floor to listen to proposals and offer suggestions. This saved time: it was more efficient for him to go to the group than for the entire group to come to him. There was no pomp or ceremony when he visited. Rather, he stood next to a person making $13 an hour and participated in the conversation as a colleague.

It's not just GE's management that touts the company's commitment to teamwork. The unions see it the same way. Jerry Carney, the local union president, remarked that if you go on the factory floor, you "can't tell a production worker from a maintenance worker from a design engineer. What we are doing is unprecedented." I had a chance to observe this firsthand. I saw one of GE's "working rooms," which resembles the common area in a college dorm: there are several cubicles, but no walled or corner offices. There's a large whiteboard in the center that has scribbling all over it. Every team member is encouraged to post ideas and also action items and deadlines. You see individuals congregated in a number of clusters in different corners of the room, engaged in animated conversation. Earl pointed to one of the groups to illustrate the diversity of interaction. "There you have someone from sourcing, from engineering, from IT, and from our assembly line," Earl stated with pride. The collaborative approach leads to faster production of prototypes, cost savings, more efficient assembly lines, and more innovative products.

GE's collaborative environment extends to business strategy. The unions cooperated with management to implement a competitive wage agreement. Jerry Carney explained the terms: although none of the existing workers took a pay cut, all new hires would begin at $13 instead of $21, a reduction of almost 50 percent. When I asked Carney why the union went for the deal, he explained that it's better to have some new manufacturing jobs, even at lower wages, than no jobs. "How many people are crying that they can't find $8-an-hour jobs?" he asked rhetorically.

Carney also credited his members for "taking a two-year wage freeze." As long as GE is willing to "put its money where its mouth is" by investing in the plant, his union is willing to do its part. In fact, Carney boasted that his union provides training in lean manufacturing for members who want it, making them far more productive than the average employee.

GE's Louisville example teaches us that while there are great rewards from manufacturing in the United States, doing so is not always easy. Manufacturers can't maintain the status quo and expect to succeed in a changed world. Rather, they need to maximize their advantage against foreign competition by creating flexible and collaborative work environments. Most critically, they need to foster a team environment, in which workers and senior management are willing to take risks and make shared sacrifices to be competitive.

SIGMA'S REVERSE JOURNEY

The last thing I expected on my trip to Monterrey, Mexico, was to speak with a leading industrialist who bragged about opening one of his company's major food processing plants in Seminole, Oklahoma. Hernan Gomez told me how Sigma, a subsidiary of ALFA, a large Mexican conglomerate, had invested $60 million to open the Seminole plant. "We're creating jobs in America!" he exclaimed. In 2004, Wrangler Jeans had closed its Seminole plant and moved to Mexico, laying off almost 600 people in a town with a population of less than 7,000. In 2008, Sigma stepped in to help fill the void, employing many of the people who had been laid off by Wrangler.

Mexico is one of the few foreign countries that I visited for work. Recognizing that Mexico is our second largest export market after Canada, the Obama administration launched a border initiative built on the Bush administration's work to improve access to the Mexican market by opening a Commerce office in El Paso.

Prior to Monterrey, I had been to Ciudad Juárez to highlight the administration's commitment to Mexico despite the drug violence. Bob Queen, the El Paso Commerce head, and I walked over the bridge from El Paso into Juárez. As soon as we were across the border, we saw motorcyclists speeding at about 150 miles an hour, and Bob explained that they were scouts for drug gangs. They didn't rattle him. They had, unfortunately, become a part of the Juárez environment that he had learned to accept. Bob told me that he'd come down every few months, often with American businessmen who were interested in selling to the *maquiladoras*, which are factories that import parts from the United States, do some assembly or manfacturing, and then often reexport them back to us. Juárez has thousands of them. Bob was concerned that China was, of late, aggressively forming relationships with the *maquiladoras*, selling electronic components to them, and even taking some of them over. He wanted to make sure that American businesses didn't lose share in a neighboring market that was of both economic and geopolitical relevance.

After my short trip to Juárez, several American business leaders urged me to go to Monterrey to get a better sense of Mexico's future. So when our consul general in Monterrey invited me to address a major venture capital conference, I accepted. Although it's much farther south than Juárez, Monterrey has seen its share of drug-related violence. When I landed there, an embassy official escorted me to a bulletproof SUV that took me to my hotel, and he instructed me not to wander the streets alone. This wasn't just paranoia. During our second night in the city, gunmen stormed into the Holiday Inn and Hotel Mission—both of which were just a few miles from where we were staying—and kidnapped six people.[14] An initial media report stated that five Americans had been kidnapped. Thankfully, this turned out not to be true, and to my knowledge, no Americans were hurt. Despite this incident, the city seemed calm, and most people went about their daily business.

Moving Jobs from Mexico to Oklahoma

My speech was at a conference hosted by Tec de Monterrey, the MIT of Mexico. At the conference, I met students and entrepreneurs brimming with passion and energy who believed that the city could model itself after Silicon Valley. They were confident that a new generation would build a new Mexico that was free of the sectarianism and violence that has plagued its recent past.

One of these young entrepreneurs told me about Sigma. "Now, Mexican companies have Americans working for *them*," she said with some sarcasm and pride. Geoffrey Bogart, our commercial officer in Monterrey, confirmed this, and then put me in touch with Hernan Gomez.

Hernan explained that although the wage in Seminole is five times what Sigma would have to pay in Mexico, locating there still makes business sense. Sigma's business is selling hot dogs and hams, which are a far cry from GE's high-tech appliances. However, the metrics that Hernan cited as justifying the company's decision to locate in the United States are very similar to the ones that Jim Campbell's team used. For instance, Hernan emphasized speed to market: it's important for Sigma to supply hot dogs and hams that are fresh. The process of shipping pork from Iowa to Mexico for processing, then shipping it back to the United States can take eight to ten days. As a result, a significant amount of meat goes bad before it gets to the supermarket, which adds huge costs for the company. In contrast, Sigma can get meat that's processed in Seminole to almost any supermarket in the United States within a few days. This speed also allows it to respond quickly to fluctuations in consumer demand. As Hernan pointed out, one of the biggest markets for Mexican-style hot dogs and hams is the United States. He repeated a number of times that the total Hispanic consumer economy in the United States is about $1 trillion. Companies such as Sigma are realizing that there's a huge advantage in locating their manufacturing close to the market that they're supplying.

Hernan also talked about the significant reduction in shipping costs from locating in Seminole. There are obvious savings from not having to transport the freight back and forth across the border, but there are also savings from eliminating the risk of cross-border inspections. When Sigma was transporting pork from Iowa to Mexico for processing, Mexican customs officials would confiscate a percentage of the supply. Similarly, U.S. customs officials would confiscate a number of processed packages coming from Mexico based on their own regulations. Manufacturing in Seminole avoids these cross-border hassles.

Perhaps the most significant factor that Seminole has in its favor is the quality of the workforce. As Hernan put it, "The quality of the people are as good as anywhere in the world. We are very happy." Sigma's executives were concerned at first because Seminole isn't a "meat city." Almost 90 percent of the workforce had no prior experience in meat processing; most had skills that were relevant to making jeans. But Sigma quickly realized that Seminole workers were adaptable and flexible. Hernan credited the culture. From the beginning, the workers were eager to learn new skills, and they adopted Sigma's best practices for doing things. Seminole's workers highlight an American advantage: in America, you don't need to come from a particular family or town to excel at an occupation. We value our family businesses, but we also cultivate individual workers that have the confidence to take on new challenges, no matter what their background or age.

Seminole's success in attracting Sigma, though, can't simply be seen through the romantic lens of American individualism. The city and state governments also played a major role. The city of Seminole passed a bond measure, raising taxes on its residents, to pay for a road that Sigma required that allowed big trucks access to the plant. Moreover, the city assigned staff members to work with Sigma's site managers in ensuring that the plant had access to electricity and clean water. The state of Oklahoma complemented the city's efforts by providing financial incentives to Sigma, including training funds so that the company could help educate its workforce on meat processing. In addition, the Oklahoma Department of Commerce signed an agreement with Sigma under its Quality Jobs incentive program, sending a paycheck to the company for every worker it hired and retained who made more than the average county wage. Sigma hired nearly 200 employees making between $10 and $13 an hour under this program. There's no doubt that the city and state's aggressive efforts to recruit Sigma made a difference, and they provide a model for how an area that is hit with a plant closure, such as the Wrangler closure, can import new jobs.

Sigma's manufacturing workforce is very diverse. Hernan emphasized that it's 65 percent Caucasian, 17 percent Hispanic, 11 percent Native American, and 4 percent African American. Although the company has had difficulty recruiting and retaining employees given the early morning shifts and "constant smell of animal flesh," the jobs provide a pathway to the middle class.[15] Take, for example, Eli Harper. Eli served for eight years in the Air Force and was stationed at a base in Oklahoma. After his honorable discharge, he had a hard time finding a job before finding an entry-level opportunity at Sigma.

Eli began as a tipper tie operator, handling machines that put the casing on hams. He soon rose to become the team leader and was responsible for all the employees and equipment involved with ham stuffing. Throughout his time at the company, Eli has received dental and medical benefits. He's grateful to Sigma because the job "kept his family going."

Eli's story can help defuse some of the political criticism of foreign direct investment (FDI). We need more of it—not less. As a general rule, foreign firms like Sigma that invest here provide our citizens with good-paying jobs. In fact, subsidiaries of foreign firms have a higher unionization rate than American-owned firms.[16]

We still lead the world in FDI, attracting almost twice as much investment as China.[17] Most of this investment comes from Canada, the United Kingdom, the Netherlands, France, Germany, and Japan. However, our FDI growth rate lags behind the FDI growth rate in emerging economies such as India, China, and Brazil.[18] More problematically, more than 80 percent of our FDI is in the form of mergers and acquisitions.[19] In other words, most foreign firms are buying and reorganizing existing American companies. Instead, what we should require is more foreign investment in new projects, colloquially referred to as greenfield investments. Sigma is a model for the type of greenfield investment that America must do a better job attracting.

SelectUSA Program

Jerry Karp, a Sigma plant manager, listed the numerous agencies that Sigma had to contact to set up its Seminole plant. Here's a partial list:

1. Oklahoma Department of Commerce (ODOC)
2. City of Seminole, Seminole Economic Development Council (SEDC)
3. Oklahoma Department of Environmental Quality (DEQ)
4. U.S. Department of Agriculture (USDA)
5. Workforce—Oklahoma Employment Security Commission (OESC)
6. Career Tech—Oklahoma Department of Career and Technology Education (ODOC)
7. Oklahoma Gordon Cooper Technology Center (GCTECH)
8. Seminole State College (SSCOK)
9. Oklahoma State University, Food and Agricultural Products Research and Technology Center (FAPC—OKSTATE)
10. Oklahoma Department of Agriculture, Food, and Forestry (ODA)
11. Oklahoma Manufacturing Alliance (OKALLIANCE)
12. Oklahoma Gas and Electric (OG&E)
13. Oklahoma State Department of Health (HealthOK)
14. Natural gas (Oneok)
15. Brad Henry (governor's office)
16. U.S. Department of Transportation (DOT)
17. Mary Fallin (congresswoman)
18. Seminole Chamber of Commerce (SEMINOLEOKCHAMBER)
19. U.S. Department of Labor (OSHA)
20. Oklahoma Tax Commission (OTC)
21. Seminole Fire Marshal (Seminole Fire Department)

22. Seminole Police (Seminole Police Department)
23. Environmental Protection Agency (EPA)
24. Telephone/Internet (AT&T)
25. Postal Service (USPS)
26. Internal Revenue Service (IRS)
27. State of Delaware (Incorporation)

"Anything the U.S. government can do to make it easier to cut through the red tape would help," Jerry explained as he sat in my Washington office. Jerry echoed Andy Grove's suggestion that the Department of Commerce should play an ombudsman role with companies that are considering establishing factories in the United States, helping them navigate through the local, state, and federal bureaucracy.

The United States has had a long history of seeking to attract foreign direct investment. Hamilton wrote that foreign capital, "instead of being viewed as a rival, ... ought to be considered as a most valuable auxiliary; conducing to put in Motion a greater Quantity of productive labour, and a greater portion of useful enterprise than could exist without it. It is at least evident, that in a Country situated like the United States, with an infinite fund of resources yet to be unfolded, every farthing of foreign capital, which is laid out in internal ameliorations, and in industrious establishments of a permanent nature, is a precious acquisition."[20] President Reagan reaffirmed this founding principle of attracting foreign investment. As he put it in more contemporary economic jargon, "Foreign investment flows which respond to private market forces will lead to more efficient international production and thereby benefit both home and host countries."[21]

Building on these principles, in 2007 the Bush administration established the Invest in America program. The program is led by Aaron Brickman, one of the most capable civil servants in Washington. His team works with about 200 foreign companies every year, helping them identify federal and state incentives for setting up factories within the United States. The problem is that Invest in America is woefully understaffed. It has a total of three employees and a budget of about $500,000. Think about that: the entire private investment promotion program of the U.S. government is currently being run by three individuals! It's time for the United States to establish an investment promotion agency with real resources and prominence. Many civil servants, including Aaron, have been calling for this for years.

President Obama took a step in the right direction by establishing the SelectUSA program by executive order and appointing an executive director who now oversees Aaron Brickman's team at the Department of Commerce. As a presidential appointee, the executive director of SelectUSA has the authority to convene high-ranking officials in other federal agencies to assist companies that are committed to establishing a presence in the United States. The executive director can also assign a staff member to serve as an ombudsperson for a particular company that is interested in investing in America. The staff member, in turn, is empowered to resolve the company's issues, cutting through burdensome federal regulations and providing access to available federal resources. The staff member is supposed to work with identified colleagues in the Departments of State, Defense, Treasury, Justice, Interior, Agriculture, Labor, Health and Human Services, Housing and Urban Development, Transportation, Energy, Education, Veteran Affairs, and Homeland Security and the Environmental Protection Agency.

The problem is that, at least for the time being, the SelectUSA program is an unfunded mandate. It's being operated by about five individuals at Commerce (Aaron Brickman's team), who are overburdened and have a minimal budget. If we are serious about the program, here is what we should do.

First of all, the SelectUSA program needs a staff of at least 30 employees and a budget of $10 million. Other nations do a lot more. Great Britain puts $25 million a year into investment promotion and has hundreds of staff members in trade offices and embassies.[22] Similarly, the Invest in France agency has a budget of nearly $30 million and more than 100 employees.[23] Even Brazil spends nearly $30 million on investment promotion and has more than 300 people working on attracting FDI.[24]

Second, on a monthly basis, the SelectUSA staff should track (1) which companies are leaving the United States and how many jobs we are losing as a result, and (2) which foreign companies are investing in the United States and how many jobs they are creating. No federal agency currently does this. Unless we begin to track these data, we can't assess whether we're making progress in stemming the offshoring of jobs.

Third, SelectUSA should partner with one of America's Internet companies through an open bidding process to launch a dynamic website. The website should provide detailed information in a user-friendly way for any company seeking to invest in the United States. This website should be the first place any company turns when making a decision about whether to build a factory in the United States. Companies should also be able to have their questions answered in a timely manner by submitting them through this website.

Critics may contend that the SelectUSA program can't change the underlying economic factors driving a company's site-selection decision. That's true. But these decisions are often made on the margins, so outreach can matter. American business leaders voice frustration that other countries roll out the red carpet for them while our own government is not engaged. Time and again, you'll hear how China takes the initiative to contact our manufacturers and, unsolicited, offer attractive packages for relocation. But when these very same manufacturers call our federal government for help, they get a runaround. As one of them put it, "Even receiving a phone call would be nice . . . just to know someone in Washington is paying attention." In a world in which countries are competing for business, we can't afford to be indifferent. We lead the world when it comes to marketing. We excel at customer service. We need a federal government that matches the skills of our private sector and promotes America, with all our underlying assets, as the best place to do business.

THE TAKEAWAY

THE ONSHORING TREND

In recent years, a number of manufacturers have been concluding that it makes economic sense to set up factories in the United States, which has led them to move production from China or Mexico back to our shores. It makes perfect sense; in addition to intangible assets such as its culture of risk taking and innovation, America offers a number of objective advantages as a place to set up shop. First, companies that have both design and manufacturing components in the United States are able to launch new products with greater speed and respond more quickly to customer requests for customized products. Second, surveys often show that the quality of products manufactured in the United States is better, as measured, for example, by customer service complaint calls. Third, shipping costs and rising wages abroad are making it less attractive to locate manufacturing overseas. Fourth, a company's intellectual property is more secure within the U.S. borders than it is abroad. Finally, America's skilled and flexible workforce enables companies to achieve higher productivity with fewer labor hours.

For years, many American CEOs and accountants simply— and wrongly—assumed that offshoring manufacturing is always profitable. It may still be the case that certain companies need to offshore aspects of their production. However, thoughtful business leaders will make such decisions after evaluating all the metrics, not simply the wage differential. Now, they can look to quite a number of models, such as GE Appliance Park or Sigma, to see how to manufacture in the United States profitably.

Our federal government can't afford to sit on the sidelines when it comes to selling America as a place for doing business. It must help remove the uncertainty regarding obtaining permits for companies that seek to set up factories here, and also provide incentives for domestic investment. Just as important, our civil servants should reach out to companies that are on the fence about where to locate. If other countries are rolling out the red carpet, we can't be indifferent. We don't need to match their subsidies, but our civil servants must, at the very least, listen to the concerns of businesses that choose to make things in America and help to solve their regulatory problems.

7

The Skills Gap

■ ■ ■

There are more than two million job openings in this country that businesses are unable to fill because they can't find candidates with the right qualifications. Many of these job openings are in manufacturing. David Altig, research director at the Federal Reserve Bank of Atlanta, argues that as businesses have improved their production processes, they require employees who have specialized skills to handle these processes.[1] Manufacturers often would like to hire new employees to increase their production and sales, but their recruiting searches are unsuccessful. Put simply, the lack of a properly trained workforce is constraining our economic growth.

The mantra we hear from policy makers is that we need more science, technology, engineering, and mathematics education. Of course, America should graduate more engineers and scientists, but the truth is that it will take a more nuanced policy to bridge our skills gap. We can't just focus on the top of the economic pyramid; we need to think about how to prepare the broader American workforce.

Mark Rice, the president of a submarine components manufacturer, put the problem in perspective. He explained that he's usually able to fill bachelor's- or PhD-level engineering positions, and also entry-level administrative positions, but he struggles to find individuals who are skilled in the trades. According to Mark, many men and women working in the trades are approaching retirement, and it's getting harder and harder to find younger folks who have the computer and information technology skills to fill their shoes. There are people who can repair or replace machine parts, but few who can diagnose problems or who excel at hands-on design. Trade unions typically have workers who meet these high standards, but they are having difficulty recruiting young people to join them.

One reason for the shortage of new talent is that manufacturing has developed a stigma. The general public isn't aware that, despite the automation and offshoring of low-skilled jobs, good careers still exist in manufacturing.[2] We need poster children for these careers. Mark shared examples of technical employees at his company who have risen through the ranks and are now making more than $100,000. Take Jim, who began right after high school at a minimum-wage job in the electronics shop. He eventually acquired machining skills and learned how to etch circuit boards. Today, he's a group manager, where he oversees both technicians and degreed engineers in electronic projects. Similarly, Nate began with Mark's company as an apprentice machinist operating complex machines. He's since risen to become a project manager responsible for producing hydrodynamic models to solve customers' needs.

America's manufacturing success has as much to do with the creativity of people like Jim and Nate as it does with brilliant scientists and CEOs. Until recently, we have excelled at matching a large number of Americans with work where they can have an impact. Our companies don't rely on a few stars, but benefit from employee excellence in every role. We mustn't lose this comparative advantage of harnessing the contribution of every employee in a world in which we can't compete on the basis of population size or scale.

This chapter looks at educational institutions and companies that are inspiring the manufacturing owners and workers of the future. Austin Polytechnical Academy and Troxler are helping us overcome the skills gap. Their success can ensure that ordinary Americans will continue to be active participants in our economic future.

PREPARING THE NEXT GENERATION OF MANUFACTURING LEADERS

Whenever I'm asked what steps are required to improve our educational system, my answer is simple: America needs more Dan Swinneys. Dan is the kind of visionary, working in the trenches, that Washington bureaucrats and policy makers should support. He doesn't just talk or write about manufacturing; he lives it. I met him one morning on the steps of Austin Polytechnical Academy, a school he founded in 2007. Austin Poly is located in a heavily African American neighborhood in Chicago and has a mission of preparing almost 400 students to become owners or employees of manufacturing companies. It's classified as a "performance school" with a focus on engineering and manufacturing, and it is part of the Chicago public school system. The school is open to any young person in the Austin community who wishes to enroll. It has partnered with both manufacturing companies and trade unions to provide high school students with the best training possible.

To enter Austin Poly, we first had to go through metal detectors and past armed guards that reminded me of an airport security screening. A group of about 10 students, all African American, were waiting for us in Austin's state-of-the-art machine room, equipped with computer numerical-controlled (CNC) machines and robotics. They had prepared coffee for us. Dan explained that the students brewed coffee every morning and sold the coffee to make some extra money for their college funds. The students use a local manufacturer's grinding equipment to roast the coffee. As Dan sees it, making and selling coffee provides these students with a basic lesson in American entrepreneurship.

The great thing about chatting with students is that they don't have talking points or give the usual platitudes that pass for Washington-speak. When I asked them what they wanted to be when they grow up, I expected them to talk about their passion for manufacturing. Instead, their answers surprised me. The vast majority wanted to do something related to criminal justice. They were practical enough, though, to understand that manufacturing credentials could be a nice backup. They could use them to get a job that would help pay for college or law school, or rely on them to start their own small business if need be. They were also determined to go to college. When I asked how many would be the first in their families to go to college, all but one in the group raised his or her hand.

It was only months later, after a conversation with my brother, an assistant U.S. attorney, that I came to appreciate why so many of these students want to pursue criminal justice. At first, I assumed that their aspirations were shaped by the slew of television shows that feature police officers, FBI agents, and prosecutors. If engineers and scientists starred in more televisions show, I thought, perhaps students would find those career choices more appealing. But my brother pointed out that my superficial analysis didn't give the Austin Poly students enough credit. He argued that in communities like Austin, where safety is often the paramount concern, law enforcement is seen as doing the most to build community. These students aspire to go into criminal justice, he surmised, because they see it as one of the most important and noble professions to improve the quality of life in their hometown.

Dan Swinney wasn't concerned that many of the students named criminal justice rather than manufacturing as their ambition. He explained to me that the school wasn't intended to track students or limit their horizons; this wasn't the German model of consigning a young person to a particular career from the time he or she is a teenager. The Austin Poly model was superior, in Dan's judgment, because it provided students with flexibility. The primary purpose was to prepare students for college, and Dan thought of manufacturing broadly. A manufacturing career could encompass being a CEO, an intellectual property lawyer, or a policy maker. Even graduates who chose careers that were not focused on manufacturing would benefit, in Dan's judgment, from learning entrepreneurship skills. Austin Poly's curriculum wasn't designed just to be technical but to teach students how to start and run a business. The schoolteachers engage students in conversations about sustainability, the innovative process, and the responsibility businesses have to create societal value.

John Torres represents the best of Austin Poly students. A young African American, John will be the first in his family to go to college. He considers Dan Swinney a mentor, and the two spend time together every week writing and reading. He often accompanies Dan to seminars and conferences and speaks about Austin Poly's mission. When I asked John what he wanted to do with his life, he shared that he'd like to be a lawyer, and also shared with me some public service aspirations. Despite John's liberal arts leaning, the manufacturing education is an enormous benefit to him. It's given him an appreciation for what his community needs and a passion for helping to bring manufacturing jobs to his hometown. Instead of having an interest in going to Wall Street or Hollywood, like many young folks, John's interest is in helping companies make things. Our future depends on graduating more people like John Torres.

As is clear from John's story, Austin Poly rejects the German approach to vocational education. The school doesn't push its students to give up on their dreams, but cultivates in them an interest in making things. As a result, its graduates, unlike most high school graduates, are employable in a competitive world and can earn a middle-class salary based on their skills. An Austin Poly diploma has economic value for students throughout their life, no matter what risks they take or what interests they pursue. John Torres, for example, could work in a manufacturing job to pay for college or law school. Just as important, some Austin graduates will choose manufacturing as a profession, taking to a career that they might never have considered as child. In this way, Austin can help the Chicago area, which currently has a shortage of 10,000 manufacturing workers and a shortage of those capable of running manufacturing companies, develop the next generation of leaders in the field.

Almost all Austin Poly students graduate with advanced National Institute for Metalworking Skills (NIMS) credentials, which qualifies them to work in precision manufacturing. These are some of the best-paid jobs in manufacturing, and employers often find it difficult to attract individuals with the right skills. NIMS has more than 6,000 employers as part of its network, and students with NIMS credentials can apply to many of them for apprenticeships or even jobs.

Austin Poly receives a significant share of its funding from private manufacturers that have an interest in cultivating a skilled workforce. But it's also precisely the type of school that should receive federal funding. Federal education funding should be linked to job preparation: we should be providing the most resources to schools and community colleges, such as Austin Poly, that are preparing students for jobs that the market demands.

The Obama administration could do more when it comes to vocational education. Although the Obama administration's Investing in Innovation Fund has supported many valuable programs, there should have been more funding directed at vocational or job-specific training.[3] The administration has been visionary in proposing greater funding for community colleges that prepare students for healthcare, information technology, or advanced manufacturing fields. But, unfortunately, in its 2012 budget, the administration actually proposed a 20 percent reduction for career and technical education.[4] If anything, this budget should be increased, not cut. Institutions with a vocational program, such as Austin Poly, should be seen not as "backwaters for underachieving or difficult students" but as a pathway to higher education that allows students to pick up important skills along the way.[5]

In a globally competitive world, we no longer have the luxury of having our youth study whatever they want, finding their calling only in their late twenties or early thirties. We need young people graduating with employable skills. Austin Poly is a paradigm for educational institutions that deserve our support.

TROXLER INVESTS IN ITS WORKERS

Schools and colleges aren't the only institutions that can help develop a skilled workforce. The best companies take it upon themselves to train workers in advanced manufacturing. They don't wait to hire individuals with the perfect set of skills—rather, they cultivate those skills in their employees. Troxler excels at helping to prepare its workers for the manufacturing future.

A Legendary Founder

William F. Troxler was in Brno, Czechoslovakia, the day the Russians invaded in 1968. Despite having four young kids, he had ventured there because Brno University of Technology was giving him an award for inventing a gauge to measure the soil moisture, water density, and compaction of asphalt. William saw it as an opportunity to market his product in Europe and among elite opinion leaders in the industry. The recognition would be a welcome break for the construction test equipment company that he'd founded almost 10 years earlier. What William couldn't have foreseen was that while he was there, Russian troops would swarm the city, "commandeer cars," and fire machine guns at civilians in the city streets.[6]

At the time of the invasion, William was staying with about 10 other Americans at the International Hotel in Brno. His son, William Troxler Jr., known as Billy, recalled that his father was a "gregarious guy" who had befriended the other Americans. William called the group together and shared a plan for escape. They would commandeer a tour bus that was parked outside the hotel and make their way to the Austrian border. Six of the ten other Americans agreed with William's plan, followed his lead, and got on the tour bus. Before boarding, they put an American flag on the front. The American flag helped ensure that not a single Russian soldier stopped them on their journey to Austria. The role the American flag had in helping to bring his father to safety is not lost on his son.

I met Billy on a trip to Raleigh, North Carolina, when I was there to present his company with an award for making construction equipment and exporting. His voice was overcome with gentle reverence when he spoke about "Dad." He shared not only the story of the Russian invasion but also some episodes from his dad's earlier life, all of which have now become part of the folklore of the company's founding.

Everyone at Troxler knows that William, the son of a Methodist minister, seemed to be born with an aptitude for configuring gadgets. In the company's early years, he fixed televisions to help supplement his family's meager income. One day he had the good fortune of fixing his future father-in-law's television set. William eventually graduated from North Carolina State in 1952 with a degree in electrical engineering and began to invent products, first for agriculture and then for the civil engineering industry, in his basement. One of his inventions was the density gauge. He recognized that the devices had commercial value for construction, and so he approached his closest friends to help fund a company. They did so on faith and handshakes. Many of his friends and professors bought stock in William Troxler's company at $1 a share. That was the beginning of a company that continues to thrive half a century later.

Taking the Company to the Next Level

Anyone who hears Billy talk about his father would understand why he feels a responsibility to ensure that Troxler remains a global leader. His family, his employees, and his community are now counting on him. Unlike the daughters or sons of many larger-than-life figures, Billy wasn't given any handouts. He started by apprenticing on the Troxler plant floor as a young teenager, working with his hands to assemble and take apart gauges. He went on to earn a business degree from North Carolina State University and an MBA from the University of North Carolina at Chapel Hill, knowing instinctively that today's manufacturers have to be savvy about marketing and management. Billy has never rested on his father's laurels. His most significant contribution to the company has been to economize the production process with the engagement of his employees.

Billy relied in part on *kaizen* methods, which are, by now, common knowledge among manufacturers. *Kaizen* requires the "successful participation of workers in the improvement" of the workplace and productivity.[7] It calls for each employee to seek incremental but continuous improvement in efficiency. Toyota made *kaizen* famous by adopting the Toyota Production System, which encourages all line workers to improve the production process.[8] Unfortunately, too many small business owners still think of *kaizen* as obscure or as relevant only for multinationals.

Billy didn't have the luxury of dismissing *kaizen* as academic. The status quo was not an option. Troxler couldn't do more of the same and expect to compete with the cheaper testing equipment that was now being made overseas. Billy had to either find ways to increase productivity or risk losing the company that his dad had spent his life building.

Billy didn't seek outside help to implement *kaizen*. He hired people with the needed skill and helped educate his own employees on the method, providing them with the proper training. As an illustrative example, during one *kaizen* event, he challenged his employees to reduce the amount of time for testing a Troxler NTO (new technology oven). If Troxler's famous gauge measures the density of an asphalt mixture once it's on the ground, the Troxler oven measures the asphalt content of a mixture before paving begins. The difficulty in quality testing this oven is that it emits a lot of dust and smoke when it is burning the mixture to measure its content. Troxler needs to maintain almost clean room conditions for its manufacturing to prevent any contamination as a result of dust in the environment. That's why the company required that the testing of the oven be done in a separate cell. Employees had to roll the oven into a different room and reignite it for testing, adding significant time and labor cost to the process. Billy asked whether there was a better way.

In a week's time, Troxler employees came up with two simple but ingenious solutions to make the testing process more economical. First, they installed an exhaust duct through the ceiling in the room where the manufacturing was taking place. They connected this duct to the oven when testing asphalt. The exhaust duct, combined with a vacuum system, ensured that no dust particles that would compromise the clean room conditions of the manufacturing space were emitted. As a result, Troxler employees now no longer need to physically roll the oven into a different room for quality control testing. Their second idea was even simpler. The employees used a microwave to heat the test asphalt until it softened. That's right: the brilliant advance in productivity was someone saying, "Hey, why don't we use a microwave to heat the asphalt first?" The use of a microwave for the initial heating greatly reduced the time and electricity needed to perform the quality control.

Billy's employees came through for him, but that's also because he came through for them. He clarifies at the beginning of every *kaizen* event that any savings in labor time won't result in layoffs. This isn't to say that he hasn't let people go during tough economic times, but he doesn't abuse *kaizen* to reduce headcount. Billy's employees trust him to make decisions with the general welfare of the company in mind. He knows which churches his employees belong to, which social gatherings they are likely to show up at, and which colleges their kids are considering attending. He shares sensitive financial information with them and consults them on big decisions.

The culture of employee involvement sets Troxler apart from many of its Chinese competitors. Chinese firms may succeed at imitating Troxler's design and then mass-producing products with cheap labor. But, according to Masaaki Imai, the founder of *kaizen*, they have had difficulty adopting a culture that motivates employees on the factory floor to make suggestions and improvements, resulting in a productivity and quality deficit for those Chinese firms.[9]

When I asked Billy whether he'd ever considered moving manufacturing offshore, he was honest. "Everyone looks at it for some part of the manufacturing process. But I am committed to keeping most of our manufacturing here. Look at how much capital equipment we already have in this place. It's been almost a 50-year investment. It just doesn't make sense to spend money buying a new factory overseas where the production process may be inefficient." Billy's metrics included the cost of capital outlays and the differential in productivity. "I'd rather invest to improve our plant." And invest he did.

In the late 1990s, Billy made the decision to buy computer numerical-controlled machines to replace the manual machines. The CNC machines allow operators to change machine parts quickly and reduce costly errors in the production process. Although buying CNC machines may be standard practice for large corporations, this wasn't an easy decision for a small business like Troxler. It meant investing millions of dollars, and Troxler was known for its frugality. As Billy put it, "Our reputation was that we would drive a car till it quits."

At the time, there were a number of folks advising Billy to give up the headaches of manufacturing altogether and let some third party do it for him. That would have been the easy out, but instead Billy decided to double down. He knew that it would take nearly three years for the CNC machines to pay back. He also knew that it would require a significant investment in training workers to operate these machines. But he was prepared to make the investment because he has never made decisions based on maximizing the next quarter's profits.

Purchasing CNC machines and training employees to use them was one of the best moves the company made. The machines have enabled Troxler to produce far more products with the same payroll. The company also has brought in-house the manufacturing of component parts that it had previously been outsourcing to another American company, which has reduced production time. By investing in Troxler's workforce to adopt the newest technology and processes, Billy has, in his own way, displayed the moxie of his father and built on his dreams.

Tax Relief for Troxler

When I asked Billy whether the government could help facilitate the investments he makes in manufacturing and in his workforce, he mentioned that there should be a tax incentive for capital expenditures, including employee training. Billy thought that he should receive a tax credit, or at a minimum a full deduction in the year of purchase, for investments in capital equipment like CNC machines and for investing in his employees. Such a policy would give small businesses across the country, like his, incentives to become more efficient.

These types of tax credits have a long history. Hamilton wrote about exempting the "materials" of manufacturers from taxes.[10] He argued that these exemptions were necessary because of the practices of other nations whose manufacturers were "competitors in our own and foreign markets."[11] In more modern times, President Kennedy called for an investment tax credit in 1962, "proposing additional incentives for the modernization and expansion of private plant and equipment."[12] President Kennedy argued that tax incentives would lead to increased "expenditures on plant and equipment," which would "immediately create more jobs." In his words, "the increase in jobs resulting from a full year's operation of such an incentive is estimated at about half a million."[13] Following President Kennedy's lead, President Reagan signed into law an investment tax credit that provided nearly a 25 percent tax credit for investment in capital equipment. Unfortunately, the Kennedy and Reagan investment tax credits were repealed by the 1986 Tax Reform Act because of a concern that corporations were abusing the provisions to avoid paying their fair share of tax.

After the Great Recession, many manufacturers called on President Obama and Congress to provide incentives to invest in America again. President Obama took a step in the right direction by reaching an agreement with Republican lawmakers in December of 2010 to allow the full expensing of equipment investments made in 2011 on a *temporary* basis. The administration's Treasury Department estimated that temporary 100 percent expensing would lead to almost $50 billion in immediate new investments, but would cost only $30 billion over 10 years because much of the revenue would be recouped, as businesses would no longer be taking deductions in later years.[14] Conservative economists Kevin A. Hassett and Glenn Hubbard predicted that the president's proposal would lead to an increase in capital expenditures of 5 to 10 percent in the year the deduction was allowed.[15]

The problem is that President Obama didn't go far enough. A bolder reform would have been to make expensing *permanent* because that wouldn't just shift investment from the future to the present but would increase domestic investment in the aggregate. Most manufacturers I met agreed. They considered temporary expensing a "nightmare calculation" and pushed for the simplicity of permanent expensing. Moreover, expenses for worker training and development should be part of the expensing.

Permanent expensing should be a bipartisan issue. After Billy had put the idea on my radar, I decided to call my friend Rob Atkinson to get the progressive perspective. It turns out he's a big advocate. Over lunch in the secretary's dining room, Rob explained to me that we need a middle ground between Keynesian economics and neoclassical economics to help American manufacturing. He called it "innovation economics," where government would provide strategic incentives for investments in long-term economic growth. Under this school of thought, we need incentives that favor "capital equipment over housing."[16] "If we can justify a mortgage interest deduction for home buyers, should there not be a tax incentive for manufacturers to buy equipment for their factories?" Rob asked rhetorically.

According to Rob, permanent expensing would raise "the level of domestic investment and the productivity of workers."[17] He argues that this hypothesis is supported by the scholarship of Larry Summers and Austan Goolsbee, senior advisors to President Obama. Although Summers and Goolsbee fear that the benefits of temporary expensing will go largely to the suppliers of capital equipment, their research shows that permanent expensing would benefit manufacturers.[18]

Rob also made a strong case for expanding the research and development tax credit for investments from 14 percent to 20 percent, seeing this as complementing permanent expensing.[19] He points out that today China, India, Brazil, and Singapore all provide more generous research and development tax credits than we do.

On the Republican side, Congressman Paul Ryan embraces permanent expensing. I disagree with many of Congressman Ryan's proposals, particularly on social security and healthcare, but he's an influential voice in the national debate on fiscal issues. In his much-publicized "Roadmap for America's Future," Ryan, the current chairman of the House Budget Committee, recognizes that capital investments should be fully expensed. As he puts it, "Expensing becomes the key element in shifting from a system that taxes income to a system that taxes consumption (i.e. income less investment). This will boost overall investment in the economy, spurring job creation, productivity and raising living standards."[20]

Ryan wants to go further than permanent expensing; he proposes getting rid of the corporate income tax and replacing it with a business consumption tax. Although Democrats are open to considering strategic reductions in the corporate tax, they aren't going to agree to eliminate it across the board. Ryan's proposal would be a windfall for, among others, financial speculators and corporate lawyers. The financial rewards in these professions are already so high that a third of our Harvard graduates—the nation's supposed best and brightest—are going into those fields.[21] Wall Street doesn't need more tax breaks at this time. Rather, any corporate tax cuts should be "narrow" and "targeted" to serve key national goals.[22] Former vice presidential nominee Sarah Palin too has talked about the importance of corporate tax cuts to help manufacturers.[23] That is why President Obama recently proposed capping the effective corporate tax on manufacturers at 25 percent.[24] At a time of large deficits, let's direct tax relief to the Troxlers of this country first. Permanent expensing and expanding the research and development tax credit are areas where we can find common ground.

Investing in Our Infrastructure

In addition to tax relief, Billy Troxler also advocated for increased spending on our highways to allow him to continue to make investments in manufacturing and his workforce. Rather than having abstract debates about whether infrastructure spending creates jobs, members of Congress should talk to business owners such as him. As Billy will tell you from his travels to China, his competitors are getting a huge boost from the Chinese government, which is spending hundreds of billions of dollars on building railways and highways.[25] In comparison, only $64 billion, or 8 percent of the American Recovery Act (the $787 billion stimulus), went to "roads, public transport, rail, bridges, aviation and wastewater systems."[26]

The United States has a far more developed infrastructure than China's, so we can't expect our government to match China's dollar for dollar. Still, we aren't doing nearly enough. Our infrastructure is ranked twenty-third in the world, behind most of our competitors'.[27] A bipartisan commission unanimously concluded that our spending on highways has fallen by about 25 percent since the 1950s.[28] The Highway Trust Fund faces both near-term solvency issues and a long-term gap of nearly $400 billion through 2015 to be able to fund the necessary road construction given the increase in our traffic.[29]

Our lack of investment in roads isn't just hurting manufacturers like Troxler compared to foreign competitors, it's also hurting our overall economy. According to the Department of Transportation, traffic congestion costs America nearly $200 billion a year because Americans are spending "3.7 billion hours and 2.3 billion gallons of fuel each year in traffic jams."[30] The American Society of Civil Engineers gives our nation's highway conditions a grade of D- in its 2009 report card.

Nearly a third of America's major roads aren't in good condition, and nearly half of the urban highways are congested.[31] So next time you're cursing during your commute home, you should know that your situation isn't unique. It's not just personal bad luck; it's our nation's inadequate planning.

To help address this problem, President Obama proposed $50 billion for an infrastructure bank to improve our roads and other infrastructure. The bank would use both federal funds and private investments to support infrastructure projects, focused initially on highways and surface transport. The disbursements would be based not on partisan politics but on the recommendations of a panel of industry experts who would assess the return on investment for economic growth and follow the lead of private investors.

The conservative-leaning U.S. Chamber of Commerce came out in support of the proposal in principle. Janet Kavinoky, transport director for the Chamber of Commerce, observed that there is a coalition of the chamber, the National Association of Manufacturers, and the truckers, all of whom believe that we need to invest more in our infrastructure.[32] This shouldn't be a partisan issue. Virginia governor Bob McDonnell, a strong conservative, has called for "investments" in transportation because it "lays the foundation for business development and gets people back to work."[33] Even Senator Rand Paul has acknowledged that "we have infrastructure needs" and that he is not reflexively opposed to government spending for such needs.[34]

This broad support for infrastructure development is rooted in American history. Hamilton argued that investment in "public roads" is important to help manufacturers transport commodities and materials.[35] To support industry, Lincoln planned the "transcontinental railroad," Theodore Roosevelt planned the "water projects that irrigated the West and generated electricity cheaply," and Dwight Eisenhower planned a "system of interstate highways."[36] President Coolidge also was a proponent of infrastructure investment, stating, "The importance and benefit of good roads is more and more coming to be appreciated. The National Government has been making liberal contributions to encourage their construction. The results and benefits have been very gratifying."[37] Most recently, George Shultz, the former secretary of state and close confidant of President Reagan, has argued that President Reagan might have "prioritized infrastructure spending today" with a clear goal of improving American competitiveness and with incentives for projects to be done "quickly and cheaply."[38]

Nonetheless, President Obama's proposal has received a lukewarm reception on Capitol Hill. Senator Mitch McConnell characterized the president's infrastructure bank as just more stimulus. As he put it, this "latest plan for another stimulus should be met with justifiable skepticism," and "Americans are rightly skeptical about Washington Democrats asking for more money."[39] Similarly, Representative Pat Tiberi, an Ohio Republican who is on the relevant Ways and Means subcommittee, cautioned, "It's important to keep in mind that increased spending—no matter the method of delivery—is not free."[40] He is concerned that "federally guaranteed borrowing and lending could place taxpayers on the hook should the proposed bank fail."[41]

There's no doubt that, given our large budget deficits, we need to be frugal and thoughtful about any government spending. But we need to distinguish between productive spending and discretionary spending. As the conservative-leaning columnist David Brooks has argued, "We must cut wasteful spending while doubling down on productive investment."[42] Infrastructure spending that meets the "market test" is a productive investment.[43] The benefits of having a strong industrial base outweigh the risks to the taxpayers of guaranteeing loans for essential projects that have already attracted private investment.

It's an issue of legacy. The Troxler family certainly has a legacy. It put resources into the plant in Raleigh, North Carolina, because it still believes that this is the best place in the world for making construction equipment. The Troxler family is eager to train its workers in the skills necessary for advanced manufacturing. If the Troxlers are willing to invest in America, is it too much to ask our leaders in Washington to do the same?

THE TAKEAWAY

UPGRADING OUR MANUFACTURING SKILLS

One of the biggest challenges for American manufacturers today is recruiting skilled workers. We have a shortage of individuals who have the expertise to operate advanced machinery, and unless we find a way to train more individuals in modern manufacturing techniques, the growth potential of even our best manufacturers will be constrained.

We need to support schools, such as Austin Poly, that provide students with skills in advanced manufacturing. We can no longer afford to underinvest in vocational education at a time when we desperately need more skilled workers. No one is advocating tracking students into the trades from a young age. But we should provide students with the opportunity to acquire mechanical skills, particularly if they display an aptitude for or interest in doing so. Schools such as Austin Poly are critical for us if we are to maintain our edge in productivity and innovation.

Companies also can help their employees develop the skills that they need for modern manufacturing. Troxler is a great example of a company that has encouraged its employees to learn the latest manufacturing practices and has also trained them in operating the latest machinery. Our government should provide companies like Troxler with tax benefits for spending on employee training and also invest in infrastructure upgrades that will allow our manufacturers, in turn, to invest in their workforce.

8

National Security

■　■　■

Wen I ask audiences what they think America still sells to the world, most people guess defense equipment. They assume that we sell primarily military aircraft, explosives, and firearms. This is simply not true. In fact, the defense sector is not even in the top 10 manufacturing export industries; it's well behind electronic devices, commercial planes, and industrial machinery. We export far more medical devices and scientific instruments than we do weapons. Total defense exports ranged from about $19 billion to $22 billion in calendar years 2005 to 2009.[1] This constitutes less than 2 percent of our total annual exports of $1.3 trillion.[2]

The defense sector, which is about $200 billion a year, does account for about 15 percent of our total domestic manufacturing output.[3] This is sizable and important, and we need to retain some threshold capability for our national security. Dr. Gerald Abbott, professor of acquisition at the National Defense University, argues that the United States must figure out how to maintain a self-sufficient "defense industrial base within an increasingly globalized manufacturing base."[4]

It is critical that, even during times of peace, we retain the capability to produce the best defense equipment in the United States. If we lose this capability, then it will be time-consuming and expensive to regain it in the future when we may have a security threat. We certainly should learn from the military advances of other nations and seek to acquire the latest technology. Our military has benefited from the "German 120mm cannon," "British armor technology," and the "Russian rocket engine."[5] But it is not prudent to be dependent on foreign nations, even allies, for our defense needs, because they can withhold supplies if they do not share our foreign policy objectives. As Dean Bartles, vice president of General Dynamics Ordinal and Tactical Systems, pointed out to me, "There is a history of countries prohibiting defense exports to the United States during times of conflict. In the past, a part supplier in Switzerland refused to supply Raytheon with certain missiles, and other allies have refused to ship certain things."

Richard McCormack, who is one of the foremost authorities on the state of American manufacturing, observes that high-ranking Pentagon officials are concerned about the "health of the U.S. industrial base."[6] According to him, the Defense Department is worried that our military is becoming too dependent on high-tech electronics made outside the United States and that there are escalating shortages of basic equipment required for tanks and weapons supplies.

Congress has already cut the Defense Department's budget by $487 billion over the next decade in the 2011 budget that it passed. If the congressional supercommittee fails to reach a compromise on how to cut another $1.2 trillion from our budget, then "the Pentagon's budget will be automatically reduced by another $600 billion over 10 years."[7] McCormack warns that those drastic cuts would "irretrievably" harm our defense capability and "result in the loss of one million jobs."[8] There is no doubt that we need to cut extraneous defense spending that is irrelevant in a post-cold-war world and to modernize our military, as Congressman Stark and former U.S. Secretary of Defense Gates have both compellingly argued.[9] But any cuts need to be in areas that do not erode our industrial base or the development of promising, new technology.

In response to a question at a 2003 technology conference about the impacts of outsourcing, Dr. Henry Kissinger, former U.S. secretary of state, explained:

> I don't look at this from an economic point of view but the political and social points of view. The question really is whether America can remain a great power or a dominant power if it becomes primarily a service economy, and I doubt that. I think that a country has to have a major industrial base in order to play a significant role in the world. And I am concerned from that point of view. . . . If outsourcing would continue to the point of stripping the U.S. of its industrial base, and of the act of getting out its own technology, I think this requires some really careful thought and national policy probably can create incentives to prevent that from happening.[10]

This chapter will highlight two successful defense equipment manufacturers. General Dynamics's Red Lion plant in Pennsylvania is one of only two facilities in the United States making tank ammunition for both training and combat. Nielsen–Kellerman is a Boothwyn, Pennsylvania–based manufacturer of weather instruments that are used by our military snipers in Afghanistan to measure humidity and deliver more accurate shots, minimizing civilian casualties and saving the lives of our troops. Commercial manufacturers like Red Lion and Nielsen Kellerman enhance our national security. The chapter concludes by proposing federal investments that can further strengthen our industrial base.

RED LION AND THE MINIMUM SUSTAINING RATE

The conclusion of our Red Lion factory tour is still seared in my memory. "We need you guys to get a radiation check," said Jeff Brunozzi, the vice president of large caliber ammunitions at General Dynamics Ordinance and Tactical Systems. "It's standard." I looked at Dan O'Brien, my colleague, with a sheepish grin. Dan and I spent most days sitting in comfortable Commerce Department conference rooms, sipping coffee and debating policy. Our jobs didn't require us to worry about health hazards. Fortunately, and as expected, our radiation levels came out normal. But the radiation check was a reminder that the men and women who make our nation's defense equipment put themselves at risk every day.

The Red Lion plant makes tank ammunition. During our walk through Red Lion's factory floor, Jeff had provided us with an overview of the company's business model. He described making the projectiles for tanks as an "art" with very high stakes. The projectiles must be reliable and lethal. Their proper functioning is a matter of life or death for our troops who are in a combat zone. When I asked whether our design for the projectiles is superior to those from foreign sources, Jeff said that this is a matter of "judgment." In his opinion, Red Lion's projectiles are the most precise (helping prevent collateral damage) and also the most potent. He further pointed out that foreign sources are often not an option for the United States if there are foreign policy disagreements.

Jeff emphasized that much of the tank ammunition that Red Lion manufactures is for training. Although simulation methods are sufficient for certain military exercises, our war fighters need to use real ammunition if they are to be fully prepared for battle. Recently, with troops deployed in both Iraq and Afghanistan, the Defense Department has cut back on ordering some of the training ammunition. The challenge for Red Lion is to maintain the capacity to produce ammunition despite these cuts. As Jeff explained, it is not easy to maintain a skilled workforce when demand for ammunition is down. During down times, many of the best welders or machine operators find alternative jobs. Workers "who have the ability to make for $10 what anyone else can make for $100" are hard to find. One of Red Lion's biggest challenges is recruiting and retaining a strong manufacturing workforce. At a recent job fair, Jeff's team attracted nearly 500 job applicants, but almost none of them had the technical skills or training to be competent.

Red Lion's commercial business, according to Jeff, helps sustain its skilled workforce. The Red Lion plant makes pipe joints for oil drilling. But during the Great Recession, Red Lion's commercial operations took a huge hit. China flooded the U.S. market with steel pipe, causing a glut in the market and leading to fewer orders from the Red Lion plant. Red Lion was forced to lay off nearly 80 employees, almost a third of its workforce. The lesson is that Chinese dumping threatens not just good-paying jobs here at home but also the industrial base necessary for our national security. Put differently, unfair trade practices that harm commercial manufacturing erode our skilled workforce and thereby hurt our defense capability. Once an ammunition plant loses its workforce, Jeff made clear, "It's not as easy to ramp up again as you would think."

After the tour, Jeff escorted us to a small conference room where Troy Franks, a senior executive at General Dynamics's

Scranton operation, joined us. Jeff and Troy explained that the Joint Munitions Command, which manages the nation's ammunition plants, has established a sophisticated tool called the Industrial Base Assessment Tool (IBAT). This tool enables the army to work with companies to come up with a "minimum sustaining rate." The minimum sustaining rate is the amount of ammunition that a defense contractor must produce annually to support a skilled workforce, an operational facility, and cutting-edge technology investment. The army uses IBAT to monitor procurement decisions and ensure that critical defense contractors are not losing capability when the demand for ammunition falls.

As Jeff put it, "We always think we can cut things and then need to pay dearly to re-create what we already had because we were chasing short-term savings over the long-term need." The army understands that short-term savings are not always in our national interest. It now uses IBAT to consider our strategic interests and to make procurement decisions based on enhancing our defense capability. Jeff is optimistic that this tool will enable the army to be efficient with our tax dollars yet sustain critical national facilities such as Red Lion. At a time when some defense budget cuts may be necessary to balance the federal budget, our leaders face the difficult task of making such cuts without eroding essential capacity.

NIELSEN-KELLERMAN AND THE AMERICAN WAY OF DOING BUSINESS

Alix James, a charismatic CEO in her forties with an athletic build, considers it her philosophical duty to manufacture in the United States. She is adamant on the subject: "We design here, we source all the parts we can in the United States, and we build here." A graduate of Yale University and the

University of Pennsylvania Law School, Alix left a lucrative legal career to return to Nielsen-Kellerman, the manufacturing company headquartered in Boothwyn, Pennsylvania, that her stepfather cofounded more than 30 years ago. The company's most famous product is the pocket-sized Kestrel weather meter line that measures critical weather conditions. Snipers use the Kestrel to take the guesswork out of long-range shooting and improve accuracy. Nielsen-Kellerman also makes many rowing products and sport performance instruments. Alix's first job was "soldering Cox Box boards" in her stepfather's basement as a senior in high school. When she returned to Nielsen-Kellerman almost two decades later, she worked in every department before rising to become the CEO.

Alix is still old-fashioned about how to do business, and Nielsen-Kellerman reminds you of the type of companies—those built to last—that is the key to America's economic greatness. The company does not chase profits but is committed to excellence in everything it makes. Alix says that many investors who have looked at the company say that Nielsen-Kellerman could make more money if it manufactured overseas. But, while this may be true in the very short term, it creates long-term drawbacks in terms of lost quality, innovation, and efficiency. As Alix put it, "The buy-and-hold philosophy is less common these days. Many investors are only in it for the short term. That's not conducive to growing a business."

This type of long-term thinking has earned Nielsen-Kellerman the confidence of its bank, which is always offering it loans, even when credit markets are tight. But Nielsen-Kellerman is careful about assuming debt obligations and sticks to the mantra of "growing organically." Alix is not judgmental about other businesses that may rely on outside investors or that outsource part of their business model. She has no idea how you could "make a laptop in the United States to sell for $398." But she insists that it is possible, particularly for niche manufacturers, to run a profitable business (earning a consistent 10 percent on the bottom line and growing at 10 to 15 percent) and make things here. She relishes that challenge.

Alix puts the company's interests ahead of her personal ones. She has limited her compensation so that she does not make more than "10 times the lowest-paid employee." She is simply "not comfortable with a salary ratio different from that." She is aware that she "could be making a lot more money in other circumstances." She could have been a law firm partner or a general counsel at some company. But it gives her more satisfaction to run a business. "When I see people who work for NK become first-time home buyers, it feels good. Five NK employees bought houses this year, and there are quite a few new cars in the parking lot. That's the manufacturing multiplier at work—every dollar in sales of products built here represents lots more dollars of economic activity." She adds, "It's incredibly satisfying to make something tangible. Our products have been in a number of movies. How do you top that!"

Under Alix's leadership, Nielsen-Kellerman is constantly innovating its Kestrel weather instruments, soliciting input from military personnel and other customers about what they would like improved. The original Kestrel model measured just wind speed. Later models added temperature, air pressure and density, and humidity. The most recent Kestrel model incorporates a digital compass for onboard calculation of crosswinds and headwinds. Crosswinds cause the largest error in sharpshooting, and the new Kestrel helps snipers take them into account before firing a shot—one Kestrel model even includes a full-blown ballistics calculator that reads out a firing solution based on the target, gun, ammunition, and environmental conditions. Military Kestrel models also feature a "night-vision-preserving backlight" that helps our troops operating in darkness maintain their night vision and avoid detection. Finally, Alix has placed an emphasis on improving the production process of the Kestrel, making it more sustainable. She has instructed her team to use recycled products in packaging whenever possible, and to come up with goals and strategies to reduce energy use in making and assembling the Kestrel product.

Alix gives credit to her employees for the innovation and the high-quality assembly of the Kestrels. The company has about 80 employees, with a handful of engineers and scientists pushing the boundaries of new designs. But Alix gives equal credit to the workers on the assembly line, who work together to improve their manufacturing process and give feedback to the engineers on how to improve their designs. Most of NK's assemblers came to work with "no prior manufacturing experience," but they work hard, and Nielsen-Kellerman devotes considerable resources to training them for their jobs and teaching them Lean techniques for eliminating waste in their own assembly areas. Alix says that she finds it hard to recruit young people with the aptitude for mechanical work and interest in making a career of it. "We need to provide interested kids with a vocational education so they can develop a particular skill set, and we need to get out the word that there are still good jobs to be had in manufacturing." She recounts how valuable her high school years assembling things in her stepfather's basement were. Her experience doing many different jobs in the company and understanding the production process is what allows her to be a good leader today.

Nielsen-Kellerman's story underscores why domestic manufacturers are critical for our national security. Often, our private manufacturers, small or medium-sized, are making innovations in equipment that can help our troops. The Defense

Department did not come up with the idea of a Kestrel. The leaders at the Pentagon did not decide that our troops would benefit from weather instruments and instruct their procurement department to find a manufacturer to design them. Rather, according to Alix, "Individual guys bought the Kestrel off the shelf. They liked the product, and showed it to their bosses and told them that they needed it." In response, the military leadership decided to order the Kestrel meters and include them with other issued equipment.

The point is that our defense innovation is not limited to the brilliant engineers and scientists in the Pentagon. In an entrepreneurial nation, manufacturers around the country are making useful products that have military applications. Having a strong commercial manufacturing base ensures that we have many laboratories for innovation. America has superior defense equipment, in part, because our military makes use of the know-how and technical ingenuity of private companies such as Nielsen-Kellerman.

INVESTING IN THE FUTURE

The federal government also has a significant role in fostering defense innovation. It must make direct investments in the next generation of defense technology, some of which will have extraordinary benefit to the private sector. The Global Positioning System (GPS) and the Internet are examples of technologies developed by the Department of Defense that made their way to the private sector and have fueled America's economic growth.

General Farrell, the CEO of the National Defense Industrial Association (NDIA), advocates for three specific investments that the federal government should make in defense manufacturing. First, General Farrell calls for increasing funding for the Department of Defense Manufacturing Technology (ManTech) program, which currently receives about $200 million annually.[11] ManTech is the Department of Defense's program for investing in cutting-edge manufacturing that is essential for our defense.[12] The program makes investments in new manufacturing processes, in sophisticated cyberspace systems, and in developing the latest generation of equipment. Second, General Farrell calls for increasing funds for the Defense Production Act, which authorizes investments in new technologies that can enhance our defense, including advanced semiconductors, superconductor wires, and, under President Obama's recent leadership, biofuels to power military aviation.[13] As the "nation's largest energy user," the Department of Defense has made it a national security priority to shift to renewable energy to meet its operational needs.[14] Finally, General Farrell argues that DARPA should continue to be fully funded because the agency helps us maintain our lead in "science and technology."[15] DARPA is innovating in finding alternative energy sources, in improving the energy efficiency of military operations, and in finding solutions to problems associated with sleep deprivation. The breakthroughs that DARPA makes can not only help our military but also spawn new companies in the private sector.

The Department of Defense is not the only federal agency making technological strides. There is the newly created Advanced Research Projects Agency—Energy (ARPA-E), which funds transformative alternative energy projects. Argonne National Laboratory, the leading nuclear energy laboratory, has done innovative work on the Integral Fast Reactor, which uses nuclear waste to generate power.[16] Moreover, three additional national laboratories—Lawrence Livermore

National Laboratory, Los Alamos National Laboratory, and Sandia National Laboratories—are engaged in cutting-edge scientific research and development. Originally, these laboratories were given the task of safeguarding and developing our nuclear weapons. But in the post–Cold War era, their mission has expanded. Although they are still responsible for ensuring the reliability of nuclear weapons, they are now also engaged in helping our nation become energy-independent, developing the most powerful and fastest computers, and providing industrial partners with technology that gives them an edge in the global marketplace.

I had a chance to visit the city of Livermore briefly during my time in the administration. The Commerce Department wanted me to recognize the iGATE program there, an effort by local leaders to foster collaboration among the Livermore National Laboratory (the Lab), local universities, venture capitalists, and businesses to help incubate new technology companies. The Lab is at the hub of the iGATE network. Innovation Tri-Valley works with iGATE to help build a regional cluster for advanced technology.

In my conversations with local leaders, what struck me is how the Lab is positioning itself as a scientific institution rather than simply a weapons laboratory. The local leadership was excited about the Lab's plan to open a Livermore Campus that will facilitate the exchange of ideas among leading scientists and academics from around the world. I learned about the Lab's commitment to commercialize more technology through industry partners and about the Lab's emphasis on critical clean energy areas such as carbon capture, energy efficiency, and fusion. The Lab sees its modern role as enabling America to be the technology leader in a range of fields in the twenty-first century. It is a no-brainer for our federal government to support this vision.

ENSURING OUR DEFENSE CAPABILITY

Our national security depends upon our having a strong manufacturing base. The United States must be self-reliant for critical defense equipment because other nations may not always share our foreign policy goals. It is impractical for domestic manufacturers to develop the capacity to produce sophisticated equipment from scratch within a few weeks or even a few months. Manufacturers require a skilled workforce and a familiarity with the latest technology in order to scale production in times of crisis.

Our military has the tools to determine the minimum sustaining rate for defense-related manufacturing. The minimum sustaining rate is the threshold amount of production of a given defense product that is necessary to ensure that the capacity for producing it remains within the United States. Even in difficult budget times, the Defense Department needs the resources to make procurement decisions that meet the minimum sustaining rate for critical equipment.

Commercial manufacturers also contribute to our defense by making products that have military applications. The strength of our commercial manufacturing sector allows for continuous innovation, enabling our military to adopt the best equipment and technology that the private sector develops. Our commercial manufacturing base also can be mobilized to ramp up production in the event of a major conflict. Although we hope that we will never need to mobilize the way we did in World War II, we should always sustain the capacity to do so as a deterrent to other global powers.

Finally, we need the federal government to make investments in our national security future. This means funding programs at the Department of Defense that focus on manufacturing the next generation of defense equipment. But, it also means thinking of national security more broadly as it relates to energy independence, economic competitiveness, and a strong computing infrastructure. We need to support DOE's scientific agencies and laboratories that secure our nation's future by keeping us the technology leader of the world.

9

What's at Stake

■ ■ ■

Charan Das Khanna, my grandfather, who recently passed away at the age of 97, grew up in a small village in India, but he had big dreams for his children. He wanted them to aspire to lead great lives and make a contribution to civilization. He saw the engineering profession as noble because, as he put it, "the engineers helped build civilization." They designed and made our skyscrapers, our hospitals, and our airplanes. So he encouraged my father to become a chemical engineer and to come to America, where he could make use of those skills.

My father came to America to pursue his graduate work in chemical engineering at the University of Michigan. He stayed not only because he fell in love with the Michigan Wolverines, but also because he realized that America was the place where he wanted to work. America valued what he had to offer. My mother stayed because she loved him.

After finishing his studies at the University of Michigan, my father joined Rohm & Haas, a Philadelphia-based chemical manufacturer. He worked there for nearly 30 years until he retired. Rohm & Haas is renowned for having invented Plexiglas in the 1930s. But the company, recently acquired by Dow Chemical, also manufactures electronic components for semiconductors and specialty materials that go into everything from paint to sunscreen.

As a kid growing up outside Philadelphia, I never really understood what my father did. Chemical engineering seemed too complicated and too far removed from my world. All I knew was that what he did was important. He would leave at 5:30 a.m. every weekday morning to be at work. He would speak about the company's "professionalism," its emphasis on "precision," and its "bottom-up" philosophy of considering the perspectives of every team member on a project. In social conversations, I would often hear him say, "That's not how we approach things at Rohm & Haas," and then proceed to outline what he considered improved processes for management or manufacturing. Rohm & Haas, in his eyes, had the highest standards. He loved working there. To this day, he is as partisan about Rohm & Haas as he is about his Wolverines.

Many of the manufacturers I met during my travels remind me of my father. They go about doing their work, without fanfare, without headlines, without looking for a fast buck. They do it collaboratively with their colleagues, with no consideration of rank, and with joy at being part of a team. They are committed to excellence, constantly challenging the status quo, conventional assumptions, or sloppy thinking. What motivates them is not profits, but perfection. They simply do what needs to get done. They take satisfaction in helping to improve a product's design, in figuring out how to make their business or production more efficient, and in helping to meet a customer's request. These are ends in themselves.

I've tried to label these guiding values, taken collectively, as America's entrepreneurial spirit. No economist can quantify them. No statistician can measure them. But they matter. When I hear all these cynics prognosticating about America's decline, I am convinced that they are missing what this son of immigrants can see so clearly. Our country and our best companies flourish because they provide individuals with the opportunity to make the most of their God-given talent. That's why the best and the brightest come here. That's why my father came here. It was not just to chase the dream of a good salary, a nice house, and a decent education for his kids. It was because he wanted to make his own contribution to civilization, however modest it might be. This country let him. The greatness of America is that it provides many individuals, regardless of surname or class or religion, with the chance to do meaningful work.

What's at stake today is how the American enterprise can continue to prosper in the twenty-first century. We face strong competition from a number of countries in Asia that are hustling to build their own manufacturing and technology base. Some of these countries do not share our values of empowering ordinary individuals. China is of particular concern because of the sheer size of its population and the zeal with which its government is following, in many ways, a mercantilist policy that favors its own elites.

The manufacturers profiled in this book are showing us how to compete in this global economy, demonstrating that the American entrepreneurial spirit is still a winning formula. But a common mantra that I heard is that it is not fair or wise, in the long run, to expect "our companies to compete against countries." We cannot afford to ignore the calls of our manufacturers for policy reform, and thereby risk losing our manufacturing competitiveness to China. To do so would be to sacrifice millions of potential American jobs. We would also tarnish our historical legacy, jeopardizing one of the greatest engines for technological advancement and scientific progress that the world has ever seen.

The policy reforms that many of our manufacturers are requesting are not radical or transformative. They do not require reinventing our entire economy. For the most part, as I have argued, their policies are grounded in historical precedent dating all the way back to Alexander Hamilton and are consistent with the principles of both recent Republican and Democratic administrations.

I take a stab here at summarizing the central policy ideas that I heard on my travels. They are not meant to be silver bullets. I am certain that there are manufacturers out there who would have constructive additions, subtractions, and revisions to this list. The final version of a manufacturing agenda may look different from what follows. But what is inexcusable is to do nothing. Democrats and Republicans must find common ground to keep America a manufacturing leader.

A MANUFACTURING AGENDA

Fair Trade

1. *Currency.* As Paul Krugman points out, twice a year the U.S. Treasury Department must issue a report identifying nations that "manipulate the rate of exchange between their currency and the United States dollar for purposes of preventing effective balance of payments adjustments or gaining unfair

competitive advantage in international trade." It's
time for the Treasury Department to label China
a currency manipulator and also make a factual
determination about other nations that are not
allowing a free-floating currency.[1]

2. *Dumping and subsidies.* The United States needs
to take a much firmer line against other nations
that engage in unfair dumping or that provide
illegal subsidies for their indigenous industries.
Dumping and illegal subsidies are hurting our
steel manufacturers, our domestic solar panel
manufacturers, and our private jet manufacturers,
to name just a few affected industries. We need
to be more aggressive in bringing World Trade
Organization (WTO) actions against these practices
and enforcing the laws that are on the books.

3. *Tax credit for exporters.* The United States should
call for revising the WTO's archaic distinction
between indirect and direct taxes, which
discriminates against U.S. exporters. Either the
United States should be allowed to offer a tax
credit to its exporters or other countries should be
prohibited from doing so.[2]

4. *Restraints on raw material exports.* The United
States should seek the elimination of export taxes
and restraints imposed by Russia, China, and
Ukraine on raw material suppliers. Other nations
should not prevent our manufacturers from
accessing raw materials, such as scrap metal, that
are necessary for production.

5. *Piracy and forced technology transfers.* The United
States should take a hard line to prevent any foreign
government from *subsidizing* the illegal copying

or reverse engineering of American products. We should demand that these countries crack down on piracy, instead of aiding it. We also should aggressively bring trade enforcement actions against nations that force American companies to sign "joint venture agreements" or transfer technology as a condition for selling into their markets.

Tax Reform

1. *Tax credits*. The U.S. Congress should offer tax credits or five-year tax holidays for manufacturers that want to set up or expand factories in the United States. The revenue from these factories should be exempt from the corporate tax for a limited period. This will help level the playing field, given the incentives that many Asian countries are offering, and also help manufacturers finance expensive new factories.

2. *Repatriation*. The U.S. Congress should offer a deal to companies with foreign earnings. They can repatriate foreign earnings at a reduced corporate tax rate provided they use that money to invest in either expanding their factories or creating a net number of new jobs.

3. *Permanent expensing*. The U.S. Congress should make the temporary expensing of equipment permanent, allowing manufacturers to take an immediate deduction for capital expenditures in any tax year. Manufacturers should also be able to expense worker-training programs as part of this deduction. The U.S. Congress should also expand the research and development tax credit to 20 percent and make it permanent.

4. *Alternative energy incentives.* The U.S. Congress
   should continue to provide broad-range tax credits
   for alternative energy manufacturers. These tax
   credits are not specific to any individual company
   and do not involve the government's picking
   winners or losers. The Treasury Department's
   Section 1603 program offering tax credits for solar
   manufacturers and the production tax credit for
   wind manufacturers help our clean tech sector grow.

Federal Support

1. *Manufacturing Extension Partnership (MEP).* The
   U.S. Congress should double the funding of the MEP
   from $120 million to $240 million and insist that
   regional centers have more authority to administer
   programs rather than the centralized Washington
   bureaucracy. The MEP helps small and medium-
   sized manufacturers become more competitive,
   and every manufacturer should have access to this
   program.

2. *SelectUSA.* The U.S. Department of Commerce
   should strengthen the SelectUSA program to help
   American manufacturers expedite the permitting
   process, cut through bureaucratic red tape, and
   navigate complex regulations. This should be the
   one-stop shop for manufacturers that want to build
   factories in the United States. The U.S. Congress
   should fund this program and should demand
   that the SelectUSA program have metrics about its
   success in retaining American manufacturers. The
   Select America program should measure how many
   jobs we are losing to offshoring each month, and

how many we are gaining because of new factories that are set up in the United States.

3. *U.S. and Foreign Commercial Service (USFCS)*. The U.S. Congress should increase the budget of the USFCS, the principal export promotion agency of the United States. A 25 percent increase from the current $250 million will help the USFCS add essential headcount and upgrade its technology. The USFCS should focus these resources on the top 50 countries for exports and allocate resources domestically in cities and rural areas that have the highest export growth potential.

4. *Vocational education*. The Obama administration has proposed nearly $8 billion for community colleges to fund skills training programs. But, it should not ignore vocational educational at the high school level. The administration's Investing in Innovation Fund should support schools such as Austin Polytechnical Institute. Moreover, the Obama administration should propose increased funding for career and technical education, instead of 20 percent in budget cuts. Vocational education can be a pathway to the middle class. As Austin Poly shows, students can gain practical skills from vocational classes but still go on to college or graduate school.

5. *Technology investment*. The U.S. Congress should fund investments in the next generation of defense through the ManTech program, DARPA, and the Defense Production Act. It should make sure that the Defense Department has the resources to maintain the minimum sustaining rate in its decisions on procurement of essential defense equipment. Finally, Congress should provide

funding to institutions such as ARPA-E and our national laboratories, which promote national security by helping us become energy independent and remain the technological leader of the world. These institutions should also reach out to private industry to partner on projects.

6. *Infrastructure investment.* The U.S. infrastructure ranks twenty-third in the world. President Coolidge, President Reagan, and President Obama have all recognized the need for greater investment in our infrastructure. The U.S. Chamber of Commerce has come out for greater investment. It's time for Congress to recognize that strategic spending on infrastructure is what David Brooks would probably consider a "productive investment."

7. *Undersecretary for manufacturing.* The U.S. Congress should create an undersecretary for manufacturing who can raise the visibility of issues that are important to manufacturers and coordinate federal support. The undersecretary of manufacturing could lead a public relations campaign to inform young Americans of the strong opportunities that still exist in manufacturing careers. This position should be housed in a reorganized Commerce Department that consolidates all the federal agencies that promote trade and business.

My hope is that these proposals will become part of a national dialogue on manufacturing. I realize, of course, that talking about manufacturing does not make for light-hearted dinner conversation. When I shared my project at one dinner party, the reviews were not encouraging. Acquaintances mockingly suggested that they would read my book to fall asleep. "Write instead about America 2020," said one well-meaning software executive who was convinced that the modern world was not so much about making as about branding. "Why not describe the social media and the information technology revolution?" others inquired. "Manufacturing is just not sexy," said a business school graduate, seeking to end the discussion. They thought I was defending a relic from the past, arguing for an industry that automation and offshoring would soon render obsolete. At its core, this book is a rejoinder to such stereotypical thinking about manufacturing. I hope readers have come to appreciate that manufacturing is critical to innovation, and that America is still home to millions of exciting manufacturing careers.

But, in a deeper sense, our manufacturers are more than economic contributors. They speak to who we are as a people. Their ability to adapt to globalization and go toe to toe with foreign competitors is a testament to our resilience. At a time when many pundits are asking what has gone wrong with America, they wake up each day figuring out how to make things right. Those who warn that America is in decline are correct to identify major challenges, including an unfair trading regime, our deficit, and Congress's inability to pass an economic growth agenda. Self-criticism is a hallmark of a great democracy. But far away from the noise in Washington, undeterred by the recent failings on Wall Street, everyday citizens, like the Freese brothers, Keith Busse, and Alix James, are hard at work, with a sense of purpose and ingenuity. They are the soul of America. They give us reason to be optimistic about our future.

Notes

■ ■ ■

INTRODUCTION

1. Larry Summers's remarks at Harvard Business Review-McKinsey Awards Ceremony, September 28, 2010.
2. Ibid.
3. In 2008, the U.S. share of world manufacturing output was 17.9 percent. China's share was 17.2 percent, Japan's was 10 percent, Germany's was 7.3 percent, Italy's was 3.6 percent, and the United Kingdom's was 3.1 percent (UNCTAD, *Handbook of Statistics*, 2008 [not adjusted for inflation]). See also Mark J. Perry, "The Demise of America's Manufacturing Sector Has Been Greatly Exaggerated" (blog), January 20, 2011, http://blog.american.com/?p=25164. This article analyzes 2009 UNCTAD data, adjusted for inflation to 2005 levels, to conclude that U.S. manufacturing output was $2.15 trillion to China's $1.48 trillion, a larger difference even than 2008. See also Mark Perry, "The Truth About U.S. Manufacturing," *Wall Street Journal*, February 25, 2011, http://online.wsj.com/article/SB10001424052748 703652104576122353274221570.html; Paul Wiseman, "Despite China's Might, U.S. Factories Maintain Edge," Associated Press via msnbc.com, January 31, 2011, http://www.msnbc.msn.com /id/41349653/ns/business-us_business/#.T0okSXJSSFd; David Brooks, "An Innovation Agenda," *New York Times*, December

7, 2009 (arguing that America remains the world's leader in nearly every cutting-edge sector), http://www.nytimes.com/2009/12/08/opinion/08brooks.html. But see Mark J. Perry, "UN Data: China Is Now World's No. 1 Manufacturer, But It Requires 9-10 Times as Many Workers as U.S." (blog), December 21, 2011, http://mjperry.blogspot.com/2011/12/un-data-china-is-now-worlds-no-1.html. This article analyzes 2010 UNCTAD data to conclude that China in 2010 accounted for 18.89 percent of manufacturing output compared to the United States at 18.24 percent. The recent data suggest that China and the United States are neck and neck and that we may see the lead go back and forth in coming years. See also Robert D. Atkinson, "Commentary on Gregory Tassey's 'Rationales and Mechanisms for Revitalizing US Manufacturing R&D Strategies,'" *J. Technology Transfer*, 2010, http://www.itif.org/files/2010-Atkinson-JTT.pdf; Daniel Luria and Joel Rogers, "Manufacturing, Regional Prosperity, and Public Policy," in *Retooling for Growth: Building a 21st Century Economy in America's Older Industrial Areas*, ed. Richard M. McGahey and Jennifer S. Vey (Washington, DC: Brookings Institution Press, 2008); Alan Tolenson, "Wall Street Journal Chooses Manufacturing Pollyanism over Reality" (blog), March 14, 2011 (blog), http://www.americaneconomicalert.org/blogger_home.asp?Prod_ID=37. Atkinson, Luria, Rogers, and Tolenson argue that our manufacturing output is a misleading statistic because its strength is due almost entirely to unprecedented growth in computers and electronics in the last couple of decades. It does not reflect, in their view, the decline across most other manufacturing sectors. They also claim that the aggregate U.S. output statistic inaccurately counts raw materials that have been imported from overseas, and that currency manipulation understates China's output. They are right to caution against an overly rosy view of the state of manufacturing, and this book argues for a comprehensive manufacturing agenda. But, even if you take issue with some of the methodology in accurately comparing us to China, the fact that we are in the same ballpark despite population size differentials is extraordinary.

4. In 2008, manufacturing constituted more than 42 percent of China's GDP. In comparison, manufacturing was a little over 13 percent of the aggregate U.S. GDP in 2008. UNCTAD, *Handbook of Statistics*, 2008.

5. The average American worker produces $65,480 of value a year. In comparison, the Japanese worker produces $45,587, the German worker produces $42,588, the Russian worker produces $18,702, the Brazilian worker produces $13,230, the Chinese worker produces $10,378, and the Indian worker produces $7,445. International Labour Organization, International Labour Office, "Key Indicators of the Labor Market," September 7, 2009, http://www.ilo.org/public/english/employment/strat/kilm. Manufacturing is one of the top five sectors that are responsible for this extraordinary productivity advantage. See McKinsey Global Institute, "Growth and Renewal in the United States: Retooling America's Economic Engine," p. 5, http://www.mckinsey.com/mgi/publications/growth_and_renewal_in_the_us/pdfs/MGI_growth_and_renewal_in_the_us_full_report.pdf.

6. John Jelacic, an economist at the Department of Commerce, concluded based on public data from the Bureau of Economic Analysis that from 1980 to 2007, total U.S. manufacturing product has grown almost 136.5 percent. See also OECD, "Structural Analysis (STAN) Database"; "A Framework for Revitalizing American Manufacturing," Executive Office of the President, December 2009.

7. According to John Jelacic's analysis of public data from the International Bank for Reconstruction and Development Indicators, China's growth rate from 2000 to 2007 averaged roughly 10 percent, while ours averaged 0.8 percent. Moreover, Stephen J. Ezell and Robert D. Atkinson have pointed out that the majority of U.S. manufacturing sectors "have seen absolute declines in real output over the last decade," and that the growth stems from "over-inflated estimates" of the computer and electronics industry. See Stephen J. Ezell and Robert D. Atkinson, "The Case for a National Manufacturing Strategy," Information Technology & Innovation Foundation, April 2011, p. 19.

8. Dana Marshall, a senior advisor at Dewey & Loboeuf, suggested this clever paraphrase for framing the challenge for American manufacturing during one of our many breakfasts. The original Churchill quote is from his February 9, 1941, BBC speech: "Give Us the Tools, and We Will Finish the Job."

9. Alexander Hamilton, "Report on Manufactures," presented to Congress December 5, 1791.

10. Thomas Jefferson, Letter to Benjamin Austin, January 9, 1816, in *Thomas Jefferson Writings*, ed. Merrill Peterson (New York: Li-

brary of America, 1984), p. 1407; Thomas Jefferson, Letter to John Dortie, October 1, 1811, in *Thomas Jefferson's Garden Book: 1766–1824: with Relevant Extracts from His Other Writings,* ed. Edwin M. Betts (Philadelphia: American Philosophical Society, 1944; repr. Charlottesville, VA: Thomas Jefferson Memorial Foundation, 1999), p. 462. These Jefferson sources are cited at http://www.monticello.org/site/jefferson/quotations-manufacturing.

11. Michael Lind, *Hamilton's Republic: Readings in the American Democratic Nationalist Tradition* (New York: Free Press, Simon & Schuster, 1997). See also E. J. Dionne Jr., *Our Divided Political Heart: The Battle for the American Idea in an Age of Discontent* (New York: Bloomsbury, 2012), ch. 7.

12. Lincoln was influenced by the writings of Henry Carey, his economic advisor. Henry Carey, *Excerpts from the Harmony of Interests: Agricultural, Manufacturing, and Commercial* (1851).; see also Morrill Land Grant Act of 1862, 7 U.S.C 304.

13. Arthur M. Schlesinger Jr., ed., *The Federal Aviation Administration* (Philadelphia: Chelsea House Publishers, 2002).

14. Alan S. Milward, *War, Economy, and Society, 1939–1945* (Berkeley: University of California Press, 1979).

15. Louis Uchitelle, "Ron Bloom Is Obama's Manufacturing Emissary," *New York Times,* September 9, 2010, http://www.nytimes.com/2010/09/10/business/economy/10manufacture.html?pagewanted=all.

16. President Ronald Reagan, State of the Union address, January 27, 1987.

17. Bill Clinton, *Back to Work: Why We Need Smart Government for a Strong Economy* (New York: Alfred A. Knopf, 2011), pp. 169–171.

18. "Remarks by the President on the Economy," May 26, 2010, http://www.whitehouse.gov/the-press-office/remarks-president-economy-0.

19. President Obama, "Remarks at the Signing of the Manufacturing Enhancement Act," August 11, 2010; Uchitelle, "Ron Bloom" (observing that "not since Ronald Reagan has an American President spoken so emphatically about the importance of manufacturing").

20. "Remarks by the President on the Economy."

21. A bipartisan poll of 1,000 likely 2010 general election voters, conducted by the Mellman Group and Ayres McHenry Associates, Inc., April 22–26, 2010, showed that manufacturing was viewed as the most important sector for overall economic strength (37

percent ranked it number 1, and 57 percent ranked it number 1 or number 2). It was followed by healthcare and then finance. The same poll showed that manufacturing was considered the most important for national security (23 percent ranked it number 1, and 40 percent ranked it number 1 or number 2). It was followed by finance and high tech. The poll also showed that 39 percent believed that the government should do "whatever is required to revitalize" manufacturing, and 47 percent said that the government should help in a limited way through incentives and trade policy. Even 70 percent of Tea Party supporters were in favor of a national manufacturing strategy.

22. When discussing my project with E. J. Dionne, he pointed me to Richard McGregor's insightful column, "Why Can't America Be More Like, Well, America?" *Financial Times*, September 30, 2011 cited in E. J. Dionne Jr., *Our Divided Political Heart*.

23. Senator Rand talks about being a "big fan of Ayn Rand," http://liberty maven.com/2009/05/20/rand-paul-talks-about-his-name-and -ayn-rand/5796/.

24. Rand Paul, "A Modest $500 Billion Proposal," *Wall Street Journal*, February 7, 2011, http://online.wsj.com/article/SB1000142405274 8703956604576110431794539522.html?KEYWORDS=rand+paul.

25. Jagdish Bhagwati, "'Made in America' Is Not Way Out," *Financial Times*, August 9, 2010, http://www.ft.com/cms/s/0/54a03eb6 -a3eb-11df-9e3a-00144feabdc0.html#axzz1nUUXJhDz.

26. Robert B. Reich, "Manufacturing Jobs Are Never Coming Back," *Forbes*, May 28, 2009. See also Reich's blog, http://robertreich blogspot.com/2009/05/future-of-manufacturing-gm-and -american.html.

27. Ibid.

CHAPTER 1

1. Andy Grove, "How America Can Create Jobs," *BusinessWeek*, July 1, 2010, http://www.businessweek.com/magazine/content /10_28/b4186048358596.htm.

2. Steven Johnson, *Where Good Ideas Come From: The Natural History of Innovation* (New York: Riverhead Books, 2010), p. 171.

3. Gary P. Pisano and Willy C. Shih, "Restoring American Competitiveness," *Harvard Business Review*, July–August 2009.

4. Andrew N. Liveris, *Make It in America: The Case for Re-inventing the Economy* (Hoboken, NJ: Wiley, 2011).

5. In 2006, manufacturing R&D in the United States was $172,728.6 million, and total business R&D was $247,669.0 million. "The R&D Expenditure in U.S. Industry," OECD, "Structural Analysis (STAN) Database," 2006.

6. "A Framework for Encouraging American Manufacturing," Executive Office of the President, December 2009. Almost 90 percent of patents are utility patents, as opposed to purely design patents.

7. Mark Boroush, "NSF Releases New Statistics on Business Innovation," National Science Foundation, October 2010, http://www.nsf.gov/statistics/infbrief/nsf11300/.

8. See Christina Romer, "Do Manufacturers Need Special Treatment?," *New York Times*, February 4, 2012, http://www.nytimes.com/2012/02/05/business/do-manufacturers-need-special-treatment-economic-view.html. Romer argues that manufacturers do not need to be subsidized because those that invest in early production usually reap the financial rewards. Even if this is true, the United States still has an interest in making sure that these companies are locating and innovating here rather than abroad. We may not want to subsidize manufacturers, but we do want to have a competitive economic environment that gives companies incentives to make some production investments in the United States. Otherwise, we risk losing a significant part of our innovative capacity over the long run and ceding good-paying jobs. As Clyde Prestowitz argues, our nation has an interest in keeping *both* innovative manufacturing and services in the United States. We should not write off either sector. For an additional response to Romer, see Clyde Prestowitz, "Why Economists Don't Get It on Manufacturing" (blog), February 6, 2012, http://prestowitz.foreignpolicy.com/blog/12503.

9. Steve Chapman, "Manufacturing an Economic Myth," reason.com, March 19, 2012. http://reason.com/archives/2012/03/19/manufacturing-an-economic-myth.

10. U.S. Bureau of Economic Analysis, "U.S. International Trade in Goods and Services: Exhibit 8" (2010).

11. BEA Current Account Data 2009. See also Laura D'Andrea Tyson, "Why Manufacturing Still Matters," February 10, 2012, http://economix.blogs.nytimes.com/2012/02/10/why-manufacturing-still-matters/.

12. A recent *New York Times* article makes the case that we need more emphasis on service exports. Catherine Rampell, "Some Urge U.S.

to Focus on Selling Its Skills Overseas," *New York Times*, April 10, 2012. Rampell makes the case that the United States has the potential to "more than double" service exports, creating $800 billion more in revenue and potentially 3 million jobs. http://www.nytimes.com/2012/04/11/business/economy/should-us-services-companies-get-breaks-abroad.html?pagewanted=all.

13. Foreign Trade Statistics (2009), U.S. Census Bureau, Foreign Trade Division. See also Stephen J. Ezell and Robert D. Atkinson, "The Case for a National Manufacturing Strategy," Information Technology & Innovation Foundation, April 2011, p. 11. The authors argue that even if the U.S. service surplus grew at a staggering and unrealistic 10 percent a year, it would take 15 years to balance the trade deficit. To balance our trade, we need growth in manufacturing.

14. Michael Spence and Sandile Hlyatshwayo, "The Evolving Structure of Global Growth," Project Syndicate, February 14, 2011, http://www.project-syndicate.org/commentary/spence20/English.

15. The average weekly pay for manufacturing in July 2010 was $933.13. In comparison, the average weekly pay for services was $736.48. U.S. Department of Labor, Bureau of Labor Statistics, "Current Employment Statistics (CES, 2010)."

16. Kathleen Madigan, "Giving Tax Edge to Manufacturers Carries Risks" (blog), *Wall Street Journal*, February 23, 2012, http://blogs.wsj.com/economics/2012/02/23/giving-tax-edge-to-manufacturing-carries-risks/.

17. Dana Frank, "Once They Started, Sit-Downs Spread Like Wildfire," Labor Notes, July 2009. See also Foster R. Dulles and Melvyn Dubofsky, *Labor in America: A History*, 4th ed. (Arlington Heights, IL: H. Davidson, 1984).

18. "Framework for Revitalizing American Manufacturing." Robert Reich, "The Factory Jobs Aren't Coming Back," *Salon*, February 17, 2012, http://www.salon.com/2012/02/17/the_factory_jobs_arent_coming_back/singleton/. Reich points out that "in the 1950s more than a third of American workers were represented by a union. Now, fewer than seven percent of private-sector workers have a union behind them."

19. Bureau of Labor Statistics data from 2010 Employment Statistics Database. The average real wage for nonsupervisory workers in manufacturing was $384.60 per week in 1978 and is only 6 percent less today.

20. For example, in December of 2010, the unemployment rate for those with just a high school diploma was 9.8 percent, the rate for those with some college or an associate degree was 9.1 percent, and the rate for those with a bachelor's degree or higher was 4.9 percent. The unemployment rate for those without high school was a staggering 15.3 percent. These percentages were about the same for most of 2009 and 2010. See Bureau of Labor Statistics, "Employment Report," Table A-4, "Employment Status of the Civilian Population 25 Years and Over by Educational Attainment," January 7, 2011.

21. Bureau of Labor Statistics data, "Federal Reserve Economic Data," http://research.stlouisfed.org/fred2/. See also Andrew N. Liveris, *Make It in America: The Case for Re-Inventing the Economy* (Hoboken, NJ: Wiley, 2011), p. 38, citing Robert E. Scott, "Manufacturing Job Loss: Productivity Is Not the Culprit," February 21, 2007, http://www.epi.org/economic_snapshots/entry/webfeatures_snapshots_20070221/.

22. Global Insight database, Bureau of Labor Statistics data, "Monthly Employment by Major Industry" (seasonal adjustment). See also Floyd Norris, "Manufacturing Is Surprising Bright Spot in U.S. Economy," *New York Times*, January 5, 2012. http://www.nytimes.com/2012/01/06/business/us-manufacturing-is-a-bright-spot-for-the-economy.html.

23. "Framework for Revitalizing American Manufacturing."

24. According to John Jelacic based on public BLS data, manufacturing jobs declined nearly 34 percent from 1998 to 2010. As a comparison, manufacturing jobs increased 4.7 percent from 1993 to 1998, declined 6.7 percent from 1989 to 1993, increased 2.5 percent from 1986 to 1989, and declined 9.7 percent from 1979 to 1986.

25. Bureau of Economic Analysis, "GDP by Industry Accounts," 2009.

26. Louis Uchitelle, "Obama's Strategy to Reverse Manufacturing's Fall," *New York Times*, July 20, 2009, http://www.nytimes.com/2009/07/21/business/economy/21manufacture.html?_r=1.

27. According to Global Insight Database, BLS data, in the period between December 2007 and November 2010, the manufacturing sector lost 2,084,000 jobs and the construction sector lost 2,360,000 jobs. As a comparison, wholesale and retail trade lost 821,000 jobs in the same period. Fortunately, today manufacturing is helping to lead the economic recovery. From December 2009 to July 2011, the United States created more than

238,000 manufacturing jobs. Data from St. Louis Fed, http://
research.stlouisfed.org/fred2/graph/?chart_type=line&s[1]
[id]=MANEMP&s[1][range]=5yrs#. Moreover, in March 2011, the
Institute for Supply Management's factory index stood at 61.4,
the highest in nearly seven years. A rate of above 50 indicates
growth, whereas a rate below 50 indicates contraction. Comparatively, China's index was 52.2 the same month. See Timothy
R. Homan and Robert Willis, "U.S. Economy: Manufacturing
Expands by Most Since 2004," *Bloomberg Businessweek*, March
1, 2011, http://www.businessweek.com/news/2011-03-01/u-s
-economy-manufacturing-expands-by-most-since-2004.html.
See also Leah Schnur, "Manufacturing Strongest in Nearly Seven
Years," Reuters, March 1, 2011, http://www.reuters.com/article
/2011/03/01/us-usa-economy-idUSTRE71R3OO20110301. See
also "Rustbelt Recovery," *The Economist*, March 10, 2011 (pointing out that manufacturing output has grown dramatically since
June 2009), http://www.economist.com/node/18332894?story
_id=18332894; Paul Krugman, "Making Things in America,"
New York Times, May 19, 2011 (arguing that the manufacturing
trade deficit is coming down and companies are moving production to the United States), http://www.nytimes.com/2011/05/20
/opinion/20krugman.html.

28. Jeff Immelt, chairman and CEO of GE, "An American Renewal,"
remarks to Detroit Economic Club, June 26, 2009.

29. Paul Krugman, "China, Japan, America," *New York Times*,
September 12, 2010, http://www.nytimes.com/2010/09/13
/opinion/13krugman.html. Robert E. Scott, "U.S. Jobs De-
pend on China Revaluing Its Currency Now," Economic Policy Institute, June 23, 2010. See also Irwin M. Stelzer, "Time for
a Dose of Protectionism? The Case for Giving China a Dose of
Its Own Medicine," *Weekly Standard*, November 30, 2009 (de-
tailing China's policies that are hurting American workers),
http://www.weeklystandard.com/Content/Public/Articles
/000/000/017/253vzcbq.asp; Alan Tolenson, "The Overwhelming Case for Ending Chinese Currency Manipulation Now"
(blog), May 21, 2010, http://www.americaneconomicalert.org/
view_art.asp?Prod_ID=3517.

30. Krugman, ibid.

31. Krugman, "China, Japan, America." See also Paul Krugman,
"China Goes to Nixon," *New York Times*, January 20, 2011, http://

www.nytimes.com/2011/01/21/opinion/21krugman.html. Kalpana Kochar, a senior economist at the World Bank, mentioned to me during a panel discussion that according to OECD data, Chinese consumption is only approximately 35 percent of GDP. This is well below the average for most countries. Comparatively, India, most European nations, and the United States have consumption rates of about 50 percent of GDP. In short, China's policies are depriving its own consumers of a high standard of living.

32. Ibid.

33. Alexandra Petri, "Pete Hoekstra's Bad Ad" (blog post), February 6, 2012 http://www.washingtonpost.com/blogs/compost/post/pete-hoekstras-bad-ad/2012/02/06/gIQABnY4uQ_blog.html.

34. Thomas Friedman, "Unusual Uncertainty Stands in the Way of a Recovery," *New York Times*, August 17, 2010.

35. Robert B. Reich, "Manufacturing Jobs Are Never Coming Back," *Forbes*, May 28, 2009. See also Reich's blog, http://robertreich.blogspot.com/2009/05/future-of-manufacturing-gm-and-american.html.

36. David Barnoza, "After Suicides, Foxconn Will Outsource Its Workers Dorms," *New York Times*, June 25, 2010, http://www.nytimes.com/2010/06/26/technology/26foxconn.html.

37. Richard McCormack, "The Plight of American Manufacturing," in *Manufacturing a Better Future for America*, ed. Richard McCormack (Washington, DC: Alliance for American Manufacturing, 2009). McCormack cites Judith Banister's excellent report "Manufacturing and Employment Compensation in China," for the U.S. Department of Labor, Bureau of Labor Statistics, November 2005, http://www.bls.gov/fls/chinareport.pdf.

38. In 2006, manufacturing firms that employed less than 500 workers accounted for a little over 6 million of the total manufacturing workforce. Data from U.S. Census Bureau, "County Business Patterns," 2006. For more information, see http://www.census.gov/econ/susb/introduction.html; See also *The Facts About Manufacturing*, 8th ed. (The Manufacturing Institute), p. 5, http://www.nam.org/Resource-Center/Facts-About-Manufacturing/~/media/0F91A0FBEA1847D087E719EAAB4D4AD8.ashx.

39. John Maynard Keynes, "Economic Possibilities for Our Grandchildren," in *Essays in Persuasion* (London: Macmillan, 1931).

40. Employment Report from Bureau of Labor and Statistics, Ta-

bles B2 and B7, January 7, 2011. See also "The Real Reasons You Are Working So Hard and What You Can Do About It," *Business-Week*, October 3, 2005 (pointing out that since 1991, the average annual work hours are down only 2 percent, including for lower-skilled employees), http://www.businessweek.com/magazine /content/05_40/b3953601.htm.

41. See Russell Roberts, "Obama v. ATMs: Why Technology Doesn't Destroy Jobs," *Wall Street Journal*, June 22, 2011, http://online .wsj.com/article/SB10001424052702304070104576399704275939640.html?mod=WSJ_Opinion_LEADTop.

42. Peter F. Drucker, "The Manufacturing Paradox," *The Economist*, November 1, 2001.

43. Paul Krugman, "Degrees and Dollars," *New York Times*, March 6, 2011, http://www.nytimes.com/2011/03/07/opinion/07krugman .html?_r=1&src=me&ref=homepage.

44. Peter F. Drucker, "The Manufacturing Paradox," *The Economist*, November 1, 2001.

45. Thomas Friedman, "Made in the World," *New York Times*, January 28, 2012, http://www.nytimes.com/2012/01/29/opinion /sunday/friedman-made-in-the-world.html.

46. Harold L. Sirkin, Michael Zinser, Douglas Hohner, and Justin Rose, "U.S. Manufacturing Nears the Tipping Point, Which Industries, Why and How Much?" Report by the Boston Consulting Group, March 22, 2012; https://www.bcgperspectives.com /content/articles/manufacturing_supply_chain_management _us_manufacturing_nears_the_tipping_point/.

47. Robert B. Reich, "Manufacturing Jobs Are Never Coming Back," *Forbes*, May 28, 2009, http://www.forbes.com/2009/05/28 /robert-reich-manufacturing-business-economy.html.

48. "Pass the Ammunition: Army Taking Action on Small-Cal Shortages," *Defense Industry Daily*, July 14, 2005, http://www .defenseindustrydaily.com/pass-the-ammunition-army-taking -action-on-smallcal-shortages-0859/.

49. Ibid. General Paul Izzo was director of the Program Executive Office for Ammunition during the beginning of the Iraq war. He confirmed during a phone interview in October 2010 that we relied on foreign nations to supply us with ammunition at the beginning of the war because of insufficient domestic supply.

50. This phrase comes from Stephen Moore's Op-Ed distinction between a nation of takers and one of makers. See Stephen Moore,

"We've Become a Nation of Takers, Not Makers," *Wall Street Journal*, April 1, 2011, http://online.wsj.com/article/SB100014240 52748704050204576219073867182108.html. Moore argues compellingly that we need to grow "the economy that makes things." He is right to observe that this sector has declined over the years. However, I imagine that he would find these stories to be evidence of America's enduring strength and "productivity improvements."

CHAPTER 2

1. Daniel Luria and Joel Rogers, "Manufacturing, Regional Prosperity, and Public Policy," in *Retooling for Growth: Building a 21st Century Economy in America's Older Industrial Areas*, ed. Richard M. McGahey and Jennifer S. Vey (Washington, DC: Brookings Institution Press, 2008).
2. Allison Arieff, "The Future of Manufacturing Is Local," *New York Times*, May 27, 2011, http://opinionator.blogs.nytimes .com/2011/03/27/the-future-of-manufacturing-is-local/?scp=2& sq=manufacturing&st=cse.
3. Ibid.
4. Susan Helper, "Renewing U.S. Manufacturing Promoting a High-Road Strategy," Economic Policy Institute, February 13, 2008.
5. Testimony of Roger D. Kilmer, director of the Hollings Manufacturing Extension Partnership, U.S. Senate Committee on Banking, Housing, and Urban Affairs, Subcommittee on Economic Policy, August 5, 2010, http://www.nist.gov/director/ocla/upload/NIST -Kilmer-testimony-Sen-Banking-Final.pdf.
6. Alexander Hamilton, "Report on Manufactures," presented to Congress December 5, 1791.
7. Ibid.
8. Paul M. Hallacher, *Why Policy Issue Networks Matter: The Advanced Technology Program and The Manufacturing Extension Partnership* (Lanham, MD: Rowman & Littlefield Publishers, Inc., 2005), pp. 55–56.
9. Ibid.
10. Detailed Summary: H.R. 408, The Spending Reduction Act of 2011, January 2011, http://rsc.jordan.house.gov/UploadedFiles /SRA-Extended_SummaryFINAL.pdf.
11. Ibid.

12. "Cochairs' Proposal for Cutting $200 Billion in Federal Spending," November 10, 2010, http://www.fiscalcommission.gov/sites/fiscalcommission.gov/files/documents/Illustrative_List_11.10.2010.pdf.
13. Lisa Lerer and John McCormick, "Why Business Does Not Trust the Tea Party," *Bloomberg Businessweek*, October 13, 2010, http://www.businessweek.com/magazine/content/10_43/b4200066170117.htm.
14. Big Think, "Interview with Dick Armey," November 16, 2009, http://bigthink.com/ideas/17331.
15. Tim Loh, "Former Congressman Dick Armey Visits Local Conservatives," *Fairfield (CT) Citizen*, November 13, 2009, http://www.fairfieldcitizenonline.com/news/article/Former-Congressman-Dick-Armey-visits-local-216912.php.
16. "Federal Budget Request for NIST Includes Science and Technology Investments," *Quality Magazine*, February 14, 2011, http://www.qualitymag.com/Articles/Industry_Headlines/BNP_GUID_9-5-2006_A_1000000000000996016.
17. See Stephen J. Ezell and Robert D. Atkinson, "The Case for a National Manufacturing Strategy," Information Technology & Innovation Foundation, April 2011, p. 28.
18. Roger S. Ahlbrandt, Richard J. Freuhan, and Frank Giarratani, *Renaissance of American Steel: Lessons for Managers in Competitive Industries* (New York: Oxford University Press, 1996), p. 15.
19. Richard McCormack, "U.S. Steel Industry Says Get Ready, Chinese Government Companies Are Coming to America," *Manufacturing and Technology News* 17, no. 16 (October 19, 2010).
20. Chris Isidore, "Bethlehem Steel in Chapter 11: No. 3 U.S. Steelmaker Blames Imports, Slowing Economy, Labor and Retiree Costs," CNNMoney, October 15, 2001, http://money.cnn.com/2001/10/15/companies/bethsteel/index.htm.
21. Chris Suellentrop, "Why Are Bush's Steel Tariffs Legal?" *Slate*, March 5, 2002, http://www.slate.com/articles/news_and_politics/explainer/2002/03/why_are_bushs_steel_tariffs_legal.html.
22. Lisa Bergson, "Heroes of Industry," May 21, 2005, http://money.cnn.com/magazines/fortune/fortune_archive/2005/03/21/8254856/index.htm.
23. Bureau of Labor Statistics index (1998 to 2009), "Iron and Steel Mills and Ferroalloy Manufacturing, Labor Productivity." The

output per hour increased by 21.6 percent from 2002 to 2009. Charles Bell at the Department of Commerce assisted in tracking down a lot of this public data about the steel industry.

24. According to Charles Bell at the Department of Commerce, steelworkers have lost nearly 30,000 jobs in the Great Recession from 2007 to 2009 (Bureau of Labor Statistics data). At a forum hosted on CNBC by Maria Bartiromo entitled "The Future of 'Made in the U.S.A.,'" part of the *Meeting of the Minds: Rebuilding America* series (aired December 2, 2009), Darryl Parker of Steelworkers Local 1375 talked about the idling of a Severstal mill in Warren, Ohio, and about his fellow steelworkers who were facing personal bankruptcy and standing in food lines.

25. American Iron and Steel Institute Annual Report (2009). In 2009, 21 percent of our steel was imported, and nearly 79 percent was made in the United States.

26. The price of steel per net ton averaged $227 in 2001 and $602 in 2010. This information was collected from Tom Stundza's monthly columns on steel prices for *Purchasing* magazine. Charles Bell at Commerce aggregated this public data for me.

27. World Steel Association, "Crude Steel Production, Major Countries," *Steel Statistical Yearbook*, 2009, http://www.worldsteel .org/?action=publicationdetail&id=104

28. Ibid.

29. Rick Farrant, "Man of Steel," *Greater Fort Wayne Business Weekly*, July 23, 2010.

30. Ibid.

31. Quoted in Richard Preston, *American Steel* (Quill, 1992). Keith Busse slightly updated the quote, but it's largely unchanged from what he said 20 years ago.

32. See Statement of Keith Busse, president and CEO of Steel Dynamics, Inc., chairman of the board of directors of the Steel Manufacturers Association, before the Congressional Steel Caucus, March 16, 2005.

33. American Society of Civil Engineers, Policy Statement, Rail Infrastructure Investment, March 12, 2009.

34. Jia Lynn Yang, "Companies Pile Up Cash but Remain Hesitant to Add Jobs," *Washington Post*, July 15, 2010 (pointing out that nonfinancial companies are sitting on nearly $1.8 trillion in cash), http://www.washingtonpost.com/wp-dyn/content /article/2010/07/14/AR2010071405960.html.

35. McCormack, "U.S. Steel Industry Says Get Ready, Chinese Government Companies Are Coming to America," *Manufacturing and Technology News*, Volume 17, No. 16, October 19, 2010.
36. Alan H. Price, Timothy C. Brightbill, Christopher B. Weld, Charles L. Capito, and Robert E. Morgan, "Raw Deal: How Government Trade Barriers and Subsidies Are Distorting Global Trade in Raw Materials," prepared for American Scrap Coalition, November 2009.

CHAPTER 3

1. Wichita was named the top-ranked metropolitan area for aerospace manufacturing by *Business Facilities* magazine in 2010, http://www.businessfacilities.com/Rankings/BFJulAug10_METRO_RANKINGS.PDF. The magazine ranks only U.S. metropolitan areas. However, given the United States' commanding global lead in aerospace manufacturing, it is safe to assume that Wichita is the global leader. As I discuss later in this chapter, the United States provides 48 percent of global aerospace manufacturing, compared to only 39 percent for the European Union. See also "Sunny Forecast for Airborne Economy, The Wichita Equation," an initiative of the Wichita Metro Chamber of Commerce, 2007 (highlighting that Wichita has more than 48,000 aerospace manufacturing employees and an estimated aerospace payroll of $2.7 billion).
2. "Wichita Engineers Participate in Optimizing the A380's Wing," Airbus news release, March 10, 2006, http://www.wingsover kansas.com/news/article.asp?id=590.
3. *Business Facilities* ranking, http://www.businessfacilities.com /Rankings/BFJulAug10_METRO_RANKINGS.PDF.
4. Wichita had 68,401 manufacturing employees out of a total of 303,173. Brookings Institution, "State of Metro America Report," 2010, http://www.brookings.edu/~/media/Files/Programs /Metro/state_of_metro_america/metro_america_report.pdf. The study relies on ACS Table C24030, Census 2000 SF3, Table P49.
5. Remarks of R. Thomas Buffenbarger, National Business Aviation Association, October 20, 2009 (nationally 30,000 laid off). See also Molly McMillin, "Layoff Notices Go Out at Cessna," *Wichita Eagle*, October 8, 2010; "Hawker Beechcraft Boss: Layoffs a Result of 'Flat to Slightly Down' Market," *Wichita Eagle*, September 24, 2010.

6. Josh Levs, "Big Three Automakers Flew Private Jets to Ask for Taxpayer Money, CNN, November 19, 2008, http://articles.cnn .com/2008-11-19/us/autos.ceo.jets_1_private-jets-auto-industry -test-vote?_s=PM:US.

7. Ronald Green helped me with statistics for some of my speeches and collected this public information from Bureau of the Census and Aerospace Industries Association (AIA) data, 2009. An economist by training, his official title is senior international trade specialist, Office of Transportation and Machinery, Aerospace Team, U.S. Department of Commerce. See the Department of Commerce aerospace page for detailed data: http://trade.gov /mas/manufacturing/OAAI/aero_stats.asp.

8. Ron got country-specific revenue data from two public sources: The European Association of Aerospace Industries (2009) and the Aerospace and Defence Industries Association of Europe (2009).

9. Ron got country-specific revenue data from public sources such as the Aerospace Industries Association of Canada (2009), Society of Japanese Aerospace Companies (2009), Aerospace Industries Association of Brazil (2009), Israel Aerospace Industries, Ltd. (2009), and Korea Aerospace Industries (2009). He got the Chinese data, which are from 2007, from http://www.marketavenue.cn /upload_en/ChinaMarketreports/2010-03/REPORTS_984.html.

10. See "Key U.S. Aerospace Statistics," U.S. Department of Commerce, International Trade Administration, http://trade.gov /wcm/groups/public/@trade/@mas/@man/@aai/documents /web_content/aero_stat_keyqtr.pdf.

11. In 2009, petroleum products accounted for $204 billion of the total trade deficit of about $375 billion. U.S. Bureau of Economic Analysis, "U.S. International Trade in Goods and Services: Exhibit 8," June 2010.

12. Michael Porter, "Clusters and the New Economics of Competition," *Harvard Business Review*, November–December 1998.

13. Lawrence Lessig, *Remix: Making Art and Commerce Thrive in the Hybrid Economy* (New York: Penguin Press, 2008).

14. Steven Johnson, *Where Good Ideas Come From: The Natural History of Innovation* (New York: Riverhead Books, 2010), p. 245. Johnson describes planes as being made in quadrant two, which is a market, networked environment (p. 229). But a visit to Wichita suggests that aerospace manufacturing also has quadrant four innovation.

15. Ibid., p. 220.
16. Sedgwick County Workforce Development website, National Center for Aviation Training page, http://www.sedgwickcounty .org/workforce_development/.
17. Mark Muro and Bruce Katz, "The New Cluster Moment: How Regional Innovation Clusters Can Foster the Next Economy," Metropolitan Policy Program at Brookings, September 2010.
18. Molly McMillin, "Contract at Spirit Could Change the Industry," *Wichita Eagle*, July 4, 2010.
19. Clyde Prestowitz and Kate Heidinger provide an excellent account of how the trading regime has been stacked against America since World War II. Clyde Prestowitz and Kate Heidinger, "The Evolution of U.S. Trade Policy," in *Manufacturing a Better Future for America*, ed. Richard McCormack (Washington, DC: Alliance for American Manufacturing, 2009).
20. Robert J. Samuelson, "The Danger Behind China's 'Me First' Worldview," *Washington Post*, February 15, 2010, http://www .washingtonpost.com/wp-dyn/content/article/2010/02/14 /AR2010021402892.html. See also Andrew Batson, "U.S. Handicapped in Indigenous Innovation Spat," *Wall Street Journal* (blog), May 21, 2010, http://blogs.wsj.com/chinarealtime/2010/05/21 /us-handicapped-in-indigenous-innovation-spat/.
21. Rich Karlgaard, "Cessna Refutes the Decline of Capitalism," Forbes.com, October 5, 2009, http://www.forbes.com /forbes/2009/1005/opinions-rich-karlgaard-digital-rules.html.
22. Molly McMillin, "NetJets' Embraer Order Is Bad News for Wichita," *Wichita Eagle*, December 5, 2010. See also Thomas B. Haines, "Embraer Market Share Grows, Forecast Robust Jet Market," *Aircraft Owner and Pilot Association Online*, September 13, 2010, http://www.aopa.org/aircraft/articles/2010/100913embraer.html.
23. Mary Saunders, Statement Before the U.S.-China Economic and Security Review Commission Hearing on "China's Emergent Military Aerospace and Commercial Aviation Capabilities," May 20, 2010, http://www.uscc.gov/hearings/2010hearings/written _testimonies/10_05_20_wrt/10_05_20_saunders_statement.phpar.
24. Molly McMillin, "Brownback Seeks Trade Commission Investigation of Embraer," *Wichita Eagle*, September 9, 2010.
25. Alan Tonelson, "Ronald Reagan: Trade Realist," American EconomicAlert.org, June 7, 2004, http://www.americaneconomic alert.org/view_art.asp?Prod_ID=1134.

26. President Reagan, "Radio Address to the Nation on Free and Fair Trade," September 7, 1985, http://www.presidency.ucsb.edu/ws/index.php?pid=39072. See also Alan Tonelson, "Beating Back Predatory Trade," *Foreign Affairs* 73 (1994), p. 123.

27. Ibid.

28. President Barack Obama, State of the Union address, 2012, http://www.whitehouse.gov/state-of-the-union-2012.

29. Testimony of Jack J. Pelton, chairman, president, and CEO of Cessna Aircraft Company, Hearing on "Made in America: Increasing Jobs Through Export and Trade," House Subcommittee on Commerce, Manufacturing, and Trade, March 16, 2011, http://republicans.energycommerce.house.gov/Media/file/Hearings/CTCP/031611/Pelton.pdf.

30. F. Robert van der Linden, *Airlines and Air Mail* (Lexington: University Press of Kentucky, 2002), pp. 10–16.

31. Calvin Coolidge, "Address to the International Civil Aeronautics Conference," Washington, DC, December 12, 1928, http://www.presidency.ucsb.edu/ws/index.php?pid=24178.

32. Boeing Company, "Heritage of Innovation," http://www.boeing.com/history/index.html. See also "Where Good Technology Comes From: Case Studies in American Innovation," Breakthrough Institute, December 2010, http://thebreakthrough.org/blog/Case%20Studies%20in%20American%20Innovation%20report.pdf.

33. W. James Antle III, review of "Toward Reviving Manufacturing," *Washington Times*, February 11, 2011 (arguing that between 1995 and 2002, Japan lost 15 percent of its manufacturing jobs, China 15 percent, and Brazil 20 percent, all more than the United States lost during that same period), http://www.washingtontimes.com/news/2011/feb/11/toward-reviving-manufacturing/.

34. "Entrepreneurship in China: Let a Million Flowers Bloom," *The Economist*, March 10, 2011, http://www.economist.com/node/18330120?story_id=18330120.

35. Alexander Hamilton, "Report on Manufactures," presented to Congress December 5, 1791.

36. Andy Grove, "How America Can Create Jobs," *BusinessWeek*, July 1, 2010, http://www.businessweek.com/magazine/content/10_28/b4186048358596.htm. I respectfully disagree with Grove's recommendation that this bank be funded by levying a tax on companies that are offshoring. That will put U.S. companies that

are exporting and need some overseas presence for sales at a disadvantage, and might force them to sell their foreign subsidiaries.

37. Andrew N. Liveris, *Make It in America: The Case for Re-inventing the Economy* (Hoboken, NJ: Wiley, 2011). See also Peter Engardio, "Can the Future Be Built in America?" *BusinessWeek*, September 21, 2009, pp. 46–51 (arguing that Washington should offer low-cost loans for companies that want to build U.S. factories and meet market criteria), http://www.businessweek.com/magazine/content/09_38/b4147046115750.htm.

38. Bill Clinton, "It's Still the Economy, Stupid," *Newsweek*, June 19, 2011, http://www.newsweek.com/2011/06/19/it-s-still-the-economy-stupid.html.

39. See Henry R. Nothhaft with David Kline, *Great Again: Revitalizing America's Entrepreneurial Leadership* (Boston: Harvard Business Press, 2011), pp. 114–115 (proposing that U.S. manufacturers be given tax holidays or some form of meaningful tax reduction on revenue from new factories). Paul Otellini, CEO of Intel, also made that argument when I met with him in the fall of 2011.

40. Alexander Hamilton, "The Examination," *New York Evening Post*, December 24, 1801.

41. Josiah Ryan, "Senate Starts Debate on Amendment to Slash Aviation Spending to 2008 Levels," *The Hill* (blog), February 15, 2011, http://thehill.com/blogs/floor-action/senate/144305-senate-starts-debate-on-amendment-to-slash-aviation-spending-to-2008-levels.

42. Ibid.

43. See Wichita Workforce Alliance for South Central Kansas, "Workforce Alliance for South Central Kansas Receives Additional Training Funds for Dislocated Workers," press release, February 2, 2010, http://workforce-ks.com/Index.aspx?page=49&recordid=117&returnURL=%2FIndex.aspx.

44. John Russo and Sherry Lee Linkon, "Social Costs of Deindustrialization," in *Manufacturing a Better Future for America*, ed. Richard McCormack (Washington, DC: Alliance for American Manufacturing 2009).

45. Vivek Wadhwa, "Top-Down Tech Clusters Often Lack Key Ingredients," *Bloomberg Businessweek*, May 4, 2010, http://www.businessweek.com/technology/content/may2010/tc2010053_047892.htm. See also Muro and Katz, "The New Cluster Moment."

46. The Department of Commerce Budget in Brief, Fiscal Year 2011, pp. 41, 46, http://www.osec.doc.gov/bmi/budget/11BiB/2011_BiB.pdf.
47. See Andrew Reamer and Mark Muro, "Congress Directs EDA to Act on Clusters," *The Avenue*, a blog of *The New Republic*, December 17, 2009, http://www.tnr.com/blog/the-avenue/congress-directs-eda-act-clusters.
48. Daniel Isenberg, "Cluster Buster, Can Policy Makers Create an Ecosystem for Entrepreneurship?," *The Economist*, November 16, 2010, http://ideas.economist.com/blog/cluster-bluster.
49. "Where Good Technology Comes From."
50. Ibid.

CHAPTER 4

1. Brookings Institution, "State of Metro America Report," 2010. The total number of workers in the San Jose–Sunnyvale–Santa Clara area was 913,420, of which 184,039, or about 20.1 percent, were in manufacturing. The Brookings report is based on 2000 census data, so these percentages may have dropped after the Great Recession, but there still remains a sizable manufacturing presence in the Valley. The study relies on ACS Table C24030, Census 2000 SF3, Table P49.
2. Ibid.
3. John Doerr, Bing Gordon, Chi-Hua Chien, and Ellen Pau, "John Doerr: The Next Big Thing," *Tech Crunch*, April 5, 2010, http://techcrunch.com/2010/04/05/john-doerr-the-next-big-thing/. See also Sunshine Mugrabi, "John Doerr Touts 'Greentech,'" *Red Herring*, October 2, 2006, http://www.climos.com/news/articles/johndoerrtouts.htm. (Doerr is quoted as saying, "Greentech is here to stay. It's the next big thing.")
4. Vivek Wadhwa, "Top-Down Tech Clusters Often Lack Key Ingredients," *Bloomberg Businessweek*, May 4, 2010, http://www.businessweek.com/technology/content/may2010/tc2010053_047892.htm. See also AnnaLee Saxenian, *Regional Advantage: Culture and Competition in Silicon Valley and Route 128* (Cambridge, MA: Harvard University Press, 1996).
5. Wadhwa, "Top-Down Tech Clusters."
6. Tom Foremski, "Vinod Khosla: How to Succeed in Silicon Valley by Bumbling and Failing," *Silicon Valley Watcher* (transcript

and video of Vinod's remarks), http://www.siliconvalleywatcher.
com/mt/archives/2009/06/vinod_khosla_to.php.

7. "Top 50 VC-Funded Greentech Startups, Greentech Media An-
nounces the Top 50 Startups in Greentech," greentechmedia,
March 8, 2010, http://www.greentechmedia.com/articles/read
/Top-50-VC-Funded-Greentech-Startups/.

8. Leigh Buchanan, "Entrepreneur of the Year: Kevin Surace of
Serious Materials," *Inc.*, December 1, 2009, http://www.inc
.com/magazine/20091201/entrepreneur-of-the-year-kevin
-surace-of-serious-materials.html; Michael V. Copeland, "My
Business Is Booming," *Fortune* June 8, 2009, http://www
.seriouswindows.com/FortuneFeature2009.pdf; "Kevin Surace
Invents Eco-Friendly Drywall," speech at TED, February 2009,
http://www.ted.com/talks/kevin_surace_fixing_drywall_to
_heal_the_planet.html.

9. Kevin Surace referred me to his address to the House Democratic Caucus, which is worth reading. "Kevin Surace's Comments at the 2010 Democratic Caucus Job Summit," *Serious
Materials* (blog), January 14, 2010, http://blog.seriousmaterials
.com/?p=1001.

10. Andrew W. Savitz with Karl Weber, *The Triple Bottom Line: How
Today's Best Run Companies Are Achieving Economic, Social, and
Environmental Success—And How You Can Too* (San Francisco:
Jossey-Bass, 2006).

11. Michael Porter and Mark R. Kramer, "Creating Shared Value:
How to Reinvent Capitalism—and Unleash a Wave of Innovation
and Growth," *Harvard Business Review*, January-February 2011.

12. Kevin Surace, "Green Tech and How It Must Save America," Strategic News Service, October 5, 2009. (Kevin cites all the statistics
on energy in this article.)

13. Mary Ellen Podmolik, "Government Raising Bar on Windows,"
Chicago Tribune, January 15, 2010, http://articles.chicagotribune
.com/2010-01-15/entertainment/1001130913_1_storm-windows
-energy-department-energy-saving.

14. John Stossel, "A Little Company Praised by President Obama"
(blog post), http://stossel.blogs.foxbusiness.com/2010/01/14/a
-little-company-praised-by-president-obama/.

15. "Update: Innovation, Guts, Better Products, and Transparency,"
Serious Materials (blog), January 15, 2010, http://blog.serious
materials.com/?p=1007.

16. This public data was compiled by Keith Curtis, senior energy advisor, Office of International Operations, International Trade Administration at the U.S. Department of Commerce. He requested the data from the U.S. Green Building Council for 2010.

17. Leslie Guevarra, "Serious Materials Reopens Failed Factory, Restore Jobs for Workers," GreenerBuildings, Greenbiz.com, March 18, 2009, http://www.greenbiz.com/blog/2009/03/18/serious -materials-reopens-failed-factory-restores-jobs-workers.

18. Ibid.

19. Students and Scholars Against Corporate Misbehavior, "Workers as Machines: Military Management in FoxConn," October 12, 2010, http://www.scribd.com/doc/46941357/Report-on-FoxConn; "New FoxConn Employee Commits Suicide in Shenzen," *Global Times*, January 15, 2011, http://china.globaltimes.cn/society /2011-01/612970.html; Chris Chang, "New Suicide from FoxConn, Worker Jumped Because of Insult," *M.I.C. Gadget*, January 13, 2011, http://micgadget.com/10864/new-suicide-from-foxconn -worker-jumped-because-of-insult/; Joel Johnson, "1 Million Workers. 90 Million iPhones. 17 Suicides. Who's To Blame?" *Wired*, March 2011, http://www.wired.com/magazine/2011/02 /ff_joelinchina/all/1.

20. Sharon Cornu and Cindy Chavez, "Manufacturing Tomorrow's Economy," *San Francisco Chronicle*, April 9, 2010, http://www .sfgate.com/cgi-bin/article.cgi?f=/c/a/2010/04/08/EDNC 1CROCL.DTL. See also Cindy Chavez, "California Working Families Say: Yes to Good Jobs—No to Prop 23," *greenforall.org* (blog post), November 2, 2010.

21. John Chambers and Safra Catz, "The Overseas Profits Elephant in the Room," *Wall Street Journal*, October 20, 2010, http://online .wsj.com/article/SB1000142405274870446900457553388032893 0598.html.

22. Robert Atkinson, "Timely, Targeted, Temporary and Transformative: Crafting an Innovation-Based Economic Stimulus Package," Information Technology & Innovation Foundation, October 2008.

23. Dhammika Dharmapala, C. Fritz Foley, and Kristin J. Forbes, "Watch What I Do, Not What I Say: The Unintended Consequences of the Homeland Investment Act," April 2010, http:// www.people.hbs.edu/ffoley/HIA.pdf.

24. Jesse Drucker, "Dodging Repatriation Tax Lets U.S. Companies Bring Home Cash," December 29, 2010, http://www

.bloomberg.com/news/2010-12-29/dodging-repatriation-tax
-lets-u-s-companies-bring-home-cash.html.

25. This is also consistent with Greg LeRoy's work. See http://www
.greatamericanjobsscam.com/index.html and http://www
.goodjobsfirst.org/. I am not sure that Greg would ultimately en-
dorse any form of repatriation, but he certainly would be for strict
safeguards on any incentives.

26. Ezra Klein, "Forum: Andy Stern's Plan to Create 12 Million
New Jobs," *Washington Post,* September 9, 2010, http://voices
.washingtonpost.com/ezra-klein/2010/09/forum_andy_sterns
_plan_to_crea.html. See also Bill Clinton's repatriation proposal,
in Bill Clinton *Back to Work: Why We Need Smart Government for
a Strong Economy* (New York: Alfred A. Knopf, 2011), pp. 134–135.

27. Stephen Lacy, "Bush Admin Pushed Solyndra Loan Guarantee
for Two Years," *Grist,* September 14, 2011, http://www.grist.org
/solar-power/2011-09-13-bush-admin-pushed-solyndra-loan
-guarantee-for-two-years.

28. Darren Samuelsohn, "Risk from DOE Guarantees Less than Expected," *Politico,* February 10, 2012, http://www.politico.com
/news/stories/0212/72733.html.

29. Youngme Moon, *Different: Escaping the Competitive Herd* (New
York: Random House, 2010).

30. Candace Lombardi, "Robots Meet Solar at Solyndra Fab 2," *Green
Tech,* December 9, 2010 (using the word *futuristic* to describe
Solyndra's plant), http://news.cnet.com/8301-11128_3-20025156
-54.html.

31. "Remarks by the President on the Economy," Solyndra Inc., Fremont, California, May 26, 2010, http://www.whitehouse.gov
/the-press-office/remarks-president-economy-0.

32. Gary P. Pisano and Willy C. Shih, "Restoring American Competitiveness," *Harvard Business Review,* July-August 2009.

33. Keith Bradsher, "On Clean Energy, China Skirts Rules," *New
York Times,* September 8, 2010, http://www.nytimes.com/2010
/09/09/business/global/09trade.html.

34. According to the Solar Energy Industry Association's interpreta-
tion of a GTM Research study, China supplies about $430 million
in solar panels of a $2 billion industry, http://seia.org/galleries
/default-file/Trade_Balance_Factsheet.pdf. See also "The Expo-
sure of Chinese PV Suppliers to Global Markets," *Greentech Solar,*
July 16, 2010 (citing GTM research on China's global solar panel

production). Based on GTM studies and his own research, Brian O'Hanlon of the U.S. Department of Commerce, Office of Energy and Environmental Studies, also estimated that China supplies about 25 percent of the U.S. market and 40 percent of the global market.

35. Todd Woody, "Silicon Valley's Solar Innovators Retool to Catch Up to China," *New York Times*, October 12, 2010, http://www .nytimes.com/2010/10/13/business/energy-environment/13solar .html.

36. Dana Hull, "Solyndra Paid Bonuses as Bankruptcy Neared," *San Jose Mercury News*, November 3, 2011.

37. See Coalition for American Solar Manufacturing, "Frequently Asked Questions," http://www.americansolarmanufacturing .org/faq/.

38. Keith Bradsher and Matthew L. Wald, "A Measured Rebuttal to China Over Solar Panels," *New York Times*, March 20, 2012.

39. Kauffman Foundation press release, "Job Growth in U.S. Driven Entirely by Startups, According to Kaufman Foundation Study," July 7, 2010. See also Tim Kane, "Firm Formation and Economic Growth: The Importance of Startups in Job Creation and Job Destruction," Kauffman Foundation Research Series, July 2010.

40. Ibid.

41. Rich KarlGaard, "What Grows an Economy," Forbes.com, November 22, 2010, http://www.forbes.com/forbes/2010/1122/focus -innovation-rules-rich-karlgaard-what-grows-economy.html.

42. "New Businesses Registered," World Bank, http://data.worldbank .org/indicator/IC.BUS.NREG.

43. Dana Hull, "Fremont's High-Flying Solyndra Hits a Rough Patch, *Mercury News (San Jose)*, January 31, 2011, http://www.mercury news.com/business/ci_17221170?nclick_check=1.

44. Alexander Hamilton, "Report on Manufactures," presented to Congress December 5, 1791.

45. The SCHOTT Solar Barometer Survey was conducted by Kelton Research between September 27 and October 4, 2010. SCHOTT Solar and Solar Energy Industry Association (SEIA) commissioned the survey, http://www.us.schott.com/english/news /index.html?NID=358.

46. I purposely do not use his last name.

47. Mark Muro, Jonathan Rothwell, and Davashree Saha, "Sizing the Clean Economy: A National and Regional Green Jobs Assessment,"

Brookings Institution, July 13, 2011, http://www.brookings
.edu/reports/2011/0713_clean_economy.aspx.

48. Arthur Miller. *Death of a Salesman* (1949).

49. "Silicon Valley Unemployment Rate Up a Tick," *San Jose Business Journal*, December 17, 2010, http://www.bizjournals.com
/sanjose/news/2010/12/17/silicon-valley-unemployment-rate
-up-a.html.

50. John Russo and Sherry Lee Linkon, "The Social Costs of Deindustrialization," in *Manufacturing a Better Future for America*, ed. Richard McCormack (Washington, DC: Alliance for American Manufacturing, 2009.)

51. Robert Reich, "The Jobs Report, and America's Two Economies," February 4, 2011, http://www.huffingtonpost.com/robert-reich
/post_1687_b_818991.html.

52. Several articles talk about the skills gap. There are apparently many manufacturing jobs that Americans currently do not have the skills to perform. I address this issue in Chapter 7. For an excellent discussion on the skills gap, see Mark Whitehouse, "Some Firms Struggle to Hire Despite High Unemployment," *Wall Street Journal*, August 9, 2010, http://online.wsj.com/article/SB1000142
4052748704895004575395491314812452.html; 52. Motoko Rich, "Factory Jobs Return, but Employers Find Skills Shortage," *New York Times*, July 1, 2010, http://www.nytimes.com/2010/07/02
/business/economy/02manufacturing.html.

CHAPTER 5

1. The export statistics are from conversations with John Jelacic and economists at the Department of Commerce. Most can be easily found on http://trade.gov/cs/factsheet.asp and the Department of Commerce website.

2. John F. Kennedy, "Special Message to the Congress on Foreign Trade Policy," January 25, 1962, http://www.presidency.ucsb
.edu/ws/index.php?pid=8688.

3. Ronald Reagan, State of the Union address, February 4, 1986, http://www.american-presidents.com/ronald-reagan/1986
-state-of-the-union-address.

4. Exports were up 74 percent, topping $1 trillion for the first time ever under the Clinton administration, "Clinton Presidency: Historic Economic Growth," April 25, 2005, http://ndn.org

/essay/2005/04/clinton-presidency-historic-economic-growth; Bill Clinton, *My Life* (New York: Knopf, 2004), p. 315.

5. Conversations with John Jelacic and economists at the Department of Commerce.

6. Ibid). See also "Top U.S. Export Markets, Free Trade Agreements and Country Fact Sheets," Summer 2008, p. 3, http://trade.gov /publications/pdfs/tm_091208.pdf.

7. John Jelacic at the Department of Commerce compiled these statistics based on International Bank for Reconstruction and Development (IBRD) and International Monetary Fund (IMF) public data for 2008.

8. Ibid.

9. Gary Locke, "Laying a Foundation to Double Our Exports, Increase Competitiveness," *The Hill* (blog), January 25, 2011, http:// www.commerce.gov/blog/2011/01/25/laying-foundation-double -our-exports-increase-competitiveness; Daniel Indiviglio, "Consumer Spending and Exports Boost GDP 3.2% in the Fourth Quarter," *theatlantic.com*, January 28, 2011, http://www.theatlantic .com/business/archive/2011/01/consumer-spending-and-exports -boost-gdp-32-in-the-fourth-quarter/70397/.

10. Gary Clyde Hufbauer and Paul Grieco, "Senator Kerry on Corporate Tax Reform: Right Diagnosis, Wrong Prescription," International Economics Policy Briefs, Number PB04-3, April 2004, http://www.iie.com/publications/pb/pb04-3.pdf.

11. The Global Enabling Trade Report of 2010 by the World Economic Forum ranked the United States nineteenth in having open markets. Comparatively, China was forty-eighth, India was eighty-fourth, Brazil was eighty-seventh, and Russia was one hundred fourteenth, http://gcr.weforum.org/getr2010/.

12. "Maria Bartiromo Interviews Former President Bill Clinton," May 17, 2010, http://www.newsonnews.net/cnbc/3090-maria -bartiromo-interviews-former-president-bill-clinton.html.

13. "Canadian Effort to Reach Trapped Chilean Miners Lags Behind Other Attempts," *Globe and Mail (Toronto)*, October 5, 2010, http://www.allvoices.com/news/6943434-canadian-effort-to -reach-trapped-chilean-miners-lags-behind-other-attempts.

14. House Appropriations Chair Hal Rogers proposed cutting the International Trade Administration's budget by $93 million. Most of the International Trade Administration's budget goes to the Commercial Service. http://appropriations.house.gov

/index.cfm?FuseAction=PressReleases.Detail&PressRelease _id=259.

15. According to Robert Stackpole, a senior trade specialist in Commerce's Birmingham office, Alabama exports grew from $12,354,803,017 to $15,504,533,318 from 2009 to 2010, a 25.49 percent increase.

16. This is according to Salim Bharbhrawala, senior international trade specialist, Office of Materials Industries, U.S. Department of Commerce. He relies on Larry Atkins, "Accelerating the Electrification of U.S. Drive Trains: Ready and Affordable Technology Solutions for Domestically Manufactured Advanced Batteries," paper presented at the U.S. DOE 2010 Annual Merit Review, Washington, DC, June 7, 2010.

17. http://ir.a123systems.com/releasedetail.cfm?releaseid=419211.

CHAPTER 6

1. Ooi Kee Beng, "The Man Who Industrialised Penang," August 4, 2010, http://www.igeorgetownpenang.com/features/640-the -man-who-industrialised-penang.

2. See Henry R. Nothhaft with David Kline, *Great Again: Revitalizing America's Entrepreneurial Leadership* (Boston: Harvard Business Press, 2011), pp. 27–29 (discusses the difficulty of obtaining permits for opening a facility).

3. Catherine Rampell, "Corporate Profits Were the Highest on Record Last Quarter," *New York Times*, November 23, 2010, http:// www.nytimes.com/2010/11/24/business/economy/24econ .html?hp.

4. Melinda Peer, "Dow Finishes 2010 Up 11%," *TheStreet*, December 31, 2010, http://www.thestreet.com/story/10957900/stock -market-story-dec-31.html.

5. Pallavi Gogoi, "Where Are the Jobs? For Many Companies Overseas," *USA Today*, December 28, 2010, http://www.usatoday.com /money/economy/2010-12-28-jobs-overseas_N.htm.

6. This is based on an analysis of BEA public data from 2004 to 2009 by Aaron Brickman, the director of the Invest in America program at the Department of Commerce.

7. According to John Jelacic's analysis of BEA public data, 90 percent of the increase in foreign employment by U.S. multinational companies over the 1999–2008 period has been in nonmanufacturing industries.

8. Brendan Koerner, "Made in America: Small Businesses Buck the Offshoring Trend," *Wired*, March 2011, http://www.wired.com /magazine/2011/02/ff_madeinamerica/all/1.

9. Michelle Dammon Loyalka, "Chinese Labor, Cheap No More," *New York Times*, February 17, 2012 (arguing that China has "experienced sporadic labor shortages, which in turn have driven up its rock-bottom costs"), http://www.nytimes.com/2012/02/18 /opinion/chinese-labor-cheap-no-more.html.

10. This statistic was provided by John M. Harris, Office of Health & Consumer Goods, International Trade Administration, Department of Commerce, based on analysis of public data provided in this spreadsheet: http://www.ita.doc.gov/td/ocg/appliance table%202010.pdf.

11. Harold L. Sirkin, Michael Zinser, Douglas Hohner, and Justin Rose, "U.S. Manufacturing Nears the Tipping Point, Which Industries, Why and How Much?" Report by the Boston Consulting Group, March 22, 2012; https://www.bcgperspectives.com /content/articles/manufacturing_supply_chain_management _us_manufacturing_nears_the_tipping_point/

12. "GE Offshores Green Manufacturing Jobs," *International Association of Machinists and Aerospace Workers Newsletter*, March 30, 2010, http://www.goiam.org/index.php/imail/latest/7091 -ge-offshores-green-manufacturing-jobs.

13. "World's Most Admired Companies," 2010, *CNNMoney*, http:// money.cnn.com/magazines/fortune/mostadmired/2010 /snapshots/170.html (GE ranked number 16).

14. CNN Wire Staff, "At Least Six People Kidnapped in Mexico Hotel Raid," April 22, 2010, CNN, http://articles.cnn.com/2010-04-22 /world/mexico.kidnappings_1_nuevo-leon-kidnapped-gunmen? _s=PM:WORLD.

15. Joel Millman, "Hot-Dog Maker, Lured for Its Jobs, Now Can't Fill Them," *Wall Street Journal*, October 1, 2010, http://online.wsj.com /article/SB10001424052748703556604575502003068891216 .html.

16. "Insourcing Facts," Organization for International Investment, http://www.ofii.org/resources/insourcing-facts.html. Overall, 12.4 percent of employees at subsidiaries in the United States are unionized, compared to 8.2 percent of employees of all businesses.

17. See UNCTAD, "Inward FDI Flows, Dollar Value of Inward FDI by Country in Millions, 1970–2008." In 2008, the United

States attracted $316,112,000 of FDI, whereas China attracted $108,312,000. The only year in which FDI flows into China exceeded those into the United States was 2003.

18. Rick L. Weddle, "Supplemental Report to Testimony Before the Subcommittee on Economic Policy," December 9, 2009, 2 p.m. hearing: "Weathering the Storm: Creating Jobs in the Recession"; "Funding for Invest in America to Attract Investment, Create Jobs and Stimulate Growth Industries: A Comparative Review of the Structure, Funding and Program Focus of Competitor Nation Investor Promotion Activities," International Economic Development Council, submitted Friday, December 18, 2009. Weddle analyzes data provided by UNCTAD, "Inward FDI Flows," to calculate growth rates.

19. Ibid.

20. Alexander Hamilton, "Report on Manufactures," presented to Congress December 5, 1791.

21. President Ronald Reagan, "International Investment Policy Statement," September 9, 1983.

22. Weddle, "Supplemental Report."

23. Ibid.

24. Ibid.

CHAPTER 7

1. Dave Altig, "A Curious Unemployment Picture Gets More Curious" (blog post), July 16, 2010, http://macroblog.typepad.com/macroblog/2010/07/a-curious-unemployment-picture-gets-more-curious.html.

2. James Sherk, "Technology Explains Drop in Manufacturing Jobs," Heritage Foundation, October 12, 2010, http://www.heritage.org/research/reports/2010/10/technology-explains-drop-in-manufacturing-jobs. Good-paying manufacturing job opportunities exist for those with some college education, but there are fewer opportunities for those who have only a high school diploma.

3. Phlissa Cramer, "How Obama's Education Grants Hinder True Innovation," August 10, 2011, http://www.good.is/post/how-obama-s-education-grants-hinder-innovation/.

4. Motoko Rich, "Tough Calculus as Technical Schools Face Deep Cuts," New York Times, July 9, 2011, http://www.nytimes

.com/2011/07/10/business/vocational-schools-face-deep-cuts
-in-federal-funding.html?pagewanted=all.

5. Ibid.

6. Guy Munger, "Raleigh Man Saw Czech Invaders Arrive," *News and Observer (Raleigh, NC)*, August 24, 1968.

7. Anthony C. Laraia, Patricia E. Moody, and Robert W. Hall, *The Kaizen Blitz: Accelerating Breakthroughs in Productivity and Performance* (New York: Wiley, 1999), p. 26.

8. Jeffrey K. Liker, *The Toyota Way* (New York: McGraw-Hill, 2003).

9. Gita Piramal, "The Father of Kaizen Speaks!," *rediff.com*, January 8, 2005, http://www.rediff.com/money/2005/jan/28spec2.htm (discussing the difficulty of implementing the *kaizen* method in China).

10. Alexander Hamilton, "Report on Manufactures," presented to Congress December 5, 1791.

11. Ibid.

12. "President Kennedy Appeals to the Congress for a Tax Cut," April 20, 1961, http://www.nationalcenter.org/JFKTaxes1961.html.

13. Ibid.

14. U.S. Department of Treasury, Office of Tax Policy, "The Case for Temporary 100 Percent Expensing: Encouraging Businesses to Expand Now by Lowering the Cost of Investment," October 29, 2010.

15. Kevin A. Hassett and Glenn Hubbard, "Obama Discovers Incentives: The President's Proposed Tax Cuts for Businesses Are a Welcome Departure from Keynesian Stimulus," *Wall Street Journal*, September 10, 2010.

16. Robert D. Atkinson, "Don't Believe Amity Shlaes (or Most Neo-classical Economists): Obama's Accelerated Depreciation Proposal Will Boost Economic Growth and Is a Good Idea," *Innovation Policy* (blog), November 19, 2010, http://www.innovationpolicy.org/dont-believe-amity-shlaes-or-most-neo-classic.

17. Robert D. Atkinson, "Effective Corporate Tax Reform in the Global Economy," Information Technology & Innovation Foundation, July 19, 2009.

18. Atkinson, "Don't Believe Amity Shlaes." See also Austan Goolsbee, "Investment Tax Incentives, Prices, and the Supply of Capital Goods," *Quarterly Journal of Economics* 113, no. 1 (February 1998); Larry Summers, "Tax Policy and Corporate Investment,"

Proceedings of St. Louis Federal Reserve Bank Conference in Supply Side Economics, 1981, pp. 115–145.

19. Robert D. Atkinson, "17 Is Not Enough: The Case for a More Robust R&D Tax Credit," Information Technology and Innovation Foundation, February 2011, http://www.itif.org/files/2011-17-is-not-enough.pdf.

20. http://www.roadmap.republicans.budget.house.gov/Plan/#federaltaxreform

21. Cliffard M. Marks, "Senior Survey 2010," *Harvard Crimson*, May 25, 2010, http://www.thecrimson.com/article/2010/5/25/percent-year-seniors-class/.

22. Andrew N. Liveris, *Make It In America: The Case for Re-inventing the Economy* (Hoboken, NJ: Wiley, 2011), p. 135.

23. Sarah Palin, Speech at Reagan Ranch Center in Santa Barbara Celebrating President Reagan's 100th Birthday, February 4, 2011.

24. Jackie Calmes, "Obama Offers to Cut Corporate Rate to 28%," *New York Times*, February 22, 2012 (noting that under President Obama's proposal, manufacturers would pay a maximum effective tax of 25 percent), http://www.nytimes.com/2012/02/22/business/economy/obama-offers-to-cut-corporate-tax-rate-to-28.html.

25. Keith Bradsher, "China's Route Forward," *New York Times*, January 22, 2009, http://www.nytimes.com/2009/01/23/business/worldbusiness/23yuan.html.

26. "False Expectations: The Historic Infrastructure Investment That Wasn't," *The Economist*, October 21, 2010, http://www.economist.com/node/17311851.

27. Charles Lane, "The U.S. Infrastructure Argument That Crumbles Upon Examination, *Washington Post,* October 31, 2011. http://www.washingtonpost.com/opinions/the-us-infrastructure-argument-that-crumbles-upon-examination/2011/10/31/gIQAnILRaM_story.html.

28. Report of the National Surface Transportation Infrastructure Financing Commission, *Paying Our Way: A New Framework for Transportation Finance* (February 2009); http://financecommission.dot.gov/Documents/NSTIF_Commission_Final_Report_Mar09FNL.pdf

29. Ibid.

30. "Reduced Congestion Strategic Goal, New Ideas for a Nation on the Move," Department of Transportation Strategic Plan, 2011, http://www.dot.gov/stratplan2011/redcong.htm

31. "2009 Infrastructure Fact Sheet," American Society of Civil Engineers, http://www.infrastructurereportcard.org/sites/default/files/RC2009_roads.pdf.
32. Transcript of Bernard L. Schwartz Economic Symposium, New America Foundation, June 23, 2010.
33. Andy Barr, "Interview with Bob McDonnell," *Politico*, February 7, 2011, http://www.politico.com/news/stories/0211/48969.html.
34. "Newsmaker Interview: Rand Paul," *PBS Newshour*, February 15, 2011, http://www.pbs.org/newshour/bb/politics/jan-june11/randpaul_02-15.html#.
35. Alexander Hamilton, "Report on Manufactures," presented to Congress December 5, 1791.
36. Burt Solomon, "The *Real* Infrastructure Crisis: The Nation's Roads and Bridges Are in Pretty Good Shape. It's the National Will That Is Suspect," *National Journal*, July 5, 2008.
37. President Calvin Coolidge, State of the Union address, December 6, 1927, http://www.infoplease.com/t/hist/state-of-the-union/139.html.
38. Nicole Gelinas, "What Would Reagan Do?," *Washington Times*, January 24, 2011, http://www.washingtontimes.com/news/2011/jan/24/what-would-reagan-do/.
39. Juliana Goldman and Lisa Lerer, "Obama Plans Business Tax Relief, Spending to Spur Growth," Bloomberg, September 7, 2010, http://www.bloomberg.com/news/2010-09-07/obama-to-propose-business-tax-relief-spending-to-spur-growth.html
40. Sheryl Gay Stolberg and Mary Williams Walsh, "Obama Offers a Transit Plan to Create Jobs," *New York Times*, September 6, 2010, http://www.nytimes.com/2010/09/07/us/politics/07obama.html
41. Ibid.
42. David Brooks, "The Next Two Years," *New York Times*, October 28, 2010, http://www.nytimes.com/2010/10/29/opinion/29brooks.html.
43. William A. Galston, "The Importance of Infrastructure Investment: A Letter to President Obama's Chief Economic Advisor Gene Sperling," *New Republic*, February 3, 2011, http://www.brookings.edu/articles/2011/0203_infrastructure_investment_galston.aspx.

CHAPTER 8

1. GAO Report to the Committee on Foreign Affairs, House of Representatives, Defense Exports: Reporting on Exported Articles and Services Needs to Be Improved (September 2010); www.gao .gov/assets/310/309800.pdf
2. Floyd Norris, "As U.S. Exports Soar, It's Not All Soybeans," *New York Times*, February 11, 2011, http://www.nytimes.com /2011/02/12/business/economy/12charts.html.
3. Mark Gordon of NCAT and John Van Kirk, president of NCDMM, both estimate $200 billion per year for the defense manufacturing sector. The total manufacturing output of the United States is about $1.6 trillion.
4. Richard McCormack, "Defense Suppliers Must Plan for a Steep Decline; The Pentagon Will Not Be Able to Revive U.S. Manufacturing," *Manufacturing & Technology News* 18, no. 11 (June 30, 2011), http://www.manufacturingnews.com/news/11/0630 /defensedownturn.html.
5. Matthew Kazmierczak and Michaela Platzer, "Defense Trade: Keeping America Secure and Competitive," U.S. Chamber of Commerce, 2007, p. 18, http://www.uschamber.com/sites /default/files/issues/defense/files/defensetrade.pdf.
6. Richard McCormack, "The Plight of American Manufacturing," in *Manufacturing a Better Future for America*, ed. Richard McCormack (Washington, DC: Alliance for American Manufacturing, 2009), pp. 52–57.
7. Richard McCormack, "Aerospace Executives Say Budget Cuts Imperil Health of U.S. Defense Industrial Base," *Manufacturing & Technology* 18, no. 18 (November 18, 2011), http://www .manufacturingnews.com/news/11/1118/defense.html.
8. Ibid.
9. Pete Stark, "Cut Defense Spending, Too, *Huffington Post*, February 2011 (blog). See also Viola Gienger, "Gates Says Defense Bureaucracy Swollen, Declares Cuts," Bloomberg, August 10, 2010.
10. Kalpana Shah, "American Jobs Must Not Be Lost, Says Kissinger," *Economic Times*, July 16, 2003, http://articles.economictimes.india times.com/2003-07-16/news/27521472_1_kissinger-technology -conference-outsourcing.
11. See Testimony of Lieutenant General Lawrence P. Farrell Jr. (USAF Ret)., President and CEO of the National Defense Industrial

Association, Senate Committee on Banking, Housing, and Urban Affairs, May 13, 2009, http://www.ndia.org/Divisions/Divisions /Manufacturing/Documents/testimony%20gen%20farrell.pdf.

12. See "The DoD Manufacturing Technology Program Strategic Plan," March 2009, https://www.dodmantech.com/related resources/DoD_ManTech_Strat_Plan_Aug_18_Final_low_res .pdf.

13. See Taite McDonald and Alex Beehler, "Defense-Funded Biofuels Can Spur Production and Lower Risk to U.S. Government," *NDIA Business and Technology Magazine*, March 2012.

14. See "Fact Sheet: DoD's Energy Efficiency and Renewable Energy Initiatives," http://www.eesi.org/dod_eere_factsheet_072711.

15. Lawrence P. Farrell Jr., "DARPA Sets the Tone for Technological Superiority," *NDIA Business and Technology Magazine*, December 2006.

16. Steve Kirsch, "Climate Bill Ignores Our Biggest Clean Energy Source," *Huffington Post*, June 27, 2009, http://www.huffington post.com/steve-kirsch/climate-bill-ignores-our_b_221796.html.

CHAPTER 9

1. Paul Krugman, "Taking on China," *New York Times*, March 14, 2010, http://www.nytimes.com/2010/03/15/opinion/15krugman .html.

2. Gary Clyde Hufbauer and Paul Grieco, "Senator Kerry on Corporate Tax Reform, Right Diagnosis, Wrong Prescription," International Economics Policy Briefs, Number PB04-3, April 2004, http://www.iie.com/publications/pb/pb04-3.pdf.

Acknowledgments

■ ■ ■

I am most grateful to the manufacturers and workers who are profiled in this book. They were gracious in allowing me to tell their stories, and they took the time to fact check drafts. They represent the best of our country.

I, of course, want to thank Mom and Dad and Vikas and Lauren, who always believed I had it in me to write a book. My closest friends pushed me to put pen to paper. They include Renato Mariotti, Chris Nichols, Sharon Cornu, John Mogg, Shefali Razdan Duggal, Mahesh Pakala, Reena Rao, John Overton, Yogi Chugh, and a few others who know who they are but do not want to be publicly mentioned. I am also blessed to have an incredibly supportive extended family.

No individuals have been more critical to my public service career than Amy Rao, Brian Wolff, Talat and Kamil Hasan, Marco Simons, and Vinod Khosla. I would not have had the opportunities I did were it not for their confidence in me.

Steve Glickman challenged my ideas throughout my time in Washington and is one of the best policy minds I know. Prerna Tomar, Etelle Higonnet, and Cindy and Alex Hilke read early drafts and helped bring out my voice. Bob Baugh, Owen Herrnstadt, and Matthew McKinnon helped me understand the biggest issues facing American workers. David Kuhn, my agent, and Grant Grinder and Billy Kingsland on his team were extraordinary in helping shape the manuscript.

I hope the work lives up to the expectations of my best teachers who shaped me, including Mrs. Gretchen Raab, Mr. Derek Longo, Mr. Ralph Rhodes, Professor Nathan Tarcov, and Professor Martha Nussbaum.

I could not have asked for a better editor than Knox Huston. He has believed in this project from the beginning. Ruth Mannino and her copyediting team helped make the writing clearer and better.

I have tremendous respect for the men and women at the United States Foreign Commercial Service. In particular, Anne Grey, Dan O'Brien, and the Network Directors taught me a lot about leadership. I also benefited from the insights of John Jelacic and Praveen Dixit, two of the best economists in government. Overseeing Commerce's domestic offices was one of the greatest privileges of my life.

Index

∎   ∎   ∎

About the Author

. . .

 **Ro Khanna** spent two years as Deputy Assistant Secretary of the U.S. Department of Commerce, where he worked with the country's most influential business and labor leaders to rebuild the nation's manufacturing sector and increase American exports. He also served on the White House Business Council. Khanna is now a visiting lecturer in the Department of Economics at Stanford University and a technology attorney at Wilson Sonsini Goodrich & Rosati.